LIVING BEYOND CONFORMITY

Owen Hardwicke

Living Beyond Conformity

AN EXPERIENCE OF MINISTRY AND PRIESTHOOD

the columba press

First published in 2001 by

the columba press

55A Spruce Avenue, Stillorgan Industrial Park,
Blackrock, Co Dublin

Cover by Bill Bolger
Origination by The Columba Press
Printed in Ireland by Colour Books Ltd, Dublin

ISBN 1 85607 308 4

Acknowledgements

This book would not have been written without the constant encouragement of the Sisters of La Sainte Union who staff the little Peace and Justice Centre which I founded in 1980, and which came into full flower when they came in 1986. Before I was sufficiently advanced with a word processor, I turned to Rita Edwards, Sylvia Holding, Mary Lloyd, Alan McDonald, David Roberts, Geoffrey Taylor and Rachel Williamson to produce draft typescripts. Angelo Edwards used his drawing skills to help me with the cartoons. I owe all of them my thanks.

And then there were those who kept asking 'How's your book going?', especially my sister-in-law, Betty Hardwicke, Fr Oliver McTernan, Michael and Priscilla Quinn, Kevin and Mary McDonald, Jim and Mary Fitzpatrick, June and Ronnie Knox-Mawer and so many of the 500 people to whom I send an annual letter – known as 'Owen's Encyclical'. Some of them have read the odd chapter and made useful comments. They must not be blamed for any remaining absurdities in the text.

I am grateful to Giles Hibbert OP of Blackfriars Publications who undertook at my request the first printing of chapter 7 for the thirtieth anniversary of *Humanae Vitae* in 1988, and, off his own bat, of chapter 14.

I gratefully acknowledge the permission of the following to quote from copyright material: Oxford University Press for Keith Ward, *Religion and Community*; Cambridge University Press for Adrian Hastings, *The Construction of Nationhood*; St Paul Publications and Clergy Review for Bernard Häring, *The Healing Power of Non-violence*; SCM Press for K. Schmidt, *Europe without Priests*; Chatto & Windus for Michael Ignatieff, *Isaiah Berlin*; Penguin Books for Jan Morris, *The Matter of Wales*; Collins Fontana for Teilhard de Chardin, *Milieu Divin*; Sheed and Ward for Karl Rahner, *Meditations on Priestly Life* and Brother Choleric, *Further Cracks in Fabulous Cloisters*; A. R. Mowbray for Dom Aelred Graham, *Contemplative Christianity*; Harcourt Brace for Dom Aelred Graham, *The End of Religion*; *The Tablet/ Priests and People* for three cartoons; John Amis for a quote. If I have inadvertently used any copyright material without permission, I apologise and will put matters right in any future edition.

Contents

*'I'm sure this collar will throttle me
now that I'm retired.'*

[Cartoon: Angelo Edwards]

Introduction

'Let me think: was I the same person when I got up this morning ... How puzzling it all is.' 'Would you please tell me which way I ought to go from here?' 'That depends a good deal on where you want to get to,' said the cat. *(Alice in Wonderland)*
'It is impossible to fathom the marvels of the Lord. When a man finishes, he is only beginning, and when he stops he is as puzzled as ever.' *(Ecclesiastes 18:1)*

Books? There are surely already too many of them. So their importance, or otherwise, depends on how we select the ones we really want to read, and also on the expectations we bring to them of their value or usefulness. So what is this one about? I hope it is difficult to categorise, because it is certainly not a logical treatise on anything. However, while deliberately anecdotal, it has a serious intent: to explore informally what it has been like to be a Roman Catholic priest in a changing world and a changing church; but to do this in a way that may command the interest of people who are not especially linked to the Catholic Church, or indeed to religion of any kind. Such people will need to be especially choosy about the chapters they read, because some of it is definitely 'in house' controversy (and not always very edifying at that). Ultimately I believe there is a close relationship between church and world; they constantly interact, and it does no harm to look at issues and problems from both perspectives. People without an explicit faith are sometimes genuinely grateful for hearing what profound significance believers can bring to the understanding of everyday events. No less should believers fail to value the comments and analysis that others can bring as, say, sociologists or psychologists, on items of religious life that otherwise overlook the factors of these disciplines.

Now I spoke of a 'changing church', and I don't want to exaggerate the situation, as though there is a massive crisis over its existence and purpose. There are far too many good and exciting things happening across the Christian world to be wholly pessimistic. In the short term we have problems galore. Yet if my personal experiences are of any consequence, as an ordinary priest of no special status or claim to authority, they indicate that it is possible to plough through some of the difficulties of holding on to one's integrity without losing touch altogether with the slow movements of an institution with roots in history.

So is this book going to be autobiography or some branch of theology? Neither in any defined sense. I just want to explore a range of issues of faith, of vocations, of ministries and priesthood in the light of some special, and occasionally documented, reminiscences. I hope thereby that people within, and especially those on the edges of, church life will find some encouragement to speak up, and perhaps hasten the discovery of ways forward in the new millennium.

I have never kept a personal diary, but from my school days of 1938 I have kept a little register of virtually every book I have read, with occasional bad lapses, together with a note of roughly where I was at the time of finishing it. How else would I recall, for instance, that I was returning by sea from Canada in July 1949 when I read Thomas Merton's *Seven Story Mountain* (published in the UK as *Elected Silence*), and Abbé Michonneau's startling *Revolution in City Parish*? I am also thereby reminded of finishing Karl Adam's *The Spirit of Catholicism* four years earlier in 1945 in the house billet in Hamburg, when I realised that, much as I disliked what I thought I knew about the Catholic Church, I had no choice but to ask for admission to membership, even though that was especially surprising since I was still involved in my war service with the Quaker-based Friends Ambulance Unit. It really does come as a surprise that among the strict quota of books allowed in one's baggage as we set off for France in 1944 (on D Day plus 92) I had included Lytton Strachey's *Eminent Victorians*, C. S. Lewis's *Screwtape Letters,* Shaw's *St Joan,* and *The Cloud of Unknowing*! This register, together with some sixteen notebooks with long extracts from the most exciting of my reading, has provided me with a record of my own intellectual development. I am certainly not very clever, which is why I have always needed to draw on the wisdom of others' minds. I have hardly a single original idea in my head, but I have digested so many rich ideas from others that the ultimate amalgam may sometimes seem to be original; but the differences stem from my trying to apply the ideas to the day-to-day issues of life. My contact with the Order of Friars Preachers – the Dominicans – so soon after becoming a Catholic, provided me with a motto for much that I have tried to do since then: *contemplata aliis tradere –*

to pass on to others the things one has weighed up. So in homilies and sermons, in lectures and informal talks I have seen my calling, if that is what it is, as one of making complex issues reasonably intelligible.

How then to offer this book to a reader? Naturally if it happens that our paths have crossed, some of the more personal facts or anecdotes may be of pleasing interest. If, without that connection, you are looking from the outside at a story of one mildly eccentric member of the Roman Catholic Church, the tangles I have got into may seem unedifying or even absurd; but I hope that the unfolding of certain issues will bespeak a conscientious journey. If you are a Catholic or a Christian of another tradition, I hope you will be prompted to ask some fundamental questions of yourself about the grounding of your personal faith and in the context of the church as the People of God.

From my earliest years, learning to read on the lap of my paternal grandfather, a retired head teacher of an Anglican Church school in Cardiff, I was taught to revere Jesus and to say my prayers. I was very happy that my Preparatory School and Public School were rooted in the Anglican tradition, with a daily act of worship. This was middle-of-the-road Anglicanism; certainly nothing 'high'. Nor did I experience the 'born again' approach of the evangelical tradition. I never wanted to embrace a knock-down theology, hardened into dogmas. They may help to make people feel secure in the conviction that there are clear answers to the mysteries of life and death, but even then it can evade the searching and questioning that marked the humanity of Jesus. The church of which I am, nevertheless, an incurable member, can sometimes be a hindrance to the exploration of God. I value enormously the following quotation from Dom Aelred Graham's *Contemplative Christianity:*

> Catholicism I believe still offers the western world the securest platform from which to launch a personal quest for ultimate religious meaning. It is also a safe resting-place for those who feel no such urge.

Maybe this helps to explain some of the tensions that exist between what are often crudely called the 'conservative' and the 'progressive'elements in the church.

I started the war-time period as a regular church-going Anglican. I was very happy to share the silence of the Quaker-style 'devotional' sessions we had, but I ended up as a Roman

Catholic. I have never lost my respect and gratitude for my
Anglican heritage and Quaker experience. Both traditions continue to illuminate some of the more awkward corners of Roman
Catholicism. I didn't leave them behind. I just discovered that
there was more to the 'universal' tradition than they displayed,
and I wanted to be part of that wider tradition. I am still mining
it. For what I picked up first of all in the Catholic Church was
only counter-reformation thinking and attitudes; and the real
tradition is far richer than that. What is sometimes thought of in
the post Vatican II world as 'new', turns out to be a revival or
re-discovery of older truths and ways. It is those labelled 'progressives' who may be nearer 'tradition'.

I have found some definite conclusions for myself, as well as
embracing what I believe to be healthy uncertainties: but I have
no axe to grind here. Taking into account all the ups and downs
of my spiritual and intellectual odyssey, I remain immensely
grateful for every aspect of the journey. It has not always been
easy or comfortable, but it has been stimulating. I could not
imagine for myself a life with more personally dramatic turning-
points. I do not think for one moment that the journey is over
simply because I am well on into my seventies. I realise that the
scriptures tell us that it is the young who have visions, leaving
the old to dream dreams. Well, that is not how I see my role.
While wholly unclear as to how the details will emerge, I am
quite prepared to offer some elements of a vision of the way the
church may go, ministries develop, and priesthood be re-evalu-
ated. Church triumphalism should by now be dead, without
waiting for the whole history of the institution and its teachings
to be understood in a global perspective. Legalism is having a
deservedly hard time but its parameters are quickly seized on for
protection when open dissent seems to threaten the institution's
foundations. Clericalism persists, not so much as a structure but
as a way of thinking; and its close connection – though emphatically not its identity – with the formalisation of ministries continues to leave us with the muddles about authority and power,
which obscure the value of the gospel's challenge to the Law,
and the many ways in which there must be witness to the risen
Christ.

Recently coming across a book on original sin (which I found
immensely difficult) I was delighted that the introduction
recommended the reader to tackle it by jumping from the first

section to the main conclusions before the hard work of the intermediary reasoning. Now my book is nothing like so learned
or complicated; but people shouldn't feel guilty about jumping
past the chapters that simply hold no interest for them. There is
no strict logical progression to this book, even though there is
vaguely some underlying chronology of my life. The headings
and the sub-headings of the chapters will give some kind of
guidance as to the topics dealt with. Some are primarily reminiscences; others are documented issues. It may turn out that the
anecdotes are the only bits worth remembering.

What is worth writing?

'There is nothing new under the sun.'
So much for any hope of originality.
Yet there is something richer in knowing
we are part of a common humanity.

All our thoughts, ideas, even flashes of inspiration
are like an awakening to a deeper wisdom,
shared by all, though largely unexplored.

The task is to capture this, or nearly so,
and clothe it with words so that we can hear
and see, and feel it together; and even then
the truth is only partially revealed.

Ideas need time and elbow room till refined,
corrected, and superseded by something more profound.
Our very being is a voyage of discovery,
an attempt to incarnate the only One who really Is.

Our life is only a quotation from the experience
and the thoughts of others; and needs
a special context to be of any value.

And in the end there are better words on the way
till we find the one Word that says it all.

'... and then he said, if there are some things
you don't agree with why don't you stay
within the church and change them?'

Author's Note, January 2001

The acute shortage of ordained men – a wholly unsurprising fact – has bitten into my diocese. Between the proof-reading and the publication of this book, the Bishop of Wrexham has asked me to take charge of the parish of Ruabon again, to which much of my story relates, though the geographical area is now much enlarged. As a seventy-six year old, I hope I can show that I have learned lessons from some of my past mistakes, and that I have a more mature vision which has been shaped by the wisdom of others.

Part One

Setting the Scene
(mainly 1946–1954)

Chapter One:
On the Fringes of Academia: A path to Rome
Here there is a focus on relevant autobiographical factors from my childhood but mainly from my student days both in Oxford and Rome.

Chapter Two:
At the Gates of the Institution: Apprentice, official and pastor
Starting in the Diocese of Menevia, I had much to learn as the bishop's secretary, exercising some surprising roles, while edging myself towards the parish work which was where I really wanted to be.

[Courtesy of *Priests and People*]

CHAPTER ONE

On the Fringes of Academia: A path to Rome

'There is no human life that is great and meaningful unless it is risked in the service of a greater cause ... The greater cause to which one must give oneself up if one's life is to be meaningful is not really a greater cause, but a greater person.'
(Karl Rahner, *Meditations on Priestly Life*)

How can you translate a name? I have never understood this, though I recognise that there are 'equivalents' available in various languages with strong etymological links. There is little problem with Anthony, Antonio and Anton being the same name. Giuseppe is recognisably Joseph, however uneasy we might be about calling the composer Joe Green, instead of Giuseppe Verdi. But some of the Latin forms strike me as far-fetched, or badly restrictive of important variations. Maria is supposed to be the equivalent of Mary, Moira and Maureen: or so I was told. It was one of my early defiances of the letter of ecclesiastical law (or the expectation of bishops, which is not quite the same thing) that I declined to fill in the parish baptismal register with anything but the 'vernacular' name a child had been given by the parents.

The Oxford academics had matriculated me into the university in 1942 under the Latin name of Audoenus – their equivalent of Owen. Ten or eleven years later, when church authorities needed some kind of authorising document of my identity before clerical tonsure and my progression through the minor orders of Porter, Lector, Acolyte and Exorcist – (some of which seem to have disappeared these days) – they nominated me as Oedenus. And by the time I was ready to be sub-deacon, deacon and then priest, this had been changed to Eugenius. I give up! And just think of the problems this would cause if someone really wanted (but I cannot imagine why) to check the 'validity' of any of these stages.

Back in those Oxford days, but now after the war, it was under the name of Audoenus that I came to be dubbed a graduate with a first degree – and only for twenty minutes. The Vice-Chancellor tapped me on the head with the New Testament, using English legal pronunciation for the words, *In nomine Patris, et Filii, et Spiritus Sancti,* and there I was, a Bachelor of Arts. In the Oxbridge system, and by what justification I know not, one is entitled to become an MA seven years after matriculation if one has acquired the baccalaureate. So I sat quietly with my white-furred hood (borrowed for the occasion) and then queued up again for another biblical bang so that I became an MA and able to don a smart red hood, which I have kept and used only to get a good seat in the Sheldonian Theatre on subsequent visits for ceremonial occasions.

But so much for Latin names. It has been hard enough to sustain my Welsh identity, the sense of which has gradually increased throughout my life, while spelling Owen thus, instead of Owain; perhaps that accurately indicates my ambivalent cultural upbringing and identity. Even today, in spite of several concentrated efforts to learn, I am not a proper Welsh speaker, though my accent, intonation and pronunciation of the few passages I regularly use in the liturgy can deceive many people. My family name of Hardwicke is no doubt Indo-European, probably something to do with dwelling among sheep: but that rather colours my father's jocular introduction of himself to strangers: 'My name is Hardwicke: I come from a long line of sheep-stealers.' Actually my paternal grandfather was a Bristol or Gloucester man who moved into Wales and married a Powell, whose mother was an Owen, I believe. He and his wife were teachers; he ended up as the head of St James's Anglican school in Cardiff. He was also the man who introduced Pitman's shorthand to the city; and to his dying day at 84 years, he kept a daily diary, in spite of acute arthritis of the hands, in immaculate shorthand. I was told he was occasionally called to the courts to identify handwriting. Alas his son, and this grandson of his, disgrace his reputation by the way our scrawl has always been a calligraphic nightmare.

My mother's parents were true South Walians. Grandpa Chappell was an experienced trade-unionist, and became a city alderman and the fifth Lord Mayor of Cardiff in 1909/1910. During his period of office Cardiff was visited by what Jan Morris (in her wholly admirable book *The Matter of Wales*) called 'that archetypally English enterprise', Scott's last expedition to the Antarctic. She continues:

'Before leaving for the south, their ship the *Terra Nova* put into Cardiff to fuel, full bunkers having been offered as a gift by the coal-owners of South Wales, and the Welsh greeted her with enthusiasm. The grimy port was hung with flags, receptions of many kinds were arranged, endless crowds made their way through Butetown to see the little vessel at the quay, and the Mayor and Corporation, in the full glory of their chains and er-mined robes, went on board to wish the crew good luck. The Englishmen of the *Terra Nova,* though, were not as taken with Cardiff, as Cardiff was with them. Edward Wilson thought the affectionate hooting of ships' horns, sirens, guns and bells no more than "a perfectly hideous din", while Oates wrote in his diary of their proud aldermanic visitors, "The Mayor and his crowd came on board, and I never saw such a mob – they are Labour Socialists".' That was my grandfather all right!

Very recently I acquired my mother's girlish autograph book, with signatures, along with that of General Booth of the Salvation Army, of Scott, Evans and other *Terra Nova* crew mem-bers. More precious perhaps is the 'thank you' postcard pictur-ing the *Terra Nova* which Scott sent from New Zealand. 'Just a line to say Goodbye. We sail south next week, and I shall take pleasant memories of Cardiff and the Lord Mayor of 1910. Kind regards to Mrs Chappell.'

My grandmother had been a Morgan, and that accounts for a whole range of Welsh cousins. It is well said that in Wales you know half the population, and are related to the other half. So I link up at this stage with familes of Chivers, Evans, Richards and Lewis. Two great-uncles, Morgans both, emigrated to Canada with about eleven of their progeny. Ontario is full of Morgans who must be related to me. In 1949, when I was there with my mother, visiting Chappell cousins, we attended one Morgan wedding in the United Church; we even sang some-thing in Welsh.

Of course the various versions of my name and the strained effort to get it into Latin might be taken as a metaphor of my journey from a Welsh Anglican background into English educ-ational culture, and the Roman Church. I never seem to fit de-cently anywhere! I seem to be an incurable nonconformist, which is not to say I have been unhappy, or that I do not value the many orthodoxies with which I fail entirely to conform. My life would not make any sense without them. As a junior school-boy I once read right through the Bible, without any great un-derstanding I need hardly say. I just wanted to know what was in this great collection of books that was such an alleged treasure. Quite early on then I realised that one has to be pretty selective if it is to be of much help. Much of the Jewish scriptures bored me to tears: it still does. Sometimes the sentiments and stories struck me as thoroughly unedifying. I was glad to break through to the stories and words of Jesus. Professor Keith Ward in a recent book *(Religion and Community)* wrote sympathetically: 'The Bible is an ambiguous guide to moral conduct, containing both injunctions to unrestricted love and warnings of primitive vengeance. Its acceptance of slavery, concubinage, polygamy, child marriage, capital punishment, and female subordination render it suspect as a literal guide to moral conduct for every human society.' Then I decided to tackle the whole business of different churches at the age of sixteen. I started my rounds at St Mary's Catholic church in the Canton district of Cardiff, where it eventuated that six years later I became a parishioner and was ordained priest five years after that. On my first call at the Priory house I asked to see a priest, and was introduced to Dom Gregory Swann, one of the resident Ampleforth monks. 'I just want to know what Catholics believe,' I innocently said. He greeted that with peals of infectious laughter, and reckoned I was very brave to put my head into the lion's den of the Catholic Church. He gave me four separate hours of his time, running through the main points of 'the penny catechism', and an outline of the Mass, giving me copies of the appropriate Catholic Truth Society booklets, with occasional notes added in his beautiful handwriting. I thanked him for the explanations, and said it wasn't for me just now, as I had other churches to explore.

I really understood very little of what Catholic Christianity meant, and what I did know had come, not in its Roman form, from my schoolfriend, Roger Newsom. He was the son of an Anglican priest, and a high churchman. It was he who put me on to reading Evelyn Underhill's fine book, *Worship*. Roger and I seemed to do things in partnership, though more accurately it was in parallel. Our very birthdays were different by only one day; after Marlborough we both registered as conscientious ob-jectors and met up again in the Friends Ambulance Unit, when I was 'training officer' (aged 19) for a new intake of members of which he was one. After the war we both had become Catholics, and had our Oxford days at New College. At the FAU Training Camp on one Sunday, four of us went to Mass in Northfield: Roger, Bruce Hunt, Mike Frankton and I. Bruce later became Dom Boniface of Ampleforth, and Mike has sustained his Anglican faith and practice. There was one period when Roger and I exchanged long letters almost weekly, exploring all kinds of philosophical and personal ideas together. I deeply regret now that, as a kind of farewell to the past, when I was setting off for studies in Rome, I burned a great pile of these. However in 1952 he wrote to me in Rome, inviting me to attend his wedding in Vienna in the Easter break. There he married another English Catholic in the presence of his widowed mother, his sister Margaret and a former fellow-student of his from Dartington, where I had visited him once and had met his enormously impressive teacher, Imogen Holst – Gustav Holst's daughter. I feel obliged to give these details because Roger was my closest friend, and plainly had an enormous influence on my development. The other influence was, as always, my reading. I see that I was moved by the letters of Evelyn Underhill, and by Eric Gill's autobiography. It was he who said, in words to this effect, 'You don't become a Catholic by joining the church. You join the church because you have become a Catholic.'

At a special training course at Selly Wood before going overseas, I read Ronald Knox's *The Belief of Catholics*. I discovered that Catholics did not believe, as I had ignorantly supposed, that all 'non-catholics' were damned. So I was free to look further. I started going to Mass, again at Northfield, and would study my little CTS booklet over and over. I wrote to Dom Gregory to tell him that I was now getting really interested. He wrote back at once urging me to take my time. He was rightly suspicious of 'Roman fever' in a twenty year old. He needn't have worried. Rush was impossible. It took time to get in! The next year or so was spent on the Unit's European adventures as the war front moved eastwards across the continent. I was still very happy to join the silent 'devotional' periods with my Quakerly colleagues; but I also slipped out to Mass when I could – in France, Belgium, Netherlands and Germany. There was something ticking over in my mind at least about the European aspect of this one church. It was in Hamburg that I read the book that was a catalyst, Karl Adam's *The Spirit of Catholicism,* and exclaimed loudly in my mind 'Damn!' For I knew I simply had to ask for admission, though much of what I understood was a bit alien to me. I started 'instruction' with Vikar Theobald Bultjer at the church across the road. His spoken English was only moderately good; my spoken German was worse; but we understood each other's language. So he spoke in German, and I replied in English. We only had time for three learned lessons on the Trinity, which I found agreeable, before I was posted to administrative work in London's personnel office. There I sought out a priest in the Oratory on Brompton Road. The lay doorkeeper was a positive dragon and nearly put me off altogether, but in due course I was assigned to the care of Fr Paul Harold Connell. He was down to earth in a friendly school-masterly way, and very systematic as we went through the Catechism. It was from him that I heard that Tommy Woodruff – still famous at the BBC for his over-genial comment one day on a programme that 'the whole bloody fleet's lit up'– had just been received into the church ahead of me. Also he explained that Alec Robertson, of the BBC's music department, was a priest, though 'returned to the lay state' at his own request, but that he could still officiate in an emergency, e.g. hearing the confession of a dying person in the street. ('Once a priest, always a priest' was how the theology ran.) Some of his stories were really funny; it was strange that one of them was prefaced with the remark 'Now this will lose something in the telling unless, like me, you had been at Marlborough.' The discovery that I had been there quite cemented our friendship. Alec Robertson emerged into my life on musical matters some fifteen years later (as I note in chapter 12), and in fact he returned to priestly ministry in his old age.

After seventeen weeks of one-hour's instruction I was given my new posting back to Germany as personnel officer for the British zone units. I had to seek out an army chaplain to continue my induction. He was a friendly Irish priest who gave his address in Ireland as Ballyjamesduff, though my subsequent letters to him never produced a reply. Long after this I discovered he had left the active ministry; and only in 1999 did I re-discover him, fifty-three years after we first met, with his wife and two of his lovely grandchildren, and not many weeks before he died. I thanked him, rather belatedly, for receiving me – adding that I doubted if everyone in authority would be so grateful! I'm not

sure how carefully I listened to what he had to teach me when I
was twenty-one; I know that I was aching to be a communicant
member. I had difficulties about the sacrament of penance – or
'confession' as we rather narrowly called it in those days; but I
swallowed my pride, and took on everything that seemed to be
required – hook, line and sinker. There was no 'hierarchy of
truths' for me in those days. If the Roman Catholic Church was
'the true church', then what she taught was true, and that was
that. To be loyal to Christ I had to be loyal to the church and I
didn't find that too difficult. What I did not like I would no
doubt come to understand in a new light in due course. This loyalty was the means to a closer union with Christ, my Lord,
whose will I had always wanted to try to do. I didn't imagine
that being a Catholic would be a bed of roses, but I was certain I
was on the right lines. The church seemed to have all the answers – provided, as I later discovered, you posed the right
questions. I was dimly aware that Jesus himself did not give precise answers to his questioners. Someone later pointed out that if
you asked Jesus a question, he either asked you one in return, or
told you a story. They say that if you ask a Catholic a question,
you get the answer. For the moment I wanted at least a clear answer to Jesus's question, 'Who do you think I am?', and there
was a sure touch of clarity in the answer the church gave. It had
the ring of truth, and I shared the feelings of those who commented about Jesus himself, 'this isn't like the teaching of the
scribes and Pharisees, but as that of one having authority'.

   I had no intention, all the same, of settling down to thought-
less membership. I was still puzzled why all Catholics were not
pacifists, given the total non-violence of Jesus. But I was almost
overwhelmed by the exciting vistas opening up for me. I adopted
the necessary rubrical protocol – signs of the cross, genuflections, taking holy water, etc., without undue embarrassment. I
do remember resolving, after accidentally dropping in at a
London church when the rosary was being recited publicly, that
I wouldn't go voluntarily to that form of prayer again. While my
respect for the rosary grew later, then waned for several years,
and has now returned as a device for private prayer, I still dislike it as a form of public worship. Some of my later parishioners
have felt it indicated a lack of devotion to the mother of Jesus;
but for me the hurried *Aves*, especially as often muttered con-
gregationally, are disrespectful and unprayerful. Somewhat

surprisingly I had no problems about the Mass being in Latin; indeed I felt perkily at ease with a language I had started on at my kindergarten at the age of seven. It was great to find that ecclesiastical Latin, once I'd switched to the Italianate pronunciation of Catholicism, was so much easier than I had found in Virgil or Cicero. I suppose my north-west-European experience of the church had shown me it was quite useful to find it the same in France, Belgium and Germany. It was some years before I realised that it was the rite, not the language, that provided the unifying link: otherwise the homily should have been in Latin. As a student in Rome I attended one unusual celebration at St Anselmo, the Benedictine house of studies on the Aventine Hill. A visiting Benedictine bishop was the celebrant of a fine Roman-rite Mass, but in Slavonic. He came, I was given to understand, from the one diocese in the Balkans where this was the tradition. One could follow the whole liturgy because the movements and gestures were those we were used to. Instead of *Dominus vobiscum* he said something strange, but as he turned and opened his hands to us, we knew what he meant. Much as I loved the Latin liturgy, and especially the Gregorian chants that went with the best monastic celebrations, it certainly made no sense to have the scripture readings in anything other than the local vernacular; at that time, however, it was not the done thing to question the universality of Latin, even though I later discovered that no less than twenty-eight languages were in use across the Catholic spectrum. It was (with that one diocesan exception) only the Roman rite, or what we should perhaps have called the west European patriarchate that tied itself to Latin. Much unnecessary grumbling about the loss of Latin might have been saved if people knew their history. The following comes from a recent study by Adrian Hastings, *The Construction of Nationhood*, page 194:

'Christianity never had a sacred language. If it had one, it would presumably have been Aramaic, that spoken by Jesus, the Word made flesh, but Christians quickly abandoned its use as they moved out from Palestine, though a few still use it. But it has never been seen as sacred. Even Greek, in which the New Testament was written, has not been. Only a sort of fundamentalism can make language sacred within the Christian tradition, but to do so goes against the whole nature of the religion. What is striking about its history is the willingness again and again to translate – into Syriac, Armenian, Coptic, Ethiopian and Latin in the early centuries: then Slavonic and finally numberless other languages. Undoubtedly there were periods of intransigence and linguistic conservatism on the part of authority, especially of the papacy, but it would be quite mistaken to see the centrality of translation to the Christian enterprise as merely a Protestant characteristic: or to doubt that the attempt to make Latin of all languages into a sort of sacred language on the part of Roman clerics was other than a deviation from the Christian norm.'

So how did I settle down in the church as it was then? Within a few months of being received into full communion, I was back at Oxford, eager to explore Catholicism more deeply, and to be an earnest student of philosophy. I missed going to the beautifully sung Evensong in New College chapel, as I obeyed the current discipline against 'mixing religions' – a view I soon rejected as unchristian. I made contact with Mgr Valentine Elwes, the new university chaplain, just returning from Navy service, and linked up with the Dominicans at Blackfriars where I went to an early Mass each day.

I realised that my Latin and Greek were not up to university standard, so I changed from 'Greats' to PPE – Philosophy, Politics and Economics, so long as I could focus mainly on philosophy and nineteenth-century British history. The idea of economics defeated me altogether, and somehow I managed to read some social and economic history to fulfil the obligation. Academically I am not very bright; never have been; just moderately intelligent and very studious within certain limits. So I tried to make up for lack of quality by getting through a great quantity of books. The idea was to swim about in the ambience of the issues, rather than master the details. I'm not sure if that isn't the story of my life!

I was lucky to have obtained a place in such a fine College in 1942, and it needs a bit of explanation, because even then there was some competition for the vacancies. I had tried for a place at Balliol first of all. My brother, two and half years my senior, had had an adventurous but academically idle period there. He was far too clever to bother to work, but he flourished at the Oxford Union and in theatrical activities. Anyway, after my interview Balliol didn't offer me a place. So I tried for New College where I had to take some written exams. I had of course obtained sufficient School Certificate 'credits' to qualify for matriculation into the university itself. Obtaining a College place was a different matter. In the course of a couple of days' stay, and in between the exams, I was interviewed by five dons. At seventeen, I didn't know who they were – not even that the chairman was A. H. Smith, whose subject was Greek philosophy. 'Now Mr Hardwicke,' he said (nice, that 'Mr' for a seventeen year old), 'if you were admitted to this college, what would you wish to read?' 'Philosophy, sir,' I replied. That was evidently a favourable start. 'Tell me, Mr Hardwicke, what do you know of philosophy?' 'Well sir, I have read three volumes of Gomperz's *Greek Thinkers*.' My goodness, this went down well. 'Really, Mr Hardwicke; tell me what is your opinion of Aristotle?' 'I have no opinion of him, sir, because he comes in Volume Four.' They all laughed and I was admitted to the college. I don't think I could have been judged on the exams, but only on the interview. Other things being equal, that's not a bad way of choosing a candidate: except, of course, that other things were not 'equal'. I was coming from one of the 'best' schools. The opportunity Marlborough had given me to browse through philosophy and other subjects was precious: I read property law in one year's spare time. Even in those days I was conscious of the privilege it gave me. 'Preparatory school' – boarding away from home at the age of seven till eleven – strikes me now as cruel, and certainly distanced me from my parents till my later twenties. 'Public school' (which of course means 'private') had begun to classify me. I enjoyed the comment made somewhere by Canon Drinkwater when he wrote: 'The right way of regarding the Public Schools, for the last hundred years at least, is as a highly successful Youth Movement created for itself by the English governing classes.' However, I never belonged to 'the governing classes', and I am Welsh!

So what was I reading, alongside all the writings of Descartes, Locke, Berkeley, Hume etc., for philosophy, and all the biographies and history around Disraeli, Gladstone, Mill and Trevelyan for politics? From my little book register I see how the influence of the Dominicans, and the occasional informal seminars with the Jesuit Master of Campion Hall, Fr Tom Corbishley, linked my studies with my development as a Catholic. I remember that, together with one or two other recent 'converts' – a word I now try to avoid as inappropriate – we made an unusual impression on several young men who had arrived at the univesity straight from Catholic schools, while we were returning from war service. After their Jesuit schooling, they were amused, and maybe even impressed by our enthusiasm for the faith. The university setting gave me an exciting and privileged way of journeying into the Catholic tradition. For some time I was secretary of the Aquinas Society when distinguished speakers were willing to dialogue with such neophytes as myself. I even hosted Gabriel Marcel, Christopher Dawson and D. J. B. Hawkins in my College rooms after meetings. These personal contacts enlivened my reading and sharpened the conviction, held ever since my Anglican days, that I wanted to serve fulltime in the life of the church, though I did not originally know that I'd end up as a Catholic priest. I was however in no great hurry, and thought I might try some further study, and maybe rise to the role of tutor for a while. A new degree course opened up which included psychology, and I made tentative enquiries about it. Personal and family events intervened, following the journey I made to Canada with my mother to see my uncle and his family, armed with the award of a second-class degree. It was only when I was well out of the university atmosphere that I recognised that there was (at least for those, like me, who were not real scholars) a fearful artificiality about the whole set-up: it was a rather unreal world. In his *Life of Isaiah Berlin*, Michael Ignatieff remarks (p. 208): 'Oxford Colleges have always served as homes for permanently arrested adolescents' – so I had a happy escape! Incidentally Sir Isaiah (as he later became) was no arrested adolescent. Our contact at New College was slight, but he was my 'moral tutor' (though I'm not sure they still have these), and had rooms on the same staircase.

During the sea voyage back from Canada, I clarified my decision to apply to Archbishop McGrath of Cardiff as a candidate for the diocesan priesthood. His reply was, 'I already have more students than I can conveniently cater for.' (I wish now I had kept his letter to confirm a remark that rouses some disbelief.) He recommended that I apply to Westminster Diocese. I was scandalised. I am a Welshman, even though most of my schooling had been in England. The Oxford chaplain was furious when I told him by letter. I gather that the archbishop, a scholar of the Welsh language though he was, didn't trust any candidates other than Irishmen. So in between attending to my mother, whose severe sickness meant transfer to a nursing home, I applied for an interview with Bishop Petit of Menevia Diocese – the only other Catholic diocese in Wales. (Menevia is the Latin form of Mynyw, the seat of St David in Pembrokeshire – and the diocese covered the whole of Wales except Glamorgan and Monmouth counties. It has since then been subdivided from the Diocese of Wrexham.) I lunched with him and, as it was now already August, the only problem was where I could start my theological studies. I was too late for acceptance for the new seminary year anywhere. I told him that I'd try to fix myself up with the Dominicans for a year, and the Provincial said I could join the philosophy year of the friars at Hawkesyard Priory where I had already made a Holy Week retreat in 1947, along with Russell Hill. I took up a room in the attached Conference Centre of Spode House and in class found myself sitting next to Russell, now Brother Edmund. It was not the only time that our paths crossed. This episode only lasted for fourteen days, because my mother's health, which had begun to break down during our Canadian visit, grew seriously worse, and I accompanied her to London's University Hospital for specialist diagnosis. It soon became clear that she had lung cancer and so returned to St Winifred's Hospital in Cardiff, as the disease spread throughout her body. I spent six to nine hours with her every day. From my wartime training, I knew a bit about nursing and have a knack of being able to make people comfortable, and I gladly did this for five or six months, as well as act as housekeeper for my father. It really was a privileged time, and enabled me to explain a little of myself to both parents before moving so acutely into a world of which they knew nothing. I never 'talked religion' to my mother; but I am confident she had been having some exchanges with the Sisters who staffed the hospital – Sister Denis Hall in particular. One day Mother said, 'You know I am dying, don't you?' 'Yes,' I said, 'and would you like to die as a Catholic?' 'Yes, but how can I, as I'm stuck here in bed?' The sisters and myself were busy at this time with a 'novena' of prayers to Our Lady of Lourdes (Feast on 11 February) that God would relieve her of the terrible pain she was suffering as cancer attacked her spine. I don't think we quite expected this turn of events. Mother was a rather reserved person with strangers; she had only once ever met a Catholic priest, Dom Charles Murtagh OSB, when he had come to tea with me at home. Charles had now left Cardiff for work elsewhere, but it so happened that he was back for a short stay. This was providential, and made it so easy for her to be received into the church on 5 February, and after receiving Communion several times, she died on 10 February, a day before the end of our novena. It was a bit startling for my mostly 'chapel' relatives to be summoned to a Requiem Mass as her funeral; my father had been happy to leave all the arrangements to me. It had been an edifying end, and I was with her as she died. Sister Denis, seeing the signs of death, brought a visiting priest to say the prayers for the dying. We went through them, in Latin of course. I then suggested that he might repeat them in English, and, almost exactly as he said, 'Go forth, Christian soul, from this world, in the name of God the Father, who created you ...', she quietly went. (This has enhanced my appreciation of Elgar's setting of these words in the *Dream of Gerontius:* the memory is vivid.) I immediately phoned my father, as it was the early hours of the morning, then stayed to say the Office of the Dead, and went home without a tear. It was two weeks later that I really started to grieve. My father was wonderful, though shattered by her going. He knew we had a rather special bond, and he shared my dear brother's attitude about her dying as a Catholic: 'You deserved it, old thing.' It was immensely consoling to me, of course.

Having settled with Bishop Petit that I was now free to go to the Beda College in Rome in the autumn, I see from my book register that I spent a week at the Cistercian monastery on Caldey Island in April, visited Roger at Dartington and had some interesting days with my father in Dublin – my first-ever visit to Ireland. That left a lot more time for reading.

It gave me a good feeling to go to Rome for studies. I soon found that the intellectual riches and freedoms I had enjoyed so far were either not the experience, nor apparently the wish, of more long-in-the-tooth Catholics. Here you read what you were told to read; and that made sense for those who read slowly and not very widely; but my mind was racing ahead, and I was already asking questions which some fellow students and professors might not have thought to be opportune. Long-standing practices, which were sincerely but mistakenly dubbed 'tradition', were not to be questioned. There was an ecclesiastically correct way of doing everything. There was even a list of forbidden books at the official level; that was the notorious Index which nobody actually mentioned. Out of curiosity I had enquired about this in earlier days; nobody seemed to have a copy, till I found one in the Anglican Pusey House in Oxford. It was an attempt at censorship, even though I had been assured that serious students had some kind of exemption, so that they could read the forbidden books without explicit permission having been given. It certainly provided no hindrance at the Beda College; and of course that sort of nonsense has gone from the church now, for nonsense it was – an arrogant attempt to monitor explorations into truth. Most of the philosophers I had studied at the university were listed there; even in those 'honeymoon' days in the church I would not have conformed to such negativity.

So was that the church I had joined so eagerly at the age of twenty-one? Was it meant to be an exclusive society with all the answers to life's questions? And am I saying that the church is now different – or that I am different? Both, I suppose. But I must emphasise that I was not totally unhappy in the church of Pope Pius XII; there was something very uplifting about Pius himself and I used to hasten down to St Peter's Square very often to catch a glimpse of him at his window or at some ceremonial occasion. The city of Rome itself was full of a wide variety of churches and shrines which, if only for historical reasons I was glad to visit; and it was possible to participate in all kinds of liturgical rites in languages other than Latin. The Catholic communion was certainly not uniform, and the relaxed discipline of the Beda College, set up to lead 'late vocations' towards the priesthood, was perfectly tolerable. We had an especially courteous and gentlemanly Rector in Mgr Duchemin. However I didn't pass through my studies as the bishop really wanted. The first year at the Beda was intellectually dreadful, as far as philosophy was concerned; nothing but 'Aunt Sallies' of disapproved writers which were quickly demolished by a kind of neo-scholastic orthodoxy. I was then asked to move to a degree course in theology at one of the Roman universities. I chose the Dominican 'Angelicum' rather than the Jesuit 'Gregorian', but it was not a good experience. The days were filled with a series of lectures, all in Latin of course, but it was too difficult for me to follow when spoken in turn by a Pole, a Sicilian, a German, a Frenchman, lecturing in their varying accents. The only one I could really understand was an American. For Mediterranean area students it all came easily; it is just possible that the three Americans in my class understood a fraction less than I did. Our

main textbook was St Thomas's *Summa Theologica;* but there
wasn't time to read it: the professors were too busy expounding
it – or that is what I think they were doing. In New Testament
studies one was occasionally called upon to translate the Greek –
but into Latin. I found a parallel version to help conceal my
weakness here. I'm afraid I learned very little in that year. At
one of the oral exams, after failing to understand the question,
let alone having an answer, I was asked, 'Will the pass mark suf-
fice for you?' 'Utique, pater,' I replied – which I gathered was
how one said 'Yes'. In the summer vacation I told the bishop of
my inadequacies, and eventually he reluctantly said I could return to the Beda course. That meant only two lectures a day, and
always in English. The theology course was much better than
philosophy; for one special term we had Alan Clarke as lecturer
(later to become Bishop of East Anglia) who was first rate. Best
of all was the fact that this left one time to read and explore on
one's own, and I see from my notebook that I read chunks of St
Thomas for myself, as well as a lot of Gilson, Maritain, De Lubac
and Congar. For a couple of years I was the student librarian
which helped me to develop a wide 'cover knowledge' of theological resources. Two wonderful books on the scriptures came
my way, by Charlier and Gelin; and a French Jesuit, Lorson, had
a new book out called *Un Chretien: Peut-il être Objecteur de
Conscience?* where I was able to begin to fathom the Just War
Theory, to explain why all Christians were not pacifists. By
providential chance I uncovered the majestic writings, especially
in ecclesiology, of Mersch and Scheeben who helped me enormously in shaping some sort of grasp of the central truths of our
faith.

A not unimportant aspect of studying in Italy was the
opportunity at the three short breaks at Christmas, Easter, etc.,
of travelling to some of Italy's glorious towns. The impact of
Siena and Assisi was enormous. I also went to S. Giovanni
Rotondo to be with the stigmatic friar, Padre Pio, and served
Mass for him one early morning. During the journeys home to
Britain in the summer, there were other chances of staying in
Germany's Maria Laach monastery, visiting Lourdes; and there
was one exciting journey to Lyons with a fellow-student where
we saw something of Bishop Ancel and the priest-worker
movement, and met several of those, later to be summarily
suppressed, who were trying a revolutionary approach to their

ministry. I see that about this time I found a book by John Coventry, an English Jesuit, *Faith Seeks Understanding*, which was enormously helpful. I later found out he got into some ecclesiastical trouble for writing it; but I was excited by it. ('That figures!' I can hear someone saying.) Most providential of all was the discovery of Dom Augustine Baker's *Holy Wisdom* which I immediately treasured, and it shaped my puerile efforts at deepening prayer for many years. I have returned to it many times.

The four years in Rome passed very quickly; the vacations were time for more extensive reading, and in the latter years involved short retreats before the ceremonies of tonsure and for minor orders and sub-diaconate – all taking place at the cathedral in Wrexham. Oddly enough, my ordination to the diaconate back in Rome, at the St John Lateran Basilica, was in my view invalid. There were so many candidates for each of the seven orders conferred at the one ceremony, it took from 7.00 am till 2.00 pm. After the 'matter'of the sacrament (presenting the book of the gospels) had been given by the presiding bishop, he went on with the ceremony, having omitted the words which constituted 'the form'. I whispered quietly to Gwilym Jones, my fellow ordinand from Wales, who was at my side, 'He hasn't ordained us properly,' which Gwilym dismissed as an impertinent suggestion. However some 10–15 minutes later some clerical official noticed and the bishop then said the correct words. In my opinion there was no 'moral unity' between 'matter' and 'form' as I had been taught there should be. I can't say I ever lost sleep over this, even in my more docile days.

Understandably I wanted to be ordained priest in the only parish I had ever known, St Mary's in Canton, Cardiff, but that was in the diocese where the archbishop had declined my application to serve. One day I asked Bishop Petit if he could come to Cardiff for the ordination. 'Of course I'd like to,' he said, 'but that wouldn't be possible – an indiscretion, in fact.' However, in the summer of 1993, when on vacation, Archbishop McGrath was in St Winifred's Hospital to check a nose-bleed, and that was where I quite often served daily Mass. After assisting him one morning I asked to see him. He was, as was his wont, personally charming. 'Now who are you exactly?' he asked. 'One of the students you turned down, actually,' I said, 'but I want to ask you a great favour. Would you let Bishop Petit come down into your diocese and ordain me in Canton?' 'Of course,' he replied, 'but you'll find he won't be willing to do this.' I said no more and kept out of his way during the rest of his stay, because he was notorious for changing his mind on his decisions within 24 hours; indeed I was told he was looking for me the following day. I gave him the slip, and it amused Bishop Petit to pull this off for me. On the same day as the actual ordination, 25 April 1954, the archbishop was tactfully busy at another ordination of another St Mary's parishioner as a monk at Belmont Abbey. In 1997, when I was staying at Belmont while attending the Hereford Three Choirs Festival, I met one of the monks who was home from serving in the Belmont foundation abbey in Africa. This was Dom Aelred Cousins, and in conversation he mentioned that he'd been ordained by McGrath. 'Was that by any chance on 25 April 1954?' 'It was,' he replied. 'So you were the fellow parishioner who provided the archbishop with his dignified and discretionary alibi!'

My pre-ordination retreat was at Downside Abbey under the guidance of Dom Sebastian Moore, whose books have intrigued me through the years since then. And after the ordination there was a celebratory party which my father generously laid on at the Park Hotel with guests including the Lord Mayor, a fellow parishioner, Fr Illtud Evans OP, an early Dominican friend, who was there also to shepherd Brother Edmund Hill (yes, again) through ordination to the diaconate on the same occasion. Then I returned to Rome, to celebrate Mass first of all at the tomb of St Catherine of Siena, several of whose aphorisms have carried me through life very helpfully; especially, 'God does not ask a perfect work – but infinite desire'. I was on cloud nine for the remaining weeks; and when the last term was over I holidayed briefly in Switzerland before returning to my Llandaff home. From there I left home for good – and it really felt like that – on 20 July to travel to Wrexham to start work as the bishop's secretary.

CHAPTER TWO

At the Gates of the Institution:
Apprentice, official and pastor

In the Catholic system, a student for the diocesan priesthood is taken on by a bishop for his diocese. At ordination he promises obedience to this bishop and his successors. You do at least know within what geographical boundaries your life will be from then on. Of course, by mutual agreement between bishop and priest, you might in fact take up a specialist post elsewhere for a probably limited period. Bishops, I soon discovered, were not insensitive; they almost always consulted the person involved before deploying him, and any particular wishes of a special kind were at least listened to. I hardly expected to be given much choice at the start of my ecclesiastical career, though I was saddened at being told that I would be the bishop's secretary to begin with.

So what had all that study and reading prepared me for? Being a bishop's secretary didn't sound very pastoral; nor was it. Yet it gave me, in three and a half years, a picture of diocesan work which I could not have gained so swiftly otherwise. There was a good deal of desk work, but most administrative affairs were handled by Fr Philip Webb who was Chancellor and Diocesan Treasurer. A very benign West Walian, he shared with me an outreach area of Overton and District in what was mostly East Flintshire, cut off from the rest of the county, to provide Sunday Mass at least. He gathered the Catholics of Bangor-on-Dee, Worthenbury and other nearby villages for Mass in the back of an adapted caravan, parked in someone's garden. It only seated about fifteen or twenty; confessions were heard on the grass outside, sometimes under an umbrella! In alternate journeys Philip and I collected up twenty children on weekdays in a Dormobile to carry them to and from the Wrexham school in term-time. That meant a round trip of thirty miles, twice a day for years. It was a chore that at least got one out of the office, and was continued until we could organise an official private bus to take over. One got to know the children quite well, and it was pleasing to find

some of them, married and with their own children, in my parish
thirty years later on.

Within a few months I had learned the role of Master of
Ceremonies sufficiently to overcome my intense inner nervousness on the first few occasions; and, regaled in purple cassock and
cincture, I found that altar servers, curates and even senior clergy
responded with alacrity to my stage directions – even if they were
wrong. I soon had confidence enough when visiting parishes with
the bishop for Confirmation, to say to the altar servers: 'Now
never mind what you have been told by the parish priest about
what to do. Just keep your eye on me and I'll indicate clearly what
comes next.' It usually lessened anxiety and worked successfully;
for the bishop was not only a bit awe-inspiring in all his various
regalia, but could be sharp in his comments in the sanctuary – not
to say sometimes alarming. Though Bishop Petit could get very
cross, he also had a good sense of humour. Having once nearly
been throttled by his Canons as they replaced his enormous *cappa
magna* at the end of a ceremony in his early years in the diocese, he
thereafter insisted that only his secretary, properly briefed,
should be allowed to drop the heavy item across his head, allowing the nearly eight feet of purple train to flow behind. However,
on one occasion in London, he took this extravagant and complicated garment for use, without his secretary attending. He duly
briefed the local curate, and told him to forbid anyone else to
touch it. At the end of the liturgy there was a slight delay when he
had doffed the chasuble, and an elderly priest near at hand said,
'Shall I get your *cappa magna*?' – trying to be helpful. 'If you do, I'll
cut your throat,' snapped the bishop; and only then remembered
he was not among his own clergy. The old priest went white, and
the bishop – who told me this story himself – laughed at his own
indiscretion.

There were many other ceremonial occasions for me to direct
as well as I could manage. One of them, within a few months of
starting as bishop's secretary, had a special resonance for me,
because of its antecedents. In my last weeks in Rome, where I returned after ordination in Cardiff, I moved around as much as I
could on free days. On one of these I went to catch a bus to
Subiaco, the original cave-like home of St Benedict before he
founded a monastery. At the bus stop I met up with a charming
little Franciscan in his friar's habit who was going the same way.
We chatted amiably as he was British, on leave from mission

work in India. 'Now that you're ordained,' he said, 'where will you be going in your diocese?' 'Oh dear,' I replied, 'the bishop has already told me he wants me to be his secretary', and I proceeded to tell him that I'd really seen enough of bishops in Rome, and that it wasn't my idea of a happy start. He laughed with me about this.

Now back in the diocese, four or five months later, I had to be MC for the ceremony of opening and blessing a new church in Rhayader in mid-Wales, which came under the care of Fr Gillespie, a Franciscan who was based at Llanidloes. He had gathered a coach-load of parishioners from a Liverpool Franciscan parish to attend, and had even unearthed a Franciscan bishop, wearing ceremonial grey, rather than the uniform black and purple which they all wear nowadays like 'secular' bishops. We were all getting ready to start when this bishop arrived; and as we shook hands he said: 'I think we have already met.' He had been my fellow traveller to Subiaco. We both enjoyed the joke, but I had to think hard to remember how offensive I might have been in my conversation about bishops.

I was also the bishop's chauffeur and bag-carrier – and I sometimes remarked that I wasn't ordained 'porter' for nothing! – since he couldn't drive. Some weeks that meant six hundred miles on the road, for our diocese stretched right down to Fishguard and St David's (which was the real Menevia). Incidentally he was one of those people who don't quickly know their left from their right, which made some of his navigating directions a bit confusing when we came to T-junctions, when he'd say 'Left here' and then at the last minute 'No! Right.'After nearly skidding on one occasion when redirecting the car sharply I resolved in future to follow his first direction only; and then, if need be, stop, reverse or turn in some convenient entrance. As a non-driver I don't think he ever grasped the danger of quick changes of steering!

On the occasions when we journeyed away out of the diocese, especially to places where the bishop had old friends, he grew more and more relaxed in his manner. That forewarned me about the problems and dangers of having so continuously a public persona; where was the private person hiding all the time? None of us can avoid playing roles altogether, but once a person is in uniform – and clerical dress, not to mention episcopal ring and purple socks is uniform – it is so easy for the role to take over. Later, much later, I came to reject wearing the uniform of a cleric outside of church worship, largely because it seemed to me to be a passport to privilege, but also because it tended to falsify the way I related to people, and – more seriously because it was not under my control – the way they related to me. Also when I had to read out from Matthew Chapter 12 I felt a shiver of embarrassment. 'Jesus said, Beware of the scribes who like to walk about in long robes, to be greeted obsequiously in the market-squares, to take the front seats in the synagogues and the places of honour at banquets…' In 1952 I uncovered a quaint anecdote in Ward's *Life of Newman*. Newman wrote in 1846, 'I had a walk in the streets with (Mgr) Talbot, who, to his or my shame, had no Roman collar on. It discomforted me a good deal, and made me a most dull companion. What a fool I am.'

Bishop Petit remarked to me one day that there was no handbook on how to be a bishop. At his own consecration (we call it ordination again nowadays) he asked Archbishop Godfrey of Liverpool if he could advise him on how to be a bishop. Godfrey said, not without a twinkle in his eye, 'Well now, if I were you I'd get a little hook inside your *zucchetto* (purple skull cap); it helps to keep it in place. And then when you wash your hands, don't put your episcopal ring on the bathroom shelf; put it in your pocket; you might forget it.' Godfrey was a nice man. I found him positively avuncular. At his dining-table, when we were staying with him in Liverpool, he listened to Bishop Petit extolling the wonders of St Winifred's well in Holywell, and how a pilgrim threw away his crutches after bathing in the waters there recently. 'Indeed,' said Godfrey, 'so there's life in the old well yet.' The following morning, after I had served Bishop Petit's Mass in the private chapel, I began to say Mass myself (that's how we did it in those days). The resident religious sisters gave the initial responses; but when I came across to the side for the wine and water, it was Godfrey himself who was there as minister. Not every newly ordained priest has an archbishop to serve Mass for him.

Occasionally there were VIPs to ferry around. We had the broadcaster Gilbert Harding to stay once in Bishop's House. He had come to open the Christmas Fayre at the cathedral parish. His conversation was, as on his TV appearances, ebullient and interesting. As he spoke of some injustice or idiocy in society, he did so with the anger that he would have shown to the perpetrator. He was a very vulnerable person because of his openness; and he wasn't afraid to look at personal matters. I remember some remarks about death and dying which showed a great sensitivity. When I drove him to Crewe for his return train, and took him onto the platform with the bishop, all eyes turned to us – even from the windows of newly arriving trains. He was approached for autographs, and if he got a bit stroppy about this, it was because he did not rejoice in his public persona. Quite unaffectedly he knelt to kiss the bishop's ring before boarding the train. I was glad to have met him, and for some time treasured one of the biro-pens he gave out, with the legend on it 'Stolen from Gilbert Harding'.

One distinctly ecclesiastical figure who came to stay was the Apostolic Delegate, Archbishop Gerald O'Hara, who somehow combined this task of being the diplomatic representative of the Holy See to the British Government, living in Wimbledon, with being the archbishop of the US Diocese of Savannah-Atlanta. Legend has it that, when asked how he justified having the hon-our, and presumably the perks, of a diocese, he replied: 'Hang it all, a guy's got to live.' I found him a thoughtful man, not least be-cause he noticed my heavy schedule on the Sunday he was with us. I said Mass at a nearby convent at an early hour, then served a private Mass in the bishop's chapel, than acted as MC for a pontif-ical Mass at the cathedral. After lunch I drove the two bishops to Bala, where the eccentric Dutch Dominican, Fr James, had set up a shrine to Our Lady of Fatima. (I still question the propriety of this dedication in the theological heart of Welsh Presbyterianism. 'Our Lady of the Welsh hills' would have given a less 'foreign' im-pression.) He was a skilful entrepreneur, and had attracted coach-loads of pilgrims from Liverpool and elsewhere for an annual big event. So we duly processed the length of this small staunchly nonconformist village with Knights of St Columba carrying aloft a statue of Our Lady of Fatima into the grounds of a hotel man-aged by a Catholic family. There I acted as MC for another pontif-ical Mass, before some public refreshments and socialising. By the time we arrived back after the thirty mile journey to Wrexham it was evening time, and I was obviously tired. 'Said your Office, Owen?' he asked. 'Not yet, your Excellency,' I replied. 'Right; I dispense you. Start with Lauds tomorrow morning.' Now that really was considerate, for I was a disciplined by-the-book priest (honestly!) and I never once failed to say the whole of the Office in Latin each day – Matins, Lauds, Prime, Terce, Sext, None, Vespers and Compline – even if on some days I had to rush down the

home straight before midnight, when the business of the day had
totally prevented me from praying at the appropriate hours. It
was twenty years before I had the guts to stop saying late morning prayers in the evening, when I had genuinely been prevented
earlier. I would now start wherever the clock said I was – Vespers
for the evening, etc. But I really felt naughty for a while, until
Vatican II of course, when its Constitution on the Liturgy and subsequent new edition of the Breviary clearly said otherwise. The
1970 General Instruction on the Liturgy of the Hours says this:
'Because the purpose of the Office is to sanctify the day and all
human activity, the traditional sequence of the Hours has been so
restored that, as far as possible, they may be genuinely related to
the time of day at which they are prayed. The modern conditions
in which daily life has to be lived have also been taken into account ... It is best that each of them be prayed at a time which
most clearly corresponds with its canonical time.'

Obvious enough and sensible, one would have thought, but it
took a General Council and its aftermath to break through the
legalistic thinking I had been presented with. Otherwise one de-
pended on thoughtful prelates to dispense one from the full
rigours.

Another remark of Archbishop O'Hara's I recall was during
one of our drives round part of the mountainous area of
Snowdonia. 'Now I know,' he said, as he admired the rugged
hills, 'why the Welsh are nationalists.' He was right. You don't
need to 'go abroad' to find such a glorious range of hills and vales.
'If you did not live in Wales,' I was asked, 'where would you like
to live?' 'In Wales,' I answered. But for all that I am a poor
Welshman, having failed to master the language even now. I have
tried several short, intensive courses, only to fail to keep it up
afterwards.

Quite early on in this, my first priestly appointment, I was
expected to respond to requests from parish priests for dispens-
ations from some of the 'impediments' to marriages to 'non-
Catholics'. With delegated authority I did this. But the bishop
kept to himself the practice of replying personally to the necessary
request that had to be sent by any non-Catholic for the use of the
organ at the wedding in these cases. He always granted it and
used to send a personal letter which was probably a helpful gesture. But what a system! No dispensation or permission, no music!
It was all part of an ecclesiastical deterrence policy to dissuade

Catholics from marrying anyone other than another Catholic. In more thickly populated Catholic areas, like Liverpool, the 'mixed marriage' had to be, not in the church, but in the sacristy. I really cringe when I think of this!

From quite early days with him, I found the bishop very trusting. One day he told me that he was due to attend a meeting of a certain Catholic society a long way from Wrexham. 'What do you think I should say?' he asked. 'I'll outline a little address for you,' I suggested. This I did, and passed it to him. But a few days later he came back to me to say that he now had to go to London on that day. 'You'll have to go for me, and read the little speech.' And that of course I did. It was amusing when a question was raised at the end: 'I wonder what exactly the bishop means by so-and-so?' 'Well,' I said, 'I think he meant ...'

The lifestyle of Bishop's House was interesting. I was of course granted the privacy of my bed-sit, when eventually I got to it in late evening. The bishop liked talking, and the two meals which we had together each day, with Philip Webb and any visiting priest, were quite lively for conversation. He wasn't exactly fun to be with, but he had quite a soft centre to his brittle exterior, and he disliked the distance his role put between himself and others. Many diocesan priests thought he was hard and uncaring, but I saw another side of him. He could be moved by the difficulties of those whom he liked, and didn't perhaps quite know how to manage his feelings; so he tended to suppress them. 'I wish chaps wouldn't act on the defensive,' he once said to me, 'it makes me feel as though I'm being aggressive.' All I could think to say in response was in Anglo-Welsh idiom: 'Well there you are, isn't it?'

The household 'staff' otherwise consisted of his two blood sisters, Norah and Molly, and the Austrian resident cook-housekeeper, Josephine. Norah was his efficient personal secretary; Molly assisted with the housekeeping. They held him somewhat in awe, though he was always nice to them. They never called him 'John', only 'My Lord'; and they came to see us off at the front door when we set off on our many journeys. Josephine was a marvellous cook with a giggly sense of humour and no-nonsense attitude to life. At Christmas and other major festal occasions she excelled herself catering for a dozen Canons at Chapter meetings, and up to fourteen priests on Christmas Day.

The Christmas festivities began of course on Christmas Eve. At about 10.30 pm we drove round to the cathedral to get ready for the midnight Mass. Not only was the place packed to the doors, but we had a small military guard of honour inside the cathedral itself, who doffed arms at the consecration. Apparently there was a local Pioneer Corps with a Catholic Major, who brought them along. It was meant well; but I should surely have objected to this if I had been a little more confident at that time. When the congregation had dispersed at the end, I then served a second Mass for the bishop – a quiet low Mass. I'm not so sure that he didn't even have the third one straight away – or was that one at noon? All this meant that we got home to the Bishop's House at about 2.30 or 3.00 am. I had to be up early again to say Mass for the convent sisters at Plas Derwen – a lovely hard-working nursing-home community. They were always very supportive to me personally, and forty years later I am still in touch with some of them, now far from Wrexham. Then I drove to Ruabon for Mass in the village room and a lively chat with those who gathered there. By lunchtime I was very tired. We had a very light and informal meal; all was being prepared 'below stairs' for an evening celebration. So I remember hurrying off to my room for a brief siesta. No chance! At 2.30 pm the bishop tapped at my door: 'Come on; drive me round the convents.' So first I drove him the 200 yards down to Plas Derwen, and while he sat in a roomful of sisters enjoying some light conversation, I'd sit outside and try to doze off. After thirty or forty minutes the next journey was to the Holy Family sisters who lived near the cathedral. They ran a fine private secondary school, taught in the primary school, and did a lot of other staffing of the cathedral, as sacristans and other tasks. Once again he disappeared into a large parlour, and I would sit outside and try to read; but soon nodded off. Although there were two other communities of sisters in town, I think even he drew the line at two visits; yet it was still about 5.00 pm when we got home.

At 6.30 or 7.00 pm the dining room table was loaded with good things, and we had a magnificent meal. Norah and Molly served it up, and then ate their own meal afterwards with Josephine. Even in those days my sensitivities about this gender role caused me some worry. It was also another clergy/lay divide; for those at the table were all priests, invited in from any of the deanery parishes where they would otherwise be on their own. That of course was kind of the bishop; but in spite of this generous hospitality the younger priests tried to flee to their family home after the last morning Mass if they possibly could. For after the meal, we assembled in the bishop's study/sitting room, where Canon Dolph Evans had set up his 118-mm film projector, and we watched a not-very-good film. The funny thing was that at the end of reel one, the lights went on, and we had to wake Dolph up to change to reel two. He was the 'administrator' of the cathedral parish of which the bishop was officially the 'parish priest' and had to defer to him, unlike the Dean of an Anglican cathedral. He was in charge of the deanery, with the customary acronymic entitlement of VF – Vicar Forane. I never came across or observed him when he was not smiling and welcoming. However harassed behind the scenes – and that was understandable – he always seemed to have time for the next caller: absolutely top marks for courtesy! He was terrified of the bishop: he had been a student at the Valladolid College when Bishop Petit had been Vice-Rector, and he responded like a frightened schoolboy to him. I'm afraid this seemed to encourage the bishop to bully him; on one or two occasions he even humiliated him in front of others. We all liked Dolph and felt sorry for him.

My job as secretary gave me huge insights into the practice and the possibilities of diocesan work, as I observed how individually the parishes we visited were run. It also introduced me to many interesting people, as we stayed with bishops and others. Once we got lost on the way to stay with Archbishop Masterson in Birmingham, getting a bit muddled in Dudley. At dinner Bishop Petit complained about the obscurity of our route. Masterson said, 'Don't you know the sixth commandment: "Thou shalt not come into Dudley".' The following morning I slipped out quietly at an early hour to go to the Birmingham Oratory, so that I could say Mass in Newman's study. 'Where were you this morning?' the bishop asked me later. 'Such piety!' he said, when I told him.

In the diocese I met some interesting and very committed priests. A fair number of them, living almost always on their own, but some with a long-term housekeeper – a genre of women who have almost faded into oblivion these days – had developed many traits of eccentric bachelors. It occurred to me that if ever any of these decided they wanted to marry – and that would mean setting aside their ministry – they would be dreadfully difficult to live with. After years of independence, making up their own minds about when, where and what to eat, what time to go to bed or get up – within the constraints of a parish timetable fixed by themselves – the sharing of decisions and the demand for less selfishness would not come easily. God help their partners!

It also became clear that each parish priest was king, nay pope, in his own domain. He took note of as little or as much of Canon Law, liturgical rules and general ecclesiastical discipline as he chose. Nothing was done to rock the boat or to draw in the attention of bishop or fellow-priest. All the same, by that special communications structure we called 'clerical bush-telegraph', there wasn't much that other priests or even the bishop did not know about all the priests. For the most part you didn't let that mean trying to enforce uniformity or even ortho-praxis. There was little or no team-spirit even within deaneries; there was little attempt to have broad lines of diocesan or deanery policy even over important pastoral methods. We never even tried to share 'good practice'. The whole notion of a single unit of leadership through the bishop and his assistant priests was absent. Priests treasured their independence of action and this could be valuable, but there was an unwritten basis of custom, sometimes mistakenly called 'Catholic tradition' which priests conformed to. A priest could be inefficient, lazy and uninspiring without interference so long as he was not innovative without authorisation. I personally never asked permission for things when I reached the status of parish priest; but I was always ready to obey a negative command if the bishop were to intervene with a 'Stop that'. I once heard a Benedictine priest in Liverpool – Dom Ogilvy Forbes, I think it was – saying that he had asked his archbishop (John Heenan at that time) for a particular permission. Heenan said: 'Certainly, Father, but why do you ask? Take my advice and do what I used to do as a parish priest – carry on until the bishop says No.'

Alongside being the bishop's secretary he had graciously given me the chance of developing Ruabon and district – five miles from Wrexham – towards being a distinct parish. He knew that such work was more nearly what I wanted to be doing. It wasn't easy to fit it all in, and I began my history of overwork. A lot of good things were done, but I am not particularly proud of my intemperance at doing them. The first thing I wanted to do was to establish a presence in the district as a focus for a growing community. The Catholics were unevenly spread across four main villages and a number of hamlets. The large village (thirteen thousand people) of Rhosllanerchrugog ('the Rhos' as we usually called it) was a mainly Welsh-speaking place, a bastion of nonconformity – especially Welsh Presbyterians and Scots Baptists. There were seven or eight resident ministers, and one Anglican priest catering for the religious needs of the villagers among whom there were only thirty-six Catholics. I say 'for the religious needs' because the chapels were already losing their influence as a cultural focus. The choirs, bible study and other classes, the music and drama, so often centred on the chapel in the past, had more attractive rivals in the growing film, TV and other entertainment markets of Wrexham and Chester. Johnstown, an outreach of the Rhos as a miners' village, had more Catholics as its housing estates grew. Ruabon itself only had a moderate number, but had been chosen some years earlier as a 'Mass centre' when there was a nearby Polish camp on the Wynnstay estate. Ruabon was also a railway junction for the Llangollen valley – it is so no longer, of course. The Wrexham cathedral priests – four of them in those days – took it in turns to travel the five miles to say Sunday Mass in the Village Room, hired for five shillings each week. The room was used otherwise for village jumble sales and as a changing room for visiting football teams.

So when the bishop said, 'You look after these people; they'll be wanting their own church and parish soon,' it wasn't as though we had great resources for buying or building a new church. To be precise the parishioners had set aside £23 from one jumble sale, and the diocese had bought a piece of land on the main housing estate as a future site. We didn't use that in the end, and I heard that the Free Church Federal Council had expressed its alarm at the threat of our arrival. How then to start on community-building? A helpful factor was the hiring of a coach to bring the people from the other villages to Sunday Mass. That cost us thirty shillings a week , which was a large chunk of the sixty or seventy shillings coming in the collection at Mass; but a good party spirit developed as the people travelled together. Often I was away for two or three days in the week, driving the bishop around. On my return I would sometimes borrow the Dormobile, after school hours, drive to Johnstown and walk a circular route through the main housing estate; then to Penycae and Ruabon for two similar routes. Chatting to people over the garden fence, and smiling amiably to anyone I passed, I really do think it was a positive process for getting to know the people and the district. I started to call on the Catholic households and to build up a proper register of names and addresses. We were soon able to see that our total numbers were around 300 – and that was a medium-sized figure for a parish in Menevia.

Even before we had found an adaptable building for a church, or had collected any substantial sums of money, I felt we needed a centre in the heart of the Rhos. I couldn't expect everyone to travel to Ruabon, except on Sunday, for meetings or groups; so we hired a shop. I gathered books together – mostly religious ones – and set up a little lending-library; and we sold rosaries, medals, etc. Parishioners staffed the shop for about four or five hours each weekday. It provided a dropping-in place for tea or coffee, and the upstairs room was used for meetings or an occasional Mass. One young girl, who later joined one of our Young Christian Worker groups, said that until our shop (entitled Llyfrfa Richard Gwyn) was set up, she'd never known anything about Catholics. It was a useful project from many points of view; it began to accustom people to working together. Here too, I began to see some of those who were expressing interest in our faith; at one point I had ten people 'under instruction'.

The strain of doing so many things, most of which I frankly enjoyed, began to take its toll at the end of three years as bishop's secretary. By the time I had found Bryn Hall, a kind of minor manor-house in Ruabon which the owner was willing to sell for £3,500, I could see that the work of its adaptation as a church and presbytery, beginning with voluntary labour, would exhaust me. I asked for time to go on a private retreat to Mount St Bernard Cistercian Abbey near Leicester. There I consulted the abbot. 'What am I to do? I'm nearly exhausted.' 'Does the bishop realise?' he sensibly asked. 'No.' 'Then you must tell him.' Good sound advice, which accorded with my general belief about openness. 'But what if,' I thought to myself, 'he were to let me go as fulltime parish priest in Ruabon? Who would replace me?' So, in the light of my knowledge of the diocesan priests, I thought of three or four moves that would be dependent on a secretarial replacement – just in case the bishop asked me. I drove back to Bishop's House and arrived as he was about to have some tea in his study. 'Can I have a word with you?' I started. 'Wait a bit,' he said, 'while you've been away, I've been thinking. I've decided you can go as parish priest to Ruabon.' This was more than I had expected, because I had never been a curate anywhere, and had still only been ordained three and a half years. 'And how are you going to manage for a secretary?' I asked; and he proceeded to list the first three moves I had worked out for myself. Needless to say I did not tell him this.

The man who came as bishop's secretary was a priest ordained in the same year as myself, but in Limerick. James Hannigan was till then one of the two curates in Llandudno. So he came to Bishop's House and never left. He served Bishop Petit, Bishop Fox, and Bishop Ward before becoming Bishop of Menevia himself. He presided over the division of the diocese, and became Bishop of Wrexham covering the northern counties of Gwynedd, Clwyd and the northern half of Powys. To these he gave strong administrative oversight – I believe he had been a civil servant before ordination; and he proved a very good friend to me personally.

Once I was living (after Christmas 1957) in the usable part of Bryn Hall as 'priest in charge' it was possible to set about some of the demolition work on an old coachhouse and barn we were to de-roof and largely pull down, to make way for a new church. We worked, the men volunteers and I, many evening and Saturday hours. I have no skills, so I mostly wheel-barrowed the rubble away from the building – all 500 tons of it.

Demolition work has a special attraction for young people, and I soon had several regular helpers from the village. One of them was a fourteen-year-old, 'Wal', who palled up with me and one of my young parishioners, John. It was a good way to get to know people, shovelling and wheeling together with frequent tea-breaks. This also helped to root me in the local community. North Walians are not so obviously welcoming as those in the south. Even after ten years in the village I might be asked, 'Well, how do you like it in Ruabon?' as though I hardly yet belonged. Working with a range of people in this informal way also made us Catholics less threatening. We were in some quarters regarded as an alien religion. Within a few years the atmosphere had changed. One or two of the younger people were even known to go to Sunday school at a nearby chapel and then come across to us for Benediction. As we were busy with our manual labour one day, Wal said to me, 'I told my uncle that I thought I might like to become a Catholic.' 'Really, Wal,' I said, 'And what did he say?' He said, 'You – a Catholic? You're not good enough to be a b… heathen.' Poor Wal. He remained a good friend always and graduated into the Youth Club when he was older.

When the builders began the work of construction, after we had taken nearly eighteen months to cover the demolition work, they only took six months to build the new church in the shell of the old buildings. Quite often when they had finished their day's work, a few of us would swoop in and tidy up the site. This made their task readier and fresher the next day. If we had helped them, albeit unpaid, on the job, we should have run into trade union difficulties – or so I was led to believe.

On the Feast of Corpus Christi 1959, we were ready for the solemn blessing of the new church, dedicated to St Michael and All Angels. Up to a few hours before the bishop arrived, some cleaning work was still in progress. I couldn't find the official key which was to be presented by the builder to the architect, and then to the bishop for the solemn unlocking. I reckoned we might just have to ask the builder to push the architect into the bishop whose weight would get the door open – but all came to hand at the last moment. Not only did we have a fine procession of servers and ministers, and a little schola of musicians (led by my friend Roger who came for the occasion), but a great gathering of parishioners, two from my home parish in Cardiff, and two representatives from the Irish Glass Bottle Company, who had helped us raise funds for the building. The ordained deacon for the occasion was Brian Jones, a Ruabon villager who was soon to complete his seminary studies abroad, and three days after the opening, was ordained priest in the new church.

We were off to an auspicious start, because we didn't owe anyone a penny for the cost of the building or furnishings. The Guild of Our Lady of Ransom had helped us, and somehow or other – I still cannot think how – we were able to pay the builder at each stage of the work, right until the end. His last certificate was for about £300, and I had to say, 'Could you wait for just a few months for this last payment?'; and sure enough, the money was there for that too. The ordinary income of the parish was still only about £6.50 (which in old money in 1959 must have been worth ten times that today) out of which all church, altar and house maintenance expenses had to be paid. There wasn't enough money for the priest's personal allowance of £40 per annum for another three years; nor anything towards car or travel expenses. My father had helped me buy my first second-hand car (which had belonged to the parents of Wrexham's David Lord, awarded the VC posthumously). I called the car Tipyn Bach (Little bit), and it got me around for several years, though I used my bicycle whenever I could. My next banger was called Brahms, and this also had some idiosyncracies. One afternoon it couldn't manage the modest hill up to Penycae until I turned it round and went up in reverse. On another occasion it sent out smoke from the dashboard; but that stopped when I brushed a swift hand across an assemblage of wires; it didn't happen again. Once again my father sent me a little allowance of £2 per week – which was riches indeed; and I used up all the savings in my bank account to cope with a holiday or two in the first years in Ruabon. I learned how to live very economically, and people often brought foodstuffs to the church porch on Sundays. There was one three-week period when they only brought eggs; but you can do a lot of different things with eggs; so I managed.

So far from finding any real hostility in my immediate neighbours, several times as I arrived home in the evening from parish visiting, the doorbell rang and the Roberts family, living opposite, handed me in some fish and chips. I began to realise that the publicised hostility to the church was a bit of a myth. If you expected it, thus affecting your own approach, you might get it. Personally I found everyone most welcoming. True, the Anglican Vicar was grievously upset when one of his former church-wardens, and his wife, decided to take a course of instruction with me and joined our community. He actually preached one Sunday against 'Roman errors'; but I got on fine with him and teased him when he became an archdeacon: 'Are you going to wear gaiters now; or perhaps preach longer sermons?' And I remember his glowing tribute to the character of Pope John XXIII.

So; a new job, a new church and place to live and a community to foster. I was already doing more than was sensible as a workload; but I was as happy as a sandboy.

Part Two

Developing a Style
1958–1964

Chapter Three: Amid the Varieties of Parish Pastoring

Tracing my efforts to build up a new parish community, I found that my methods did not commend themselves sometimes to my neighbouring priests, as I tried to take the people into fullest confidence in a collaborative ministry. Using the methods of the Young Christian Workers, establishing a diocesan youth centre, the clientele widened to mostly unchurched young adults.

Chapter Four: In the Gaps Between the Rubrics

Seeing that a sense of liturgical worship would be the focal point for a Catholic community, we built the new church with the altar 'facing the people', and tried to be imaginative with our celebrations – including house Masses.

Alarmed by Pope John XXIII's document Veterum Sapientiae, which looked as though it would pre-empt the coming Vatican Council from moving towards vernacular liturgy, I started on a 'round robin' letter, which was soon to become a habit with controversial items.

'Saved? Is that the same as respectable?'

[Cartoon: Angelo Edwards]

CHAPTER THREE

Amid the Varieties of Parish Pastoring: Collaborating within and without

The greatest objection brought against Christianity in our time and the real source of the distrust which insulated entire blocks of humanity from the influence of the Church has nothing to do with historical or theological difficulties. It is the suspicion that our religion makes its followers inhuman. *(Teilhard de Chardin)*

I was thirty-five when the new church in Ruabon was opened and blessed by Bishop Petit in May 1959, and I was inducted as the first parish priest, having done the job as a part-time activity for more than four years. Of course I had only been a Catholic for eight years when I started working in the district, and I was extraordinarily ignorant of what constituted 'parish work'. Just as for a bishop in his role, so there is no handbook on how to be a parish priest – nothing at least to compare with the contemporary American Fr Bausch's *Total Parish Manual*, which is full of sound and innovative ideas. On the whole, I rather think the model was to provide a 'religious service station'. The central idea was to find a good place for Sunday Mass, and where baptism and the other sacraments could be celebrated with dignity. I shall always be glad that we didn't start with our own building before we had a church. Discovering where people actually lived, gathering them in for organisational and practical tasks – especially when we started work on Bryn Hall, the house we bought – and the necessary efforts to raise money – all this helped to build a community. We were able early in 1958 to leave the Village Room and celebrate Mass in two rooms of the Hall which opened into each other. The kitchen door was also left open so that, together with half a dozen who sat on the staircase in the hallway, we could pack 130 people in. In 1956, while still using the Village Room, I had turned the table round so that the priest faced the people.

This might have been deemed revolutionary at that time; but I explained to the people why we would do this, and I specifically asked them to make no comment or judgement for at least a month. People need time to take on changes. When they did so, there were only expressions of gratitude. So in the new temporary house-church, it became even more 'familiar'; there were people all around me. Little children at my back could tug, and sometimes did so, at my alb during the celebration while most people were in front of me. I gave a lot of attention to preparing the six to eight minutes' homily I gave. It had to be brief and homely; there was no room for pomposity or high-flown words; it was a good introduction to preaching. I grew to love this modest-sized congregation, which fostered a sense of family. I've no idea how I would have managed with a large church in a city parish. I gave a lot of time to encouraging as whole-hearted participation in the liturgy as was allowed. The first developments were to come soon from the Vatican Council, and the construction of the new church with the altar facing the people, with a smaller and lower altar on the nave side with the Blessed Sacrament, was set to build on this. We really made something exciting of the Holy Week liturgies. A year or two later the bishop re-constructed the Wrexham cathedral sanctuary; but ours had been the first in the diocese. When several other items in parish life showed similar 'advanced' tendencies in the social or ecumenical field, it apparently upset some of my neighbouring priests. On one occasion I had a visit from two of them to tell me I was wrecking the church in North Wales. 'Dash it, you've only been a priest a few years, and a Catholic about a dozen.' I was naturally hurt by this; but I was quite confident we were close to the developing mind of the church. It did not incline me to slow down in any way.

It happened that I had already trailed my coat before leaving the role of bishop's secretary. In October 1958 Bishop Petit inaugurated an annual Diocesan Clergy Conference, held at Pantasaph Friary over three days. This was an idea which proved of enormous benefit to the priests in parish work across our scattered diocese – which, as I have explained, covered the whole of Wales except Glamorgan and Monmouth. We were able to spend time together over the meals and in the evenings, apart from our discussion exchanges in the daytime sessions following an important keynote address. It shows something of the vision that Bishop Petit had that he chose as the first theme, 'The Use of Organised

Laity in the Work of Conversion'. It shows something of my naïveté that I agreed to his request to give one of the main papers.

In my opening paragraphs I quickly referred to my inexperience as a four-year priest, but I entered a plea for fresh voices to be heard, especially if they were expressing ideas already outlined by the current Pope. I was glad to quote him when he said:

'It would be a misunderstanding of the true nature of the Church and her social character to distinguish in her a purely active element, the ecclesiastical authorities, and on the other hand a purely passive element, the laity. All the members of the Church are called to collaborate in the building and perfecting of the mystical Body of Christ. All are free persons and therefore must be active … To determine the sphere of action for each it is enough that all should have a sufficient spirit of faith, of disinterestedness, or reciprocal esteem and confidence. Respect for the priest has always been one of the most characteristic features of the Christian community. On the other hand even the lay man has his rights and the priest for his part must recognise them.'

One now cringes slightly at that word 'even' the lay man, and the firmly male identity of those who are lay. It is also true that Pius XII was thinking mainly of what he called *consecratio mundi* (consecration of the world) as the sphere of laity, which he seemed to believe was easily discerned as distinct from the sphere of the clergy. He had no doubts about who managed the church. I made one little effort to push this a bit further.

'Can we not see to it that the laity in our parishes are taken into the fullest confidence about parish matters? It is not possible or desirable to have long pulpit sessions to explain the administration or the missionary policy of the parish. So it always seems to me to be essential to have from time to time something of the nature of a "parish meeting". It is an opportunity for the laity to make suggestions, to ask questions and even to proffer criticisms. Of course it may be necessary to keep some things for the pious ears of clergy alone; but I am certain we can trust our people more. No-one suggests that we hand over the running of our parishes to a committee of lay people, but skilful priests have managed parish committees for many administrative details with success. Surely we should, however, consult them more. Parish funds, for instance, are admittedly in our charge, but the people should have some voice, or rather some understanding of the way in which the money is spent. Those priests who decline to give

their people the chance of raising their voices in criticism or enquiry can rest assured that the criticisms and enquiries will still be
made behind their backs, possibly with unfortunate innuendoes.
It makes for a lack of confidence, and thus of full co-operation in
every aspect of parish life, when there is no organ for the expression of public opinion. One considers the ordination ceremony of
a priest, and the care with which the bishop is obliged to consult
the people before proceeding to ordain. "People will render obedience more readily," he tells the congregation, "to the ordained if
they have consented to his ordination".'

All this seems so condescending now; and I am not sure
whether the notion of the people being obedient to their priests is
anything like the model we approved of even in those days; but
the point about consultation is still valid, and widely ignored. A
year after that event, when writing to the bishop from my new
parish, I remarked to him that presenting that paper to the clergy
had been an unfortunate watershed. Many priests came up to me
and thanked me, saying 'Why hasn't all this been said before?' My
reply was, 'It has; many times.' For, in my innocence, I thought
everyone would at least know something about the re-thinking of
church life going on in Europe and elsewhere. Many of the priests
who made no comment were probably grievously offended.
Recommendation for change is so often taken as condemnation of
earlier thinking and practice. Part of their annoyance was, I think,
associated with rumours that there were dangerous innovations
taking place in Ruabon. From the start I wanted a consultative
parish. As well as taking care to explain the reasons for liturgical
and other changes, I wanted a wider sharing in decision-making.

In 1960, we made several attempts in Ruabon at whole-parish
meetings: they were lively but not a roaring success. So we tried a
more selective system, asking for two representatives from any
existing organisation, plus two people elected by vote. Our
Catholic organisations were few and only lightly supported,
sometimes falling into disuse. So we divided the parish into four
geographical areas, and we had an annual election for two (later
three) representatives from each area. To prevent this from becoming an 'in group', I encouraged any parishioner who had a
special concern to raise, to attend – even though the whole parish
was invited to submit items for the agenda; and they all had a report on the decisions and findings of the meetings. The system
was called 'must and may': the elected representatives must attend;

any parishioner may attend. I regarded my work as parish priest to be accountable first to the parish council, while remaining canonically answerable to the bishop of the diocese. To mark my passionate wish to be open, I gave an account of every penny received and spent – this, I reckoned, was the most convincing proof of openness. The whole parish had copies of the annual statement, and anyone could call it into question.

Within a few years I had several other priests staying with me in the large Bryn Hall; sometimes as curate, or on temporary placement. One of them was present when the accounts were being examined by the council. 'You seem to have spent an awful lot on postage,' said one lady. It infuriated my colleague – that anyone should offer an implied criticism. 'And there'll be a lot more spent on it when I get going,' he said. It was some years before I discovered that a Finance Committee is a requirement of Canon Law; for some priests it is used more as a fund-raising team, without any real involvement, or as assistants with bookkeeping or collection-counting. Ours was rolled into one with the parish council.

I really wanted the council to help plan, and have oversight of, the whole work of the parish. Taking on this responsibility did not come easily to some parishioners who had inherited a totally different model of priest/parishioner relationships. Could they criticise me personally? One day a council member, whose co-operation was constant and unstinting in every way, said he wanted to say something a bit harsh. 'Father; you always seem to be in a hurry. We know you have a lot to do apart from the parish work, but you do sometimes give the impression that you haven't enough time for people.' It was an accurate picture of my home visiting. I was rather proud of my record of home visits. I had started at the rate of one visit to each Catholic household every four to six weeks, across the six villages that made up the parish. But to ensure this, I would make a daily list of six, seven or eight visits, and then charge around to complete the schedule. If anyone really had a problem to discuss, I knew how to shut off steam and really listen; but people clearly did not feel able to indicate quickly enough that they had a problem. It wasn't only that I was impatient (though I am) but that I think quickly myself and seemed to expect others to do so also. I often declined to sit down when I called, to show I hadn't all day to spend and that of course was sufficient to prevent anyone raising any issue that would take time. The criticism was fair, and important too. Did I mind it being made ? Well, I didn't exactly enjoy it in the presence of others; but afterwards I rejoiced that someone felt safe enough to make it. I continue to work at speed, to get through a quantity of things which would defeat many colleagues whose metabolic rate is obviously slower than mine; but I hope I have learned to notice other people's need for time and space. I suppose I shall always be battling with an inner impatience, and the self-regarding tendency to want to tick off a list of tasks completed. It is valuable (or do I mean in-valuable?) to have people who will with honesty remind me occasionally of my social faults; I certainly need that help with my examination of conscience. And what is the real meaning of all my busyness? I remember one shrewd friend, a very competent professional counsellor, saying to me: 'With all that is going on in your busy life, what are you running away from?' Now and again I think I have come up with some answers.

At parish council meetings we never resorted to a vote: that was a vestige of my Quaker-influenced background. The idea was to try to reach a genuine consensus. I was sometimes unable to achieve a unanimous reaction to my ideas. For instance, I was adamant about not having a football pool or Bingo to raise money for ordinary parish expenses. It seemed odd to some parishioners that I should object to this, when it was standard practice in many Catholic parishes, including our immediate neighbours. I felt (and continue to feel today) that even this form of light gambling is an unsuitable way for the church to raise money for its own needs. It wasn't just that there was this puritanical streak in me – no drinking, no smoking, no gambling – but in a largely nonconformist area, I didn't wish to give even this much scandal, since we were a newly arriving community.

I asked those members who disagreed with me – about four of them – to continue to raise it at meetings, so long as it grieved them; and when they asked me to explain more fully to the whole parish why I took this stand, I prepared a little typed statement which I read out one Sunday at Mass in October 1959. In this I was careful to say that I didn't believe Bingo or Pools were morally wrong in themselves, but that I felt they were unfitting ways of finding the money necessary for the work of the church. If we couldn't give, we shouldn't have. Bingo and Pools concealed our responsibility of shouldering the financial implications of the work of the parish. Too many people might feel that once they had bought a pools ticket they had contributed adequately to the parish. Apart from that, such activities needed time and energy to administer properly, and these commodities were necessary for other more urgent and apostolic work.

Fortunately the statement was typed out and in the files; for only a few days later I received a letter from the bishop that he had heard 'you have come out against Pools from the pulpit.' He continued:

'How true this is I do not know, but I hope you will not let your convictions in this matter spoil other work, as it can so easily do if you turn your brethren against you. You see, any pronouncement of this sort is by implication for them a condemnation, and it hurts; and so they almost automatically oppose any work which you may be trying to do along youth lines like the YCW. I need the help of all the clergy if the ideas I have on the need for Youth Leadership training are to be successful; and this to me is a most important work, as it is to you. But knowing them like I do, I know I have to go quietly to secure their full co-operation and not merely their obedience. Since Bryn Hall, Ruabon, is to be the centre for trainee leaders for the YCW principally, very much will be centred around you personally, so however strongly you feel about such money-raising efforts like Pools in a nonconformist world, having said your say, say no more.'

I thanked him for his note of warning, but assured him on the basis of the actual text of my statement that I had been careful to say that I was not declaring Pools or Bingo to be against the law of God or the church, but just unsuitable in our circumstances. Then I continued:

'I realise with regret that I may upset neighbouring clergy, and I know how important it is to work in unison. But if one took note of every criticism, little progress would ever be made in anything. To hear (as I have heard it said, by no means in reference to Ruabon necessarily) that it is "protestant" to consult the laity, or to wear a long cotta without lace; "anglican" to sing a good hymn tune even when it is in the Westminster Hymnal; "nonconformist" to decline to have Tombola; "nationalist" to say even occasional prayers in Welsh, and "uncatholic" to say Mass facing the people …To hear these remarks is no encouragement to listen to criticism. Incidentally the clergy are invariably kind to me, but I have been made aware recently of a certain undercurrent of feeling. You have always given me more encouragement and support than I deserve, and I sense the impression that I am too prominent in diocesan affairs for a junior priest.'

I then asked to be withdrawn from two diocesan tasks he had given me. He replied by saying that he had no intention of giving anyone the impression that he disowned me, and he went on to share his own difficulties with his reputation outside the diocese for moving the cathedral altar to the centre of the sanctuary. I am fairly sure that it was a visitor to the parish Mass from elsewhere who must have falsely or inaccurately complained about what he had heard. It was a tiny indication of how one could be watched if one dared to be even slightly different, from whatever motive

The last of the objectors to my ruling on Bingo and Pools was a wonderful ex-Liverpool lady. With great humour and good temper she tried to stop me being so puritanical. Then one day she was arriving in Wrexham by bus. When it reached the bus-stop by our cathedral, the conductor shouted 'Bingo stop'. She came to me soon after. 'You're right,' she said, 'that's how they think of us Catholics.' Objection not so much over-ruled as overcome!

What I have been referring to, if not precisely describing, is the sense in which I disliked the clergy/lay distinction, with the shades of clerical domination that were behind it. I felt that my parishioners were my family; that it really was 'our' parish. Formal 'ministerial' involvement was not officially recognised yet, but what I had my eye on in the 1960s was what we now call 'collaborative ministry'. It is still an uphill struggle to establish it in many places. Of course priests know the value of having people help them in their priestly work – eucharistic ministers taking communion to the sick, catechists teaching the children, etc.; but the mindset of priests is still very often one of delegating tasks, rather than sharing responsibility. I think it was Bishop Fox who helpfully made the distinction between decision making, where there should be wide consultation, and decision taking at the end of the process, which may have to be undertaken by the priest alone. Only the priest had to answer to the bishop, whose assistant he is meant to be for the pastoral care of the parish. But especially in these days, when large numbers of the parishioners are certainly as educated as the priest, it is a nonsense to leave all the discernment on pastoral policies and methods to someone who has simply been ordained priest.

At the end of my time in Ruabon in 1969, that is after fifteen years of work there in increasing stages, I tried to sum up, at my farewell party, what had been happening.

'If ever you've been invited to a meal with me in Bryn Hall,
you will remember that it was best just to eat it, and only ask afterwards what it is you have had. My work as parish priest is now
over here; and perhaps I should try to tell you what I think we've
been doing in these years.' I then outlined the three stages we had
gone through. The first, to try to organise and build a community
of Catholics in the new parish area. Then to try to be more aware
of our fellow Christians in the other churches, and to work in
warm co-operation wherever we could. Thirdly, we were trying
to remember that the church exists for the world, and that we
should register our presence positively in the local community.

Work with young people
In particular I believed that our contact with local young people,
including my rather specialised work with those in trouble with
the law, was an important contribution. Even before we had completed the work of demolition on that part of the property which
was to be re-shaped to become the new church, we had already
started work with young people. It was one of the providential elements in my training that in 1949, before going to Rome, I had
somehow come across literature on the Young Christian Workers.
I was given this by a young enthusiast in my Cardiff parish, Peter
Rees, who disappeared from my sight soon afterwards. I wish I
could tell him how grateful I still am for this. This was a movement started in Belgium by Joseph Cardijn, a priest who had
sensed the cultural divide that arose as he left home and returned
as a seminary-trained priest. He realised that the best principle for
true evangelisation was from like to like; and also that it was necessary for everyone, young people especially, to see the relevance
of the gospel to the details of ordinary life – at home, at work, at
school, in leisure. I discovered that there was a five or seven day
residential opportunity for seminarians at Newcastle upon Tyne
to learn about YCW and its methods of apostolate. They let me in,
even though I hadn't actually started in a seminary. It was my
first contact with some of the finest priests I have ever known.
Edward Mitchinson and Eugene Hopkins were the YCW national
chaplains, and we had talks also from Vincent Whelan of Salford
Diocese, whose gifted insights were a real treasure trove. That
valuable experience remained with me through my seminary
years, and gave me the confidence to approach two groups of
young parishioners to start the YCW and later a pre-YCW group.

We met weekly for our Gospel Enquiry and Social Enquiry, led in turn by the members, after they had had a one-to-one preparatory session with me. We went to rallies in Liverpool and elsewhere, and to a residential week in the summer; and we began to draw in quite a number of young people whom we had contacted locally, some of whom had been part of the gang working on demolition on the church site. We decided to start a Sunday evening youth club, since there was so little going on in the district at weekends. It was to be a purely social event, with records (45s), some dancing, dart-playing and refreshments. We named it after an early YCW hero, the Callo Club. For myself it was tiring at the end of Sunday's work, to have a crowd – 30, 40, maybe 50 young people aged 16–20 – filling the downstairs rooms and kitchen, and a games room upstairs. They were noisy, rough and ready, but I grew very attached to them. It was those (by far the majority) who were not Catholics who seemed to like to call me 'Father'. I began to learn a lot about the inadequacies for many of them in their experience of family and working life. Occasionally they went overboard and abused the openness of the house. On one occasion a couple of them got out onto the roof and began to strip away bits of loose lead. I caught them at it. As I began to berate one of them – a very likeable though cheeky eighteen year old – he said, 'Hit me, hit me; but don't tell me off like that.' He was prepared for physical punishment which I would not provide, but really couldn't stand my being personally angry with him; it hurt him too much. That was a valuable lesson for me in personal relationships, and the exercise of discipline. The result of all this was that, when we later had a proper church building, we got to work on the old stable outbuildings, which were about 300 years old, and made an unusual setting for a regular club. This part of the village was 'Brynfields', so we decided to call it Brynfields Club, which met not only on Sunday night, but then on Tuesdays and Thursdays as well. Membership rose to over 100, of whom there were never more than about 8 Catholics. It attracted by personal contact young people from all the surrounding villages, and became a notable local feature. We made no attempt at proselytism; it did not turn people into church-goers. Indeed the majority had no church or chapel connections at all, but informally there was a growing maturity of relationship between the rebellious young people of the 60s and a range of adults, drawing in some wonderful parishioners and others to help in the canteen and kitchen, and to lead special activities. A growing number of regular attenders were lads – the girls were rarely in this category – who were in trouble with the law. I found myself in the magistrate's court with them many times. We had a system in the club of introducing new members as 'probationer' members for one month, until we noticed that it was not a good term to use – so many of them were 'on probation' already! Indeed my growing contact with the Probation Service led to them recommending some young people to join our club. On more than one occasion I was told that Lord Maelor, chairman of the magistrates, would ask a young defendant if he belonged to the club, with a suggestion about joining. I began to take very seriously the role of youth leader, and the potential of youth club work and read a good deal to improve my understanding. I attended a number of Youth Service training sessions. I established an excellent management team of adults from the village with regular meetings, and the club members had their own policy-making committee. I found that the members could be more censorious of bad behaviour than I was prepared to be – another interesting lesson. Some of those adults who lent a hand were professional people who themselves, after perhaps an initial shock at the rough language often used, learned a lot about relating to young people. The parish by now had enough income, though it was still small, for us to employ for a few hours each week, someone to come and clean the youth premises and the publicly used parts of Bryn Hall itself. Mrs Ethel Martin was a gem. She came faithfully for over ten years, and the great thing was that, while her task was officially 'domestic', she met up with so many of the youth club members that she became a great ally in helping them. Occasionally I would arrive back from some parish task to hear that she hadn't had time to do much cleaning because someone had been along very depressed or worried, and she had spent the time listening to him. This was excellent, because it was just this adult/youth interplay that I believed was so healthy and important in local life. There grew up a wide bond of affection between young people, their families and the adults they came into contact with in the club. It was a pleasure to walk round the housing estates and hear people over the fence saying, 'My George goes to your club – he likes it.' Although the club was officially called 'Brynfields', most of the members called it 'Father's'. I recall being shouted at across the road one day by one of the members: 'Hey Father, is there "Father's" tonight, Father'?

In course of time I developed my own 'philosophy' of youth club work, as well as improving my psycho-social understanding of adolescence. Since childhood I had a great interest in 'education' in its widest sense – not just schooling. My notebook shows me that in the thirtes and forties I had been reading books by Richard Livingstone, Cyril Norwood, Percy Lunn, Richard Nettleship, H. C. Dent and others. Now I was picking up strong leads from James Halloran, Richard Hoggart, Brian Wicker. I learned a huge amount about young people both theoretically and practically, though I never discovered just how explicitly to incorporate a religious vision. It seemed to me that many of those I spent time with – mostly 16–25 year olds (no one younger was eligible for membership) had a need to explore their humanity first, and to experience a mature and reliable relationship with some adults who were totally non-judgemental, very personal and tender, yet starting from a firm conviction of values. If such relationships could be established, then maybe they could be less defensive or aggressive in their relationships generally with adults, with the world at large, and maybe even with God.

When the Youth Service Report came out from the committee chaired by Lady Albemarle, I was full of admiration for its wisdom. The following extracts will illustrate this:

> One thing is sure: in the next few years young people will be entering employment in conditions of change and fluidity which will add to the strains of adolescence and the problems of adjustment to the adult world.
>
> 'We are particularly conscious of the lack of opportunity which ... industry in general provides for any working girls and for many boys to have continued educational experience or to develop their personality at work. It is to young people such as these that society owes a special debt, since they leave the educational system earlier than many of their contemporaries.

The three point purposes of Youth Service were to be Association, Education and Challenge. The report gave strong pointers to ways of fulfilling them.

> We should like to see more responsibility for activities and programmes turned over to the young wherever this can be made possible, and real and actual charge of things within their compass (or just enough outside it to make them stretch their minds) given to them. We believe too that such groups

will evolve their own discipline which they will accept the more readily because it grows out of the needs of real situations.

Among my other wise sources was a Youth Review which (in October 1964) had a brilliant piece by Harry Webb:

But how to pitch it when we first start? How to remain at one with the youngsters, accepted as a mate of theirs, and yet not be childish or immature? How to be firm and yet friendly, loving but not sloppy, dignified but not ' on our dignity'? How to know when ragging is healthy and when it is wise to call a halt? I recall my first evening as a helper at a settlement boys' club in the centre of Birmingham. The lads were banging away on an old piano with a great crashing of discords on the battered ivories. Should I stop them and insist on the instrument being properly used? Or was the old piano there for the purpose of letting the lads let off steam? I asked the warden. 'Sometimes this crashing on the piano is a healthy noise,' she said, 'Allow it! Sometimes it is an unhealthy noise. When it is, stop it!' The advice, I must confess, made at that time no sense at all to me. But I know now what she meant. A youth leader somehow develops an extra sense.

The Albemarle Report was equally sound when it said: 'Youth work is peculiarly challenging precisely because it requires a tense day to day walking on a razor-edge between sympathy and surrender.'

We worked hard at it through the years – the Management Committee, the club members' committee, the assistant leaders and myself. By 1957 the annual Club Leader's report was seen and used as a model at Youth Leadership Training courses at Leicester College and the N. E. Wales Institute.

There were as many girls in the club as boys, and a fair amount of time was spent easing the pain of their romantic attachments and such like. Language was occasionally apt to be 'strong', but they made special efforts in my presence. I recall one good-hearted but rough-edged girl arguing in a corner with three of the lads, making a great shindy. I came up behind her and tapped her on her shoulder to attract her attention, and she spun round and shouted in my face 'F … off' and then suddenly realised I was not another lad trying to control her flow of words. She immediately winced and said, 'O God, Father, I didn't know it was you.' All I could do was double up with laughter with the others standing round in fits. 'Tell you what, Mo, just to show me that you really are sorry, will you have a ten-minute discussion with the lads to decide what, if anything, was wrong with what you just said to my face?' When I came back, they all agreed that bad language was often silly – 'why call a chair a f...ing chair, when it can't! But words could be unpleasant to other people, and usually were a sign of bad temper – that's all.' A reasonable conclusion?

Moral advice? Well in small groups they would often ask what behaviour could be tolerated – sexually, I mean. To the general question 'How far can you go ?' I offered a bit of sound advice to start with – which I think I picked up from Fr Whelan in YCW (or was it Lewis Carroll?) by saying. 'That depends where you want to get to.' Pointing a finger of scorn was stupid and unhelpful; moralising was no good either. So I used to say, 'Look, if you start having whole-hearted sex with a girl, what do you think you are really saying? "You mean everything to me, and I am totally safe in your love" – and unless you are engaged and on the way to marriage, that's not true, is it?' They could see more readily that they were acting a lie than they could estimate its wrongness in another sense. But I also found – at least as far as the lads were concerned, who talked more openly to me – that it wasn't really intercourse they wanted (and certainly not needed) so much as an intimacy with someone who could hold them like a child – though I didn't suggest that analogy to them. Lots of them were touch-hungry, even though they were big macho lads. They knew sharply enough what it was to be touched inappropriately, and yet they wanted to experience and express touch. They reckoned I was safe enough and did so by physical brawling from time to time. I learned a lot from this, which came in useful in my later work. The girls were always completely at ease with me. They seemed to trust my celibacy (though they wouldn't have put it like that), and were not in the least defensive. I wish we priests always deserved such trust. Attitudes to sexuality have become more brash since that time.

As the years went by, the YCW groups faded, but their influence remained. Two of the members, Douglas and Thelma, had actually been received into communion with the church. In 1957 there had been a national YCW pilgrimage to Rome. Bishop Petit was accompanying them. By this time the national YCW prayer had been put into metrical form (by me!) and set to the tune of Finlandia.

Lord Jesus Christ I offer thee this day
My work, my hopes, my pleasures, griefs and pain
Grant me the grace that I may with thee stay
In every instant by thy side remain
Grant me and all my friends the grace to give
Ourselves to others that thy truth may live

Make me to love thee now with all my heart
With all my creature-strength, with all my soul
Christ's love must flow through me to every part
Reaching from east to west, from pole to pole
Thy kingdom come beyond our church's domes
Into our factories, workshops, schools and homes

May those who run the risk of sin today
Hold to thy grace, and fall not from thy love
On labour's battlefields we'll fight and stay
All sons of God, then live with thee above.
Our role as Christian workers not denied,
May we by Jesus' heart be sanctified.

Not exactly Gerald Manley Hopkins, but it served well
enough when sung. (I should certainly substitute 'children' for
'all sons' in the last verse, if I dared publish it today.) As we assembled in London for the journey, we had a great Mass, all 1,200
of us, in Westminster Cathedral, where I exercised my penchant
for choral conducting – very amateur, but full of expressive gestures – to lead the singing of the assembly. In Rome itself, Bishop
Petit and I stood on the steps of the papal altar under Barberini's
baldachino, and repeated the performance. He laughed with me
at our audacity. The return journey on the special YCW train was
badly marred by a mild train crash in France at 2.00 am. Our particular carriage remained upright; but we were all de-trained into
a turnip field because there was another special train due to follow us, and the warning of the crash might not have reached
them. Our engine was lying on its side, and somehow I climbed
into the driver's cab to see if he was hurt. He had of course already
dismounted and had gone ahead with the alarm. We were eventually collected by another train, and after a few hours we were
shunted into a siding, because rumours had gone ahead that we
were going down like flies with Asian flu. True enough some people did pass out and were obviously very sick, and eventually we
insisted on being taken to the port. All this excitement rather put

into the shade the stories of happy experiences of a worldwide youth movement in Rome; and it took us all several weeks to get over it.

Bryn Hall and its complex of outbuildings, you will have gathered, was far too large a place to live in on my own, which was why it had facilitated the local youth work development. For several periods I had other priests either lodging with me or spending a period as assistants. These had included Fr Cyril Schwarz and his housekeeper, while they were building up a new church and presbytery in neighbouring Llangollen; and then Fr Breen who was a qualified teacher at work in St Joseph's School, Wrexham. Before that, while that school was still being built, the newly appointed head teacher, Martin Cleary, who came from my 'home' parish in Cardiff, often lodged from Monday to Friday while he was shaping up his new team of teachers.

On one of the YCW residential weeks, we were at Roscrea Abbey in Ireland, where I met Fr Joe Loran of Salford; he was a talented priest who was, I am told, not averse to taking a ventriloquist's doll into the pulpit to liven up catechetical teaching. One of his YCW parishioners was Joe Dickson, who, soon after our Roscrea meeting, joined the Marist brothers and lasted with them for a year or so. When he decided to leave them, he came to stay at Bryn Hall – a stay that lasted about three years. He still had a real leaning for some kind of religious community, so when we had drawn in David Muir, a Scot who had also left the Marists, and later again John, a forty year old who had been a Dominican brother, we shaped ourselves up as Third Order Dominicans, and said the Little Office together, and they were otherwise variously deployed as parish assistants. Chris McKean came to us for ten months as someone to build up the YCW. I simply cannot remember how we managed to finance ourselves, because there was absolutely nothing surplus in the parish income; I know we shared any personal money we had according to practical needs.

After a while we had developed more of the outbuildings, and were able to offer 35 residential places on bunk beds. This serviced a major annual YCW leaders' training week. This brought me into close contact with two more top quality priests, who by now were the national chaplains, Canon Arbuthnott and Fr John Foster. It was priests like these who gave me the wish to carry on in the priesthood imaginatively. Joe, Mrs Martin and I quickly learned how to cater for that number of people and I was glad to gain experience in larger-scale housekeeping. I also hosted occasional youth weekends from North Wales parishes, but, perhaps because of the rather flexible nature of our liturgies and the openness in discussions, some priests thought it unwise to send any of their parishioners along. I had by now become the Diocesan Youth Officer for the north of the diocese. This gave me the opportunity to link up with other diocesan officers and benefit from their knowledge and experience, and especially that of Jimmy James of the National Catholic Youth Association. The formal Chairperson was Lady Albemarle, already renowned for the Report named after her, so I knew there was going to be a visionary approach to policies.

By this time I was becoming an 'expert' on youth apparently – which was not quite how it felt to me as endless problems were thrown up. It was especially difficult to lay down some kind of time and space boundaries for myself, so I managed to arrange a 'flat' within the large house, which could be locked off, leaving the rest of the house for more communal use, including five bedrooms. The openness of the house surprised some people, and even alarmed some colleagues who had serious doubts about the menagerie of people who resided for short or long periods, or just seemed to make their way around the place without permission. I am absolutely certain that such unprotected sharing would be ruled out nowadays; quite rightly so.

What impact did all this make on the young people who came and went – more than 400 through Brynfields Club altogether? It certainly disposed many of them to look more kindly than they otherwise might have done on the Catholic Church. I have said that it didn't make them church-goers, though a few might turn up at the back for Christmas midnight Mass. I am sure they genuinely liked and respected the church-goers whom they met as helpers in the club, and a few became quite active in the YCW for a short period of its life. Several later asked me if I could officiate in our church for their weddings. I don't think I actually did so, and might have had difficulty with church requirements in those days. I would have no hesitation today. I have kept in touch with a number of the club members through the years. One visit I recall making, some twenty years after leaving the parish. The lad was very monosyllabic, but had a warm heart and pleasant smile. He had married another club member, and one of his children had borne a child at the age of fourteen. He and his wife had taken the baby on very bravely. As we sat in the lounge by the fire, he gruffly said, 'It's her you should talk to,' indicating the daughter, now sixteen. 'Hey girl,' he said, 'you've heard about God, haven't you? Well this (pointing to me) is the next best thing.' What I think he meant was that I was the nearest he had come to 'religion' in any meaningful sense. But 'next best thing to God' would be a trifle flattering on one's tombstone! Alas, he died a year or two later from cirrhosis, and I joined the Vicar for the funeral – another good friend of mine. So many of the former youth-clubbers poured through the lytchgate for the service and greeted me warmly that the Vicar said, 'I think you'd better take the lead in this service.'

I say that the church as such didn't make much impact on them, but they certainly made an impact on me. It was for them that the Good News was given us. How do you get past the superficial aspects of 'church' to the heart of it? Nonconformity – I say it with regret – had given them a negative image: no drinking, no swearing, no Sunday jollity. Anglicanism seemed – again, I mean no offence – to portray respectability. These boys and girls were out for some fun, and were certainly not 'respectable'. The way was open for something fundamentally different. I am sure our parish community conveyed acceptance, caring and even love. We became a point of reference, and with more commitment maybe I could have led them to a sense of God that really inspired. How I wish the development of the Taizé community had come earlier! What did St Paul write? (Colossians 3): 'Be tactful with those who are not Christians and be sure you make the best use of your time with them. Talk to them agreeably and with a flavour of wit, and try to fit your answers to the needs of each one.' As it was I took several small groups – but mostly of my own parishioners – to Italy or Spain on holiday, helping them to save up their money, learn a bit about the language, the money, etc. Otherwise many of them hardly went anywhere. We came back from Spain once, and I found two or three of them, about 19–20 years old, sitting on my doorstep. They had failed to save the necessary money, and they had spent their whole work break from the coal mines just mucking about locally. 'Come on; let's go out now for a ride.' I simply took them on to the panorama above Llangollen, a matter of five or six miles. We then romped about on the hillside in the bracken, chasing one another and so on. I don't suppose they had had such innocent and inexpensive fun since they were children – if then. There was a kind of apathy in their lives, and no sense of family enjoyment. One of the best events in club life was travelling to that spot on a late summer evening, climbing to the top of Dinas Bran to the ruined castle, charging around on a kind of hide-and-seek game, and then cooking sausages and eating strawberries. Maybe a bit late for childhood, but it was as though they had somehow missed out on it.

The relationship between time used for simple socialising in the club, and 'activities' was a delicate one. If one just had 'records and canteen', you'd hear the comment 'Boring! Nothing happens here.' So we'd put together a programme of small-scale events, optional for those present. Very few would actually take part, but it made them speak well of the club. When I issued a list of possible future events, asking them to tick the ones that interested them, the greatest number always ticked 'Courtship and marriage', so we put on a series of evenings when, for example, for about half an hour we asked three fairly recently married couples in the parish to sit in a circle and the club members would stand around, while we threw into the circle some leading questions which I had elicited from the club members in advance. 'Do you think a long or a short engagement is a good thing?' 'When did you have your first really serious quarrel?' With the help of the wonderful assistant club leaders, Laura McAulay, Gwen Hurst and Bruce Howell, they were good sessions because after 20–30 minutes the group broke up but stayed around informally to share some really good conversation. Another successful evening was when a nurse or health visitor showed a film of the birth of a baby. On another occasion a bank manager (a member of the management committee) and a Building Society official came to say something about home ownership and mortgages. If I had my time again, I would work more intensely on personal relationships, on parenting and domestic economy!

Was this religion? It is a matter of perspective and conjecture. There was a TV in the canteen room – I didn't have one myself. It was 'on' once during club time, and a documentary showed Pope Pius XII being carried into St Peter's, fully vested and mitred, on the *sedia gestatoria*. I heard some quite comic comments. This man and this scene had moved me deeply when I was a student in Rome, but it was a total irrelevance to these young people. What on earth had all this to do with the gospel? Maybe the course on courtship and marriage was more realistic and evangelical?

It is odd what bits of religious practice people will pick up without one knowing it. One night at 11.00 pm I was setting off in a hurry for Chester, fifteen miles away, where Joe, one of the former YCW lads, was arriving on leave from the Navy. Brian, a club member, stopped the car as I slowed down at the main road. 'Father, I want to talk to you'– he was slightly the worse for drink. 'I haven't time to stop now, Brian. Jump in and come with me to Chester.' As we arrived at the city we passed a hot-dog seller. 'I could do with one of those,' he said But it was already late, and we drove on. The train had already arrived, but no sign of Joe. Thinking he might have moved across the city in search of a bus, we drove off again, past the same hot-dog man. 'Come on, Father, let's get a hot-dog.' 'No, Brian I must find Joe first.' I realised at the same time that it was a Friday, and if he got a hot-dog, he'd surely bring me one whether I wanted one or not. Still, no Joe at the bus station either, so back through the city again. This time I did stop for Brian to get his hot-dog. Now if he brings me one, I pondered, what'll I do? He's not a Catholic and won't understand my refusal. Heck, it'll be midnight (and thus Saturday) in ten minutes time. Right, if he brings me one, I'll take it out of charity towards his feelings. Sure enough he came with a hot-dog for me; and as I took the first bite he said, 'Mind, I don't know what the hell you're eating this for. It's still Friday, you know.' Game and match!

One of the best ways of learning is having to teach, and I found myself called upon to speak to part-time youth leaders in training. In particular I was listed as a lecturer on two six-day residential courses in Aberystwyth for the Staffordshire Youth authority – a sizeable conference of about 100 mature students. There were some wonderful people there – lecturers and students from whom I gained a lot. Since there were several ordained ministers from different churches among those attending, we agreed that there should be optional worship each morning, led turn by turn. On the first morning an Anglican priest was there to lead a service of Holy Communion. I was intrigued to note that most of the Catholic participants on the course – about eight – were present as well as myself. When it came to the reception of the sacrament, I personally was ready to go forward, but thought it prudent, as we had not had the opportunity to discuss the matter, to note what the others did. None of them moved. So at breakfast I spoke to one woman who was a teacher in a Catholic secondary school. 'Margaret, why did you not receive Communion at the service this morning?' 'Oh heck,' she said, 'only because you didn't.' Now this is a matter which I shall explore later on, but this was the early 60s, and showed how willing some Catholics already were to move beyond the accepted discipline. Karl Rahner is quoted as saying: 'The official doctrine of the church may sometimes have to adjust itself to what actually goes on in the heads and hearts of church members.' Donald Nicholl, who quotes this (*Testing of Hearts* p. 92), adds, 'Because what the people of God actually believe is somewhat ahead of the official doctrine.'

This potted history of my involvement with young people – often 'disorganised youth' as I came to call those whom others would pejoratively label 'delinquents' – will help to explain both why and where I moved on after fifteen years involvement with Ruabon parish. Some people suggested I didn't have a parish with a Youth Club attached, but that I had a Youth Club with a parish attached. If I did become what the jargon calls 'a significant adult' in the lives of a fair number of young people, it was as a 'church man', and I can think of no other way in which our community became so widely known in the district. I accept that it leaves all sorts of questions unanswered; it may be that we simply didn't get round to shaping the best questions. What, for instance, was an adequate vision of the role of a parish priest? Was he meant to be a chaplain to the local Roman Catholics, providing them with access to the sacraments? Was he meant to be a teacher of the faith and a proselytiser among non-Catholics? Was he a leader/animator of a worshipping community of lay apostles? Should he spend so much time relating to young people without any obvious 'religious' purpose? Was the church only meant to serve the present or potential Christians, or care about the needs of everyone?

Some of these questions would have implied criticism of what I had been doing. I think there were perhaps some parishioners who were not impressed by the 'secular outreach', if that is what it was, but in general people gave it a benign blessing.

CHAPTER FOUR

In the Gaps Between the Rubrics:
The style and language of worship

My own enthusiasm for ecumenical development did not always command universal support. My deep interest in encouraging a better understanding of the liturgy, and a more active participation of the congregation did help, I think, in showing my commitment to the central feature of Catholic life – a lively celebration of the Mass and other sacraments. The construction of our new church building with the altar facing the people in 1958, as I have already explained, heralded our attention to the European liturgical movement. Mainly through my contact with the Dominicans of Hawkesyard Priory near Rugeley, and its attached conference centre, Spode House, I was drawn into a meeting in January 1962 to discuss the initiation of a 'Conference of Practical Liturgy'. The twelve of us who met included Frs Conrad Pepler, Illtud Evans and Edmund Hill from the Dominicans, Fr Winstone, Fr Rabnett of Ampleforth and Fr Charles Davis of St Edmund's College, Ware, all of us under the leadership of Fr Jim Crichton – who today (in his nineties) is the doyen of pastoral liturgy.

The idea was to work towards having an annual congress of priests ensuring a close co-operation between pastoral clergy, seminary professors and other specialists in all matters pertaining to the liturgy. We hoped that a permanent centre would eventually be found to foster sound liturgical understanding and development. This, of course, was prior to the Vatican Council, and we were conscious that priests, first and foremost, needed to have the benefit of an annual gathering after the manner of Glenstal for the Irish clergy, and the more thorough-going liturgical Centre de Pastorale Liturgique for the French.

I had already had a short experience of the latter in Lyons in 1947 when Illtud Evans and Russell (now Fr Edmund) Hill and I went from Oxford for a stay in France. The visit gave us time to call at the Paris HQ of the Dominican Editions du Cerf, where we met Pere Roguet and several other distinguished friars. We went on to Lyons to a conference of the Centre du Pastorale Liturgique, and heard Romano Guardini address a large assembly of bishops, priests and others. There was one great moment when he said: 'Jesus left us the precious gift of his church. And what have we made of it? – a hierarchy!' This was greeted with applause. It's hard to realise that this was in 1947.

Our first conference was called for September 1962 and was by invitation only. With some amusement now I note a letter of Fr Conrad to Fr Crichton about the propriety of adding the name of a mere seminarian to those being invited. He was, after all, not even a sub-deacon yet: his name Nicholas Lash. The theme of the conference was 'Baptism: entering the parish community'. Papers were given by Fr Henry St John OP, Dom Edmund Jones OSB, Fr Harold Winstone and Canon J. B. O'Connell. From the 220 priests invited, some 60 actually came, and the two and a half days were truly memorable. A committee was then elected to ensure further annual gatherings. I was elected secretary, John Dewis (a former colleague from the Beda College) was elected Treasurer, under the chairmanship of Jim Crichton; the group also included Charles Davis, Hubert Richards and Joseph Buckley – all priests of real note. I was privileged to work with them.

In 1963 we took as our theme 'The Parish' and related the sociological setting of a modern parish to the theology of the People of God, and the practical problems in parish liturgies. By now the Vatican Council was under way, and before we held our third conference in 1964 on 'The Christian Sunday', the first document had been issued, which was The Constitution on the Liturgy. This was not primarily about the use of vernacular languages, though that was an important element for consideration. Before the Council had begun, a document came out (actually an 'apostolic constitution') under the signature of Pope John XXIII, entitled *Veterum Sapientiae*, on the place of Latin in the life of the church. It looked like an attempt to pre-empt an open discussion at the Council, and created a great stir of disappointment, and even anger, among many priests. At a local deanery meeting I was astounded at the almost total consensus that the document was unhelpful. It seemed to me therefore that we should inform Bishop Petit of our views before he returned to Rome for the coming Council session. When I had prepared a letter, virtually none of my deanery colleagues was willing to sign it; such was the docility or fear of priests in those days. Undismayed I decided to send copies to all the priests of the diocese with the following cover note: 'I hope you will not regard as an impertinence my sending you this copy of a letter I have written to the bishop. I have no idea whether you will in any way agree with its sentiments, even in a general way. If you do agree, however, I hope you will feel able to say so in whatever way you may believe right and prudent. If you do not agree with it, I hope it will not annoy you unduly.' This was the letter:

My dear Lord Bishop,

The coming Vatican Council has been in our prayers and on our minds for sometime. My impression has been that its very announcement fostered a great wave of optimism among the clergy, and also among those of the laity who follow the life of the church at all closely. As our bishop you will presumably go to Rome to represent the church in Menevia – not exactly as our 'representative', I know; but the clergy and laity will be there by your presence. During the preparations we clergy have probably been very slow to make our views known, though everyone has been urged to make a contribution.

Recent events have given rise to much moderated hope for the Council's results. Several incidents have suggested that there will be much obstruction to any kind of reform or renewal in the life of the church. Padre Lombardi, for instance, who was so encouraged in his bold re-appraisal of church life by Pope Pius XII, now finds himself publicly rebuked in the columns of *L'Osservatore Romano* for recommending a reform of the Roman Curia. *L'Osservatore* is not the voice of the Pope, even less that of the ruling and teaching church, but it has semi-official status, and the worldwide comment on the incident has caused no disavowal. It is even reported that the Pope endorsed the criticism in an unofficial comment.

Next has come a stunning blow in *Veterum Sapientiae* on the place of Latin in the life of the church. It seems to be a complete pre-judgement of the whole issue which many of us had been led to think would be debated at the Council. We are not now permitted to hold publicly any view contrary to that expressed in *VS* on the dignity and supreme value of the Latin language. Many of us believe this to be completely non-proven. Why should such a disciplinary decision, affecting the life of the whole church be taken prior to the Council itself?

The document states: 'Latin by its nature is perfectly adapted for promoting every form of culture among every people.' This seems to me to be a gross mis-statement. It can surely be shown from history that Latin is wedded to purely European ways of rational thinking: that disasters have occurred in missionary countries where European and Latin ways have been imposed. The document states that 'Latin has a noble and characteristic conformation which contributes singularly to clarity and solemnity.' Solemnity it undoubtedly has; as the chief 'instrument of mutual communication, especially between the Holy See and the various churches of the same Latin rite' its clarity is unrivalled. But for the clarity of living thought, for the expression of those nuances of personal reflection which are thought, it is singularly inept, except possibly in the hands of supreme masters of the tongue.

Some are now assuring us that the document does not refer to the liturgy at all. I find myself unable to construe it in this way. It is plain that even if we do not speak 'moved by an inordinate desire for novelty', we are not meant to write against the use of Latin. To say that we are not discouraged from writing for the use of the vernacular seems to be a little too simple an alternative. The document applies at least to the clergy, but I have not yet met a priest who was not distressed at the whole tone of it , and dismayed by its policy in liturgical and other spheres. I have a private letter from a distinguished English theologian in which he says: 'I regard the recent document on Latin as a disaster. I think it means that the church has failed to meet the present situation, and that we are going to see perhaps several decades of feverish activity in an enterprise that is bound to be abortive.'

I know of nothing else I can do than to voice my personal distress to my bishop, in the hope that others will do likewise, and that we may represent to the Holy Father through you that this decree ill accords with his splendid desire, so often displayed, of knowing what the church as a whole thinks about vital matters. It is not merely that I believe the increased use of the vernacular in the liturgy to be a desperate necessity. Many clergy and laity disagree on this issue, even for pastoral reasons, though the witness of missionary bishops would seem to be overwhelming. Perhaps I am wrong, and it is not intended to refer to the liturgy at all. But many of us believe that Latin, as a means of communication in seminary studies is grossly over-rated in this Constitution.

No doubt it would be a tremendous advantage if all the clergy had a better grasp of the Latin tongue; but extra time given to this skill would mean less time for the study of philosophy, theology, the scriptures and the liturgy, which already are poorly mastered by most of us. Speaking for myself, the longer I use my Latin breviary, the less it means to me, and the more time I have to set aside for reading the scriptures in the vernacular. The more I reflect on the Latin textbooks of the seminary, the more I see the need to read current theology in the vernacular to follow the mind of the church. The more I try to share the life of the church's worship, the more I find Latin a desperate obstacle to its main purpose.

On all counts I believe this Constitution will put a brake on the renewal of the church which we all so urgently want. I think it is honest to voice my immense personal distress in case it finds some echo in your own mind. I am showing this letter to other priests and hope they will do something similar to indicate their thoughts.

The Tablet's editorial (3 March 1962) in general upheld the desirability of sustaining or reviving Latin culture. The writer ended: 'Some sentences in the Encyclical seem to indicate that even the campaign for the vernacular is to be considered at an end, at any rate as far as Ecclesia Docens is concerned; that Roma locuta est; causa finita est.' That is exactly what many of us worried about.

The reactions to my circularised letter were interesting. Fr Jim Donnelly of Llanrwst said: 'I couldn't agree more with anything than I do with every word and sentiment of that letter, and I congratulate you on your initiative and pluck in sending it. I am so glad you brought in the case of Fr Lombardi. The tirade against him in Osservatore made my blood boil.'

Canon J. B. O'Connell (author of the editions of *Ceremonies of the Roman Rite Described*) thanked me 'for sending a copy of your excellent, courageous and well-timed letter on *Veterum Sapientiae*. I agree that it is a very disturbing pronouncement; but I know a little of the background concerning it. It was engineered by a group of die-hards in Rome (I know their names) who hoped, I am informed, that it would be interpreted as a pronouncement on

Latin in the liturgy, when I believe and hope it is not. Time will tell.'

An elderly Canon, Joseph Geraghty, said: 'There's nothing we can do about it now. The old stagers of the Roman Curia are against what they call the modern innovations. You are young and you'll see great changes in the direction you advocate in your lifetime.' Fr Jim O'Reilly of Barmouth wrote: 'In full agreement with your letter. *Senium insipientiae,* or a load of bull. Its very inaccurate assessment of Latin's value has nothing to do with faith or morals. It is obviously an effort by the rearguard to thwart progressives. I shall drop the bishop a more temperate note with a little philological data to back you up.'

Several referred to my 'courage' in speaking up – symptomatic, I suppose, of the attitude to hierarchical structures. To me it was not a matter of precocity or disobedience. I really thought then, as I have increasingly believed since, that we have a duty to speak of our concerns. The church, as we are reminded over and over again, is not a democracy; but that can be made to allow tyranny if we are not watchful. 'My first reaction,' wrote a Carmelite, 'was one of admiration for your courage. But then I thought the bishop might be glad to know of your opinion and feeling in "the other ranks". I have written to him indicating my sympathy with your main points. Let's hope we don't finish up with offers of parishes in Alaska!'

While not entirely agreeing with my anxiety that the document was aimed obliquely at the liturgy, Fr Vaughan Roscoe Beddoes said he believed 'proper steps should be taken to discover the mind of the laity. There is too much driving and autocracy.' Fr Jim Cunnane gave a more measured response, underlining the danger of losing Latin from the liturgy altogether. Fr Jim Mitchell objected to 'the stifling of discussion and debate' but otherwise did not agree with me. An experienced missionary (SVD) priest quoted to me a saying of Cardinal Constantini (Prefect of Propaganda Fidei): 'The principal obstacle to mission work in China was not the Chinese wall, but the wall of the Latin language.' Fr Eric Green wrote anxiously to the bishop because 'Fr Hardwicke sounds as if he were speaking for the clergy as a whole whereas at least a few of us hold contrary opinions, and some of the laity are vehement against the introduction of any vernacular at all.' His view was based on personal experience of being a priest with a one-time congregation 'of Chinese,

Portuguese, English, French, German, Red Indians, and even one Parsee'. This, I need hardly say, had not been in Wales, but during wartime military internment in the East. Even so, I still wondered if the homily had been in Latin also!

It is however relevant to quote a letter in *The Tablet* which had already given the text of the Constitution. It came from H. W. J. Edwards. who wrote 'The spread of the vernacular movement could very easily be dangerous for the mission of the church within Wales; but for that matter I have suspected that the manner in which the liturgical movement has developed might also require some adjustment in Wales.' His deep concern that English would rule out Welsh had some real justification.

Bishop Petit in due course replied to me in a way that showed he did not resent my intrusion. He had other reasons for knowing I spoke my mind on issues. 'I think you are worrying unduly about the Council, and what it is or is not going to do; and also about the latest Constitution. Take it all quietly – these things have a way of working out quite satisfactorily to the good of all, even though they seem to disturb everybody of a certain frame of mind to begin with. I don't think the Constitution will affect the use of the vernacular in the liturgy any more than it has up to the present. But it will help to stop the rather contemptuous and scornful way in which some, especially on the continent, have been treating Latin, in which so much of the essential value has been preserved for the church of God ... I have lived so long now and I have seen God working in such strange ways that I refuse to regard any move now by ecclesiastics in power as a disaster or even as a set-back.'

It was a kindly and pious response; and it didn't convince me that ecclesiastics couldn't produce set-backs. The issue over the suppression of De Ricci's work of Chinese inculturation is surely enough to mention. I know of more curial ineptitudes nearer our own time. God works through an obstacle path quite often!

The little exercise of consultation did, however, set something of a precedent for me, as my tale will show. I am glad that the clergy gathering we had inaugurated had been entitled the Conference of Practical Liturgy. We were encouraging ourselves to explore the best liturgical scholarship for the sake of the people in the parishes. In Ruabon we were already celebrating baptism with a bit more imagination, starting with a knock on the church's 'west door' for a formal entry of the family, with their child, before the first question there: 'What do you ask of the church of God for your child?', followed by a different setting for a reading of the scriptures. That, at least, was one of our efforts to enliven the celebration.

But, apart from the full parish Sunday assemblies, how should we deal with weekday Mass, to which the merest handful of people were free to attend from across the several villages in the parish? For some that would involve a journey with two different buses, which would probably not coincide with Mass times. This was long before almost every family had a car. Heating the whole church for a 20–25 minute celebration was a consideration also; so I used a tiny side-chapel, which could be closed off and seat about eight people. Quite soon I suggested that on at least one day each week I might arrange to say a house Mass in one or other of the housing estates in Johnstown, Penycae or Rhos. The idea was for the host family to invite other parishioners who lived near to join us for a domestic celebration. It was not a matter only of venue, but one of trying to locate our worship in the context of that particular street or estate. Adaptations to the rite were clearly appropriate. To begin with the family would have tried to set up a table as near to the height of a church altar as possible, with a white cloth, a crucifix, and maybe even some flowers; everything was being done as if we were in a 'proper church'. I felt we had to learn a bit more about the New Testament origins of the eucharist, before ever there were 'churches'. We soon felt able to start the liturgy of the word in a sitting-room setting, and I encouraged people to share comments after the scripture readings; we might even have a brief discussion. Then I would move into a more formal 'offertory', now wearing the requisite vestments. There would be between six and twelve people packed into the small council-house rooms; and we would end up with a cup of tea and a biscuit. It became necessary to insist on no more than this, or else we might have developed an embarrassing competition in refreshments, which would quickly exclude the less-well-off families.

On these informal occasions I was learning what were the varying degrees of Catholic understanding which were around. I encouraged people to speak openly, and this revealed a range of variations in orthodoxy. 'I never really believed that' was a remark I heard more than once. One person said once, 'Ever since I came during the war as an evacuee from Liverpool, and when

Mass was only available from the occasional visit of the travelling missioners, I used to go the Baptist services with my hosts. This didn't seem wrong in any way; but of course I never told the priests.' In my view the way Catholics used their common sense, and made conscientious decisions, whatever 'the rules' said, showed a far greater maturity than we priests ordinarily admitted. In the presence of the clergy, many of them had been infantilised. They knew how to be flexible with rules, but kept this to themselves.

At one house Mass, after our liturgy of the word, I turned to my bag of ecclesiastical millinery to get ready for the eucharist. Someone said: 'Do you really have to bother with all that?' I replied: 'Why? Don't you like vestments or something?' 'Oh yes, they're fine for church, but they look a bit silly in the sitting-room.' So we had another discussion, which revealed how they could tell the difference between essentials and non-essentials. 'So what shall I wear?' 'Why not just a stole?' It was their idea; and bit by bit that is what most house-groups approved of.

To add to my respect for their maturity, it soon appeared that one of the parishioners who turned up quite frequently would have been upset if there was anything less than full vestments, 'a proper altar', etc. For her sake everyone realised that I must have the whole bag of tricks ready so as not to scandalise her. On one occasion I accidentally-on-purpose forgot to bring the little communion breads, so that I could pose an educational question – 'Would ordinary bread be all right this evening?' It was a learning experience for them as they brought bread from the kitchen; and also for me, as I had to cope carefully with the left-over crumbs. It's not any use being 'avant-garde' unless you can meet the practical snags which need to be dealt with.

The whole area of 'experimentation' was much frowned on in the Anglo-Saxon and Celtic fringes. So while one knew that in France, Germany and elsewhere all kinds of things were being tried, one didn't raise one's head far above the parapet in Britain. More than ten years after I had been celebrating house Masses, a much senior priest phoned me to ask how I managed to do this, when he had asked the bishop, and had just been refused. I could only think to say: 'Why did you think it was necessary to ask him? Are you not the pastor of your people?'

On Monday mornings it was rare that anyone other than the server, Paul, and I were there for an early Mass. For several years before the vernacular was introduced I used to say to him: 'What would you think if I said the Mass in English?' 'Could you?,' he asked. 'Well, let's just try; and if anyone else turns up, I'll switch back to Latin.' Soon I said: 'Paul, instead of kneeling behind my back, why don't you stand by my side at the eucharistic prayer? But again if anyone else turns up, back to your place !' Later again I said, 'Paul, Jesus said "Take and eat" not "Kneel down and be fed". If at communion time, I offered you the plate, perhaps you would do what Jesus says; just take and eat.' Paul was about four-teen at that time; but together we learned what was appropriate, and what 'worked'. What a pity the experiment only involved him. We might have been able to short-circuit with maturity some of the unnecessarily long drawn-out developments that eventually came our way.

When the bishop came for Confirmation I had read the official ruling that the candidates and their sponsors and any ministers, might be allowed to receive Communion from the chalice as well as the officiating clergy. Just before we processed into the church, I told the bishop that the seven candidates and their sponsors had been led (by me, of course) to expect this. 'Are you sure they are old enough?' he asked. 'Yes; they're fine,' I replied. Then as I poured the wine into the chalice at the appropriate moment, he stopped me quietly saying 'That'll be enough!' But I added, 'There'll be twenty-eight people,' because I included all the altar servers, the readers, the organist, as ministers. Fair play; the bishop made no objection. He was ready for change, so long as it was 'of-ficial', and he already knew that I would have done my home-work. 'That was nice,' Paul remarked afterwards, 'but really everyone should have the chalice, because in a way we're all min-isters.' He was well educated!

If only more people could have shared our learning activities. If this had been, as I believed, an educational process in the parish, it certainly was not programming any of us for conformity. What I discovered from our adaptations or experiments was that it en-abled people to explore and develop their personal understand-ing of sacramental worship. I had the advantage of some liturgical education – certainly not from seminary – with the help of the library I was building up, but also through the scholarly and pas-toral experience of the members of our 'conference'. Nowadays there are more lay-people with theological and liturgical knowl-edge, sometimes way ahead of priests; and once a group of people work together in, for instance, a parish liturgy group, the sense of full participation – which was one of the stated aims of Vatican II's liturgical document – is enormously enhanced.

All this was basic to a more adequate witness as Christians. We needed a rich sense of community, with proper consultative processes. We needed to stop looking inwards, only at our own structures and to find ways of reaching those outside the church. And we needed vibrant, participative worship. None of these actually demanded an ordained priest to bring them about; but it taught me that without clear-headed leadership, none of this was likely to happen.

It looked as though I was beginning to prepare a 'job description' for a parish priest, which would concentrate less on the validity of his ordination, and a lot more on the skills he should try to develop. Much would depend – or so the structures of diocese implied – on the policies and sense of direction coming from our bishops. I'm not sure we had great expectations of this in the 1960s. Each parish priest did his own thing, according to his particular interests; we had to wait another decade for various forms of 'pastoral congresses'. Alas, the famous one in Liverpool, which was such a resoundingly successful experience for participants, withered away by the time the old ecclesiastical habits drowned it. Reading Clifford Longley's *The Worlock Archive,* one realises there were pressures from the Roman Curia affecting the whole event.

Subsequent more localised attempts have been more valuable perhaps. But then, as now, we were left with one major hurdle – the choice of our bishops. Having stuck my neck out about liturgy already, I dared to question an item about this in our own diocese.

Part Three

'On Consulting the Faithful'
1965–1969

Chapter Five: Near the Edges of Ecclesiastical Politics
This is the first of three chapters, when I made three distinct efforts to confront some ecclesiastical and pastoral problems by writing round to find out what others were thinking, as well as to express my own anxieties. This chapter is about the appointment of an auxiliary bishop.

Chapter Six: Along the Boundaries of Legality
This explains my challenges to the complexities, and to me the absurdities, of some of the rules governing 'mixed marriages'.

Chapter Seven: On the Margins of Obedience
The watershed issue stemming from Paul VI's encyclical Humanae Vitae *uncovered profound matters about the nature of authority in the church. Here is a fully documented account of what was said to parishioners as guidance, of letters exchanged with the bishop; the public letter of 54 priests to* The Times, *and the manner in which we were 'disciplined'.*
Because of the thirtieth anniversary of the Letter in 1998, this chapter was published in advance, and perhaps roused some interest for the completion of this book.

'Mind you, I'm speaking of thirty years ago …'
[Courtesy of *Further Cracks in Fabulous Cloisters*]

CHAPTER FIVE

Near the Edges of Ecclesiastical Politics: The choice of a bishop

In October 1965, when Bishop Petit's health was not too good, we were informed that the Holy See had appointed Bishop Langton Fox as his auxiliary. Dr Fox was to come from Chichester, but only a few months earlier he had been appointed as the new Rector of St John's seminary at Wonersh. This was now over-ridden, and one heard the remark that some ecclesiastical left hand didn't know what its right hand was doing!

Talking informally face to face with friends, and over the phone, made me think that we should at least comment on the appointment. I tried another circular letter to brother priests in the diocese. Dated 1 November 1965, I sent this out.

> About two years ago I promised myself that I would not indulge in criticisms behind anyone's back. There is surely a constructive place for criticism. Accordingly I have written to Bishop Petit a purely personal letter saying how delighted I am that he is to have help, but expressing exasperation that the Roman authorities have insisted on appointing another bishop (this makes three out of three) with no knowledge or experience of Wales and her clergy prior to the appointment. I feel justified in sharing my sentiments with fellow-priests, for I do not want to establish a narrowly nationalist point. I have already found others who see in it a matter of principle. And it seems to me important that it should be freely discussed urgently by clergy and others – perhaps at deaneries for instance – before much time elapses. We must try to safeguard the future
>
> Dr Langton Fox sounds an admirable person; from all accounts he will be a most sensitive, approachable and valiant worker here. No-one would wish to make his task more difficult than it will already be. He must not be embarrassed by any lack of welcome and co-operation. That is why, as I see it,

the matter should be discussed before we can be accused of passing any personal judgement on him. He will probably be a godsend, and we shall be more than thankful that he has come to us. But on two counts: i. The complete lack of consultation in the diocese, and ii. The complete lack of knowledge and experience of Wales and the clergy here, the appointment is profoundly to be regretted. If you agree with any part of this letter, would you try to discuss it with others, and perhaps have it raised at your own deanery meeting. My own dean has already agreed that this might well be a suitable thing to do, if it is done tactfully, courteously and without rancour.

Not surprisingly for a matter so near the 'engine room', I did not get many replies; but of course I didn't ask for them. Some did choose to write, all the same. One religious order priest said: 'The out-of-the-blue appointment of our new auxiliary bishop – the very day after we had been speaking of such things – certainly took us all on the wrong foot. I spoke so strongly about it here for a couple of days that my superior told me to tone it down.'

Another priest said: 'Your views were already my own though I could not formulate them so aptly. I have already discussed the appointment with several priests and all share my feelings. I shall strive to introduce the matter at the next Conference, though the Vicar-General for various reasons may prohibit discussion. In the meantime, thank you for your courageous action.'

Another found my letter 'interesting and could see the point. However consultation has never been the practice no matter how desirable we might think it to be … While lack of knowledge of Welsh conditions and of the clergy seem a big disadvantage, he will on the other hand have an open mind on things and fresh ideas. From what I hear of him he's very go-ahead which is a good thing.'

Another was in favour of discussing consultation, but added 'May the Lord preserve us from all Welsh Nationalists – at least we have had a succession of first class bishops under the present system.'

Several others agreed to raise it at their deaneries, so I was very encouraged. One senior priest wrote vigorously, speaking from considerable knowledge: 'I entirely agree with your letter; but I intend to keep quiet or it will be said that I was looking for

the job myself. The whole present system of episcopal appoint-
ments revolts me. Almost without exception they are men of
similar background and education. There is not a scholar among
them. Outstanding men like the Abbot of Downside are point-
edly passed over. When Rome does break out of the rut (as in
the case of Gordon Wheeler) the poor man is sent to kick his
heels in a remote diocese where he is not needed. No attempt is
made, as far as I can see, to fit the man to the diocese. Scandalous
situations are allowed to drag on for years. But basically it is the
fault of the clergy and people. The sheep are far too sheepish.
Now, if ever, is the time for being vocal and staying that way.'

I must have sent a letter to Cardinal Heenan about something
he had said at the Vatican Council about this time which had
disturbed me – I have quite forgotten what, and have certainly
lost any copy – and I must have enclosed a copy of my circular.
A reply came swiftly where, having dealt with my first point, he
referred to the auxiliary bishop's appointment.

> 'I cannot safely comment on your second point because I am
> a member of the Consistorial Congregation and would prob-
> ably risk excommunication if I voiced an opinion on the ap-
> pointment of bishops. I am most grateful to you for your let-
> ter. I am sure you realise that one of the crosses of a bishop is
> so rarely to hear plain speaking such as yours. With an affec-
> tionate blessing and begging the help of your prayers, I am,
> Yours devotedly, + John, Cardinal Heenan.'

I sent a personal letter to Bishop Petit also at the Council in
Rome. His reply was extensive and generous.

> 'From what I hear of Dr Fox, I imagine he will become Welsh
> to the point of learning to speak and write in it. So you must
> all be very patient and understanding, and not too ready to
> voice feelings, rather than convictions, based on facts you
> have balanced. As for methods of appointments, the change
> will come, but gradually. I am old enough now to realise how
> sudden changes can upset so many people who have no
> power to vocalise these feelings, but suffer in silence. The
> silent, quiet revolution is longest lasting. So I would not, if I
> were you, write to the Apostolic Delegate; there are many
> other factors to be considered, not least of all the reaction
> such news would have on Dr Fox when he got to know, as in-
> variably he would. God's ways are not ours, but as you saw
> Pope John's appointment was not a disaster but a complete

success because sanctity of life is supranational. So obedience leads to sanctity, and even Pope John must have had his scruples when he was asked if he would accept the papacy, and replied that he would. I hope the clergy give you a very favourable reply to your last letter to them.
My blessing, + John.'

It was thoughtful of the bishop to warn me not to upset Dr Fox, and a reminder that he was not as insensitive as some of the clergy reckoned. I already knew that in fact he could be quite sentimental below his rather gruff exterior.

Bishop Fox in his turn amply demonstrated his sturdy commitment to Wales and the diocese, and he provided us, all through the long years of serious sickness and handicap because of which he had to resign the see, with a real model of fidelity and piety in a totally uncomplaining way. That such a competent and distinguished man should have his role as our diocesan bishop, following Bishop Petit, cut short so tragically must have been a very heavy cross to bear. What was very touching was that, when his physical condition made it clear that he needed another bishop to assist him in the diocese, he entered into a little process of consultation with the priests of the diocese.

This was fourteen years after my earlier intervention about the appointment of bishops, and so is out of chronological order in the telling of my tale; but it is relevant to the topic. By now, as my later chapters will reveal, I was working in a secular capacity, and it was gracious of Bishop Fox to include me in the consultation. In a way I was living in a self-inflicted isolation from other diocesan priests, so I thought it might be useful if I offered a few thoughts, in a fairly light-hearted way, as a contribution to the process. So I used my old duplicator to produce copies for all the clergy, saying that these were 'some untidy thoughts upon nominating candidates to a bishopric, which are to be treated, if necessary, with the contempt they may deserve'.

'Bishop Fox has asked for the appointment of a Coadjutor Bishop. We must regret the necessity due to his reduced activity; and we have some comfort in knowing that the coadjutor will have an apprenticeship in episcopacy under his guidance; for there is no guidance on how to be a bishop.
May I express a personal regret that the Coadjutor is to have the right of succession? Please God, we shall have two bishops for a long time yet. But what if we found that the Coadjutor

did not fill the role as Menevia needed and wanted? Would not the fact that he would then be known to us actively be grounds for offering us a free choice before his auxiliary status were changed into permanency? We will be much more likely to affirm him, which would be very encouraging.

This is of course only a tiny reflection of the way in which the church's ordained ministers are set up to 'serve' without real consultation with their 'masters', the people of God. Heaven forbid that we should seek to have a majority show of hands for ordination candidates – that is not what is meant by 'consulting the faithful'. We can surely trust the various levels of the selection process – references, adequate seminary performance and a final consensus of opinions by those best placed to know – though some of us, even then, turn out to be pretty odd fish!

Ordination, however, does not assure everyone that the recipient is in principle suitable, competent and authorised to exercise a particular ministry. He does not thereby receive an actual task or office. It is a pity that neither he, nor the people he is likely to serve, are asked whether he might be suitably placed with them. But even if we cannot devise machinery for this consultation, we could certainly work out something for his confirmation in office after a year or so.

Anyway, we start the other way round with the choice of bishops. We know there are vacancies not just before the appointment, but before any ceremony: and we flutter between calling it ordination (again) or consecration, or enthronement because of profounder uncertainties. The theology of priesthood 'of first and second rank' is not astoundingly clear: perhaps there is no real difference ... For sure, the functions have been made distinct. There has been developed a jurisdictional ranking of which it is alleged we stand in awe. In my time as bishop's secretary my impression was that parish priests were very selective in their response of obedience. What did not suit or please was usually honoured in the breach. I have not noticed that the talk about collegiality and co-responsibility since Vatican II has altered things much.

Another thought. Though priesthood is a 'calling' we nevertheless approve of a young man who offers his services of his own accord. Is not episcopacy also a calling? Yet we would question a priest's humility if he sent in his own nomination ...

I should be most sorry, however, if any volunteer, or anyone pressed into the new office, were too sure of what the role of a bishop is today. We all know what he may legitimately do. I hope we can expect someone who has a mind to sit with us and discern the signs of the times so that his episcopate may be an effective leadership, and not just a step-up in line management. Bishop Fox gives us a powerful example in one form of renewal. He doesn't only recommend it; he does it passionately and effectively; he has been moved by God's Spirit to do so. I trust his future Coadjutor will discover other desirable and necessary things that could be afoot if the Spirit were not quenched or ignored.

I am aware that my personal approval of anyone's name for bishop might be the kiss of death on his chances, so is it naughty of me to think I should perhaps recommend a list of those I really believe to be totally unsuitable?

This only produced four responses; three of them appreciative and constructive; one utterly condemnatory, starting with the sentence. 'Your circulars are so tendentious and inaccurate that it hardly seems worthwhile bothering about them' and thus thoroughly putting me in my place. 'I wish you would get on with the job you were ordained for.' There were some really tough words about my failure in obedience to my ordination promises, and it did me no harm to be so severely criticised. Indeed it helped me get my thoughts on priesthood in a different kind of order. There was no malice in the attack; it was certainly meant as fraternal correction, and some further letters were exchanged.

The impact of this belongs to a later chapter. I cannot forbear to add a note that my circular did not have such an adverse effect on Cardinal Hume. With his customary tolerance his reply came like this:

'Dear Owen,

Thank you so much for your letter. If I happen to be called along the corridors of power, then I shall remember what you have written. Thank you so much.

Yours devotedly, Basil Hume, Archbishop of Westminster

But as I look over the unfolding of my years in Ruabon, beginning in 1954 till 1958, when it overlapped with being secretary to the bishop, and thereafter through till 1969, I can see that my understanding of the life and role of a priest was developing in several ways. In large measure I had been trained to be a cultic figure, the one who offers the sacrifice of the Mass and administered other sacraments. I had quickly discovered the need to share the pastoral responsibilities with the parishioners, though we had not reached the idea of lay ministries so clearly. I had valued the role of animator of lay apostles in the YCW, and had come to see ways of not being cut off from non-church people through youth club work. This taught me so much about human relationships in and beyond the church, and the ways in which authentic leadership could be exercised.

All this was not unconnected with the celebration of liturgy which was becoming increasingly participative. My interventions on ecclesiastical matters were explorations of a more adequate perspective on the church as teacher and shepherd. The years of the Vatican Council were crucial in opening the windows of our minds to many hidden riches. No longer were we to be counter-reformation Catholics, but members of a church with a long developing tradition of doctrine, guidance and worship.

For some priests it was a frightening phase to be entering. All the old certainties were open to questioning, and that could be very uncomfortable. What I personally experienced for the most part was a liberation, with all the dangers that implies. Most of the elements of the church that I had always disliked were now seen not to be part of her essential being. But how quickly could we expect the real effects to permeate Catholic life? Of course my natural impatience was not going to make it easy for me. There were going to be some major disappointments ahead, and, when *Humanae Vitae* appeared, a conscientious conviction that I could not conform on some important issues. But that is to race ahead. One other issue was going to occupy my mind first; and it benefited from the preliminary attempt to consult over less critical issues.

CHAPTER SIX

On the Boundaries of Legality:
Marriages, mixed or confused?

In the midst of the continual exercise of diplomacy and discretion in an effort to be a good pastor, a parish priest has also to be a somewhat hard-headed official of Canon Law. That subject did not rank very high on my seminary college agenda in the 1950s. I knew roughly what legal requirements there were for Catholics to enter a 'valid' marriage. I had a rather better understanding of the sacramental implications of two baptised Christians undertaking matrimony. Some of the Canon Law requirements were, as far as I was concerned, simply disciplinary. After all, as I later discovered from our history, the involvement of a priest for the recognition of the validity of a marriage was a somewhat late requirement, and could, of course, be changed. I soon ran into problems.

I quite enjoyed spending time with couples in preparation for a wedding; marriages of any sort were not very frequent in a small rural-industrial parish in Wales. In one best-managed period, I had two couples together, when we explored the Christian understanding of marriage, discussed the way they saw their distinctive roles in the partnership. We even looked at domestic financial management, at housing ownership or tenancy; and I brought in a doctor to share any difficulties about their sexuality. I am quite certain now that the required sessions by the priest himself are totally inadequate, though it was one of the failing elements of my ministry that I never thought this through to ensure a more helpful process. Things are managed better today.

What 'the Church' mainly seemed to require was that I should give some understanding to those who were not Catholics about what it meant to be married to a Catholic. This was to be 'explanatory' rather than 'instructional', and we always had the hope that they might in due course wish to hear more, with a view to being received into full communion with their spouse and the church. In retrospect, little emphasis was given to the clear distinction we should have been making between those couples where one party was plainly without explicit faith or religious observance, and those where one party was the baptised member of the church in a different tradition. It took the second Vatican Council to remind us that two consciences were involved here. To that point, if the Catholic was to have a dispensation from the law forbidding marriage to a 'non-Catholic', the latter had to give a signed promise to allow any child born of the marriage to be baptised and brought up in the Catholic faith. The less they cared about religion, the easier it was to get the dispensation – a point to which I shall return later.

The fact remained that if the likelihood that the couple's indifference to church law would lead to them entering a mere civil marriage at the Registry Office, or if their failure in sexual continence had already led to a pregnancy, the easier it was to get a swift dispensation from the bishop, so that all should be (at least externally) well.

One important condition for a valid marriage for a Catholic was that it should take place in the presence of the local parish priest (or his authorised delegate) and two witnesses in a Catholic church. This condition had been laid down sixty years earlier in a Roman decree, known as *Ne temere*. It was designed, I believe, partly to prevent clandestine marriages, and perhaps to ensure that the couple was entering marriage responsibly. But it invalidated in the church's eyes any marriage by a Catholic, bound by Canon Law and Roman decrees, which was not celebrated in a Catholic church.

On 4 September 1967 I wrote to the bishop asking for a dispensation from this latter requirement – 'dispensation from canonical form' as it was officially called. I outlined the facts as I shall now describe them with the actual names having been changed, of course.

My dear Bishop,

James is a devout and Mass-going Irish Catholic in my parish, aged about 21, who wishes to marry Sarah of Rhosllaner-chrugog, also in the parish. Sarah is a chapel-going Baptist, also aged about 21, and a baptised Baptist at that. She is anxious in the preparation for the marriage next January to hear a full account of the Catholic faith, which she thinks she might well be able to embrace in due course. She is quite ready to give the customary undertakings about children etc. However, her father is a deacon in the same Baptist chapel. Both her parents have taken to James and do not seem to be unduly worried by his being a Catholic; but, following the laudable and understandable custom – universal in Wales – whereby marriages take place normally in the place of worship of the bride and her family, Sarah is anxious for the wedding to take place in the Baptist chapel. Since her chapel has currently no minister, I presume that one of the two ministers from neighbouring Baptist chapels would officiate, and since they are both friends of mine, I think this would be an enormously helpful ecumenical gesture for all concerned.

I trust you can grant a dispensation from the canonical form in this case, or get this dispensation from Rome. Since the wedding is not until January, there should be plenty of time.

Yours sincerely, Owen

A week later I had the bishop's reply on 12 September:

My dear Owen,

I have no power to dispense from the canonical form of marriage; the matter will have to go to Rome, but as this point will undoubtedly be considered by the Synod of Bishops, it is most unlikely that I would get any reply until the Synod, which is close at hand, has finished its work.

In any case I am very loathe to send such a case to Rome, because the answer would undoubtedly be, 'What is your votum?'; and my votum would be against the relaxation of canonical form. My reason is simple. It would constitute a precedent not only for the diocese but even for the country, and that is a responsibility I am not prepared to shoulder without consultation with the rest of the hierarchy, which does not meet until December. What is implied is an individual case of the repeal of *Ne Temere,* and I can see many reasons for not repealing it.

This case presents a conflict of 'laudable and understandable' customs, to use your own words. Laudable and understandable custom in the case of James is that he marries in the church, and I think equal consideration must be given to the Catholic as well as to the non-Catholic person. Much will depend upon how Sarah's parents are told of the normal canonical form. They may be adverse in any case: they are bound to be adverse if the case is not delicately presented to them.

May I remark *en passant* that the universal practice in Wales that marriages take place in the place where the bride and her family normally worship is also the universal practice in England: Wales is not special in this respect.

With my blessing, Yours sincerely

+ John, Bishop of Menevia

It was a clear and reasoned response, but I was shaken by it. I wanted to reply at once, and I sketched an outline of my next letter. Suddenly I realised I was about to have a wonderful chance of discussing the issue with those who would be attending a Spode House Conference, for which I had already booked in, on 'Authority in a Changing Church'. Accordingly I did raise the matter with a number of those present.

The Conference itself merits a special note, because in large measure it was a watershed event for those who attended. The findings of the Vatican Council were filtering through, and a 'crisis of identity' for Catholics, especially for priests and members of religious orders, was beginning to be noticeable. Twenty-five lay people and just over fifty priests attended, and the sessions were stimulating to the point of excitement for myself. The published papers are archive material of that time.

My little problem about a marriage dispensation related to the exercise of authority, power and jurisdiction. I began to see that I might consult others a little more formally than quiet chats at this conference. So I sent out another of my circular letters to forty of those who had attended, as well as to a scatter of my fellow diocesan priests, and some others. I gave them a copy of my first letter to the bishop and his reply, and a draft of my next possible letter to him, which went like this:

Thank you for such a swift reply to my first application for a dispensation from canonical form. So reasonably certain was I that your answer would be in an entirely opposite sense, I was momentarily stunned into silence. I really thought that out of the pastoral concern which we share, you would immediately arrange for this minor adjustment to the legal prescriptions – especially as every other 'safeguard of the faith' seems to be assured. After all, the couple administer the sacrament to each other, and the chances for the faith of the whole family are strongly favourable. What does it matter, Canon Law apart, where and before whom they exchange promises? I'll be there in any case.

Obviously we must meet and talk about this in depth; but you know me of old. I get really worked up about these things, and I must have a week or so to simmer down before coming to see you. I hope that's alright with you. You see, your answer seems simply concerned with the technicalities of some legal system; 'My reason is simple ... it would constitute a precedent'; and I thought my request was concerned with modifying the rules on the basis of a reasonable desire of two Christians, and out of the urgency of making a responsible ecumenical gesture in a matter which concerns none of the essentials of marriage. I am as anxious as Sarah and James for the marriage to be in the Baptist chapel; Sarah's family, her fellow chapel-goers and others, are as much my pastoral responsibility as anyone else.

Please give me the chance to think the case out again, and to consult some of the brethren before coming back to you. I am sure that we both want to act as the servants of our people for Christ's sake, and not as administrators of some impersonal law.

That was the material of my concern, so I asked my correspondents for their opinions. I had not concealed my personal view and the strong emotion with which I held it. Looking through some of the forty-five replies I had – some lengthy ones, and many of them challenging the pressure I was proposing to put on the bishop – I am amazed and delighted with the charitable concern expressed by so many of them. My covering letter had said:

Will you please help me with your judgement? I think the case explains itself in the copies of the letters and I am not asking you simply to tell me which 'side' you are on: that would be to reduce the matter to politics and pressure groups. I have a deep anxiety that we clergy spend much of our time administering a legal system instead of being creative with the gospel. I share all the recent criticisms of the impersonal way in which the institution works, to the fearful detriment of the message of salvation: this issue arises as another instance of the clash ... In this case do you share my view of the rightness of asking for this special dispensation? and how far should I press the matter? Under some circumstances I believe in the 'duty of disobedience' so there could be quite involved consequences. Thanks: Owen.

It may now seem like a storm in a teacup, thirty years later; that shows how far we have moved in the meantime. The replies indicated a wide range of attitudes; and I needed this to help me be a responsible pastor. I was beginning to see how differing underlying theologies of 'church' affected pastoral decisions. The replies also illustrate the fear felt by some priests about stepping out of line, and of causing unnecessary or dangerous fuss. Here are extracts from some of the letters:

(from a senior diocesan priest): 'The bishop says he will not agree to a dispensation because it has never been done under *Ne Temere*. Surely this is precisely what you are asking him to do. It is no answer to say he won't solely because it is exceptional; the point is, is the good of souls furthered? It is this "good of souls" that is made to depend on the law, and not on the individual case which is hurting the church.'

(from a young Franciscan priest): 'It seems to me necessary only that you should officially witness the marriage; where you witness it is a secondary matter. Isn't this a case of not asking for unnecessary permissions – but don't rely on my canonical knowledge. Your own personal dilemma would seem to be whether the circumstances justify taking the risk of a certain amount of trouble. As long as the couple's position is safeguarded, you may find this easy to solve.'

(from a Benedictine parish priest): 'We are caught up in the works of a system which is none of our making or wishing. Still, at present you can only accept the "No". The reason must be fully discussed with the girl's family. If they see you are suffering about this, then they will in charity help you to bear it. If we feel isolated, though immediately surrounded by the love and compassion of our people, how isolated and helpless must a bishop feel, grounded in "the system", and unable to find an obvious way out.'

(from a distinguished woman writer): 'My own impulse would have been to go ahead without even asking permission, because although there might have been a row afterwards, it wouldn't undo a perfectly valid marriage. But it's too late for that, and you did the normal thing anyway: and I expect I'm all wrong. But certainly you are right in principle, and this is exactly one of those idiotic restrictions for the sake of restriction which we should be fighting. In any case there have been cases recently in which marriages were blessed in non-catholic churches.'

(from an elderly parish priest, renowned for his pastoral concern and outspokenness): 'Granting all that you say about legal technicalities, I don't think you can expect one bishop to grant this case without consulting fellow-bishops; he can't go against 60 years of *Ne Temere* and all the people's traditions and habits on his own. Can't you soften it by inviting the Baptist minister, and even the father-deacon, to assist in an official way? To challenge the bishop in this case would be like choosing to bat on a sticky wicket.'

(a distinguished Jesuit scholar): 'I can't see what can be done at present but to accept the bishop's ruling and persuade the parties accordingly. I long to see – and will work for in ways that I can – a situation in which local bishops take these decisions without recourse to Rome; but till then, this is how those who have responsibility in the visible church decide, and good standing in communion with the church is made conditional on doing things this way. The most I can suggest is that you tell the couple that, as far as things have got in the RC Church, this church asks them to have a wedding in your church at which you will preside; and for the rest, they should follow their consciences. Taking this line, you will despise yourself, and feel ashamed to leave them in this sort of position, but it ought to be possible to explain we are in an interim stage, still debating this sort of thing, in which there are solid points on both sides, and that you can leave them free; but that you are not free yourself. I take it you want to remain in good standing so as to be able to continue in your service. This is not an end which would justify every means; but I do feel we ought to pick our battlefields very thoughtfully and prayerfully, and not find ourselves at Thermopylae until we quite definitely are there, and until we are quite sure that continued service would be at the cost of our entire integrity.'

(from a woman member of a diocesan ecumenical commission): 'It seems to me that the good *Ne Temere* was out to achieve is now counterbalanced by the harm it does. And I should like it scrapped for this country at least. I agree that this couple should be married in the Baptist chapel, if at all possible without raising Cain, and that because they might not want their wedding to be a cause of Cain-raising.'

(from a seminary professor): 'Deeply regret bishop's decision. Try renewed effort. Surely the place of marriage is not important;

only canonical requirement. Splendid precedent here; and it seems by sticking out for due canonical requirement we are missing an ecumenical opportunity.'

(from a priest-scholar): 'Your bishop is wrong about precedent – though the news won't perhaps be out just yet – a current case. Catholic boy marrying Anglican Canon's daughter. Bishop asks Rome for dispensation, believed to be with bishop's own negative votum attached; dispensation refused. Then Catholic boy's father writes to Archbishop of Canterbury and Papal Delegate. Result? Rescript from Rome gives permission for wedding to take place in bride's father's church with father officiating. Finally since this church is in another diocese from the boy, the Catholic bishop gives permission for the boy's parish priest to preach at the wedding. Do press your case. Only by cracking individual nuts will we get the principle changed.'

(from a senior diocesan parish priest): 'I lean sympathetically towards your case. Nonetheless I think the bishop is in a cleft stick; acting "unilaterally" would almost certainly arouse contention and add intransigence among the more conservative bishops … Some of us have felt pretty helpless, knowing that to have voiced non-current views would have labelled us as heretics or schismatics at worst. I cannot see that any change in Canon Law can make matters worse, as far as the status of the church is concerned, and could do much to assist it.'

(from a diocesan parish priest): 'I am no canonist to pass any sort of judgement on that aspect of things, but your arguments seem sound enough. But as far as the human side of the thing, it seems to me you are blinded to the possible consequences for the couple of being the pioneers in this country of a new look at the form of marriage; blinded by your indignation and irritation at the slow pace of the Curial establishment to implement the "spirit of Vatican II" in particular cases. This is Owen with a cast-iron case to beat the bloody fools on the head with; and you might elevate the couple to the martyrdom of publicity if you went ahead without permission.'

(from a Cistercian abbot): 'I think I can claim to feel as uncomfortable in the institutional church as anyone else so it is not difficult for me to understand your feelings over this business. Even so I think you are being unfair to the bishop. He is quite right when he says he can't grant such a dispensation. I believe he would if he could.'

(from a seminary Spiritual Director): 'You must dialogue with the bishop like mad. The sort of letter he wrote must not be allowed to be his last word on the subject. If he'll not change his mind about relaxing the canonical form, you should aim at two ceremonies – one in chapel, one in church. It is of course a crazy solution but only part of the craziness of *Ne Temere* and of a divided Christendom. After all dialogue you must obey, and suffer and be bewildered.'

(from a diocesan parish priest): 'The bishop hides a velvet hand in a rather iron glove, but after most of his priestly life in preconciliar times, when a slavish narrow obedience to the letter of the law was held by many to be good and virtuous behaviour, it is absurd and extravagant to expect him to change now. A large affair like holy church has to go gently when it wants to reverse current rules; granting your dispensation would pierce a tiny hole in a wall allowing a flood through eventually, impossible to channel again.'

Even those fourteen extracts, out of over forty, showed a variety of responses, and included some good personal advice. I took them seriously, and then went on to do something that might be thought unpardonable. I decided to consult the parishioners, and made a public request for the parish council, and anyone who felt able to do so, to meet me to discuss 'an important pastoral issue about which I am very troubled', before I approached the bishop again. I had the permission of the Catholic partner to do this. Some fifteen attended, and the specific question I put to them was this. In the light of the facts of this case, concerning James and Sarah, should I press the bishop to obtain from Rome the necessary dispensation from canonical form, so that the wedding can be in the Baptist chapel? Their replies were interesting.

(a Scottish Catholic with a non-Catholic husband): 'It is in my blood still that a marriage anywhere but in the Catholic church is all wrong; but if we say the others are Christians, we must go on to meet them in many ways.'

(a single woman from Liverpool): 'Long before the Council I disobeyed the letter of the law about attending non-Catholic churches with a clear conscience; now ecumenism has caught up with me. I am 100% in favour of the wedding taking place in the Baptist chapel.'

(married woman with non-Catholic husband): 'To refuse to go to

the Baptist chapel will only mean bitterness and complaint. We should certainly give way on this point when all else is safe.'

(a catechumen from Baptist tradition): 'I know the particular Baptist family involved, and how much has had to be overcome in accepting James as a Catholic fiancé to the daughter. It is unthinkable that they should have to give way also about the place of the wedding.'

(married man with wholly Catholic family and five children): 'Why not go to see the Baptist minister first, and then the family, and see how strongly they feel. Perhaps this might persuade the bishop to act differently.'

(married woman with wholly Catholic family and children): 'What we all suffer from is a false "guilt". Time and again we are hedged around with things that make the Christian life more difficult than it need be. Of course the law should give way in this case, so that the marriage can be in the girl's chapel.'

(husband to same family): 'The bishop plainly has a point about precedent. Personally I believe in sticking out my neck on matters where I feel strongly, especially in conscience; but family consequences sometimes hold me back. It would not be good to prejudice your work in so many other and wider spheres for the sake of one instance of marriage law. What about getting the Baptists to let you officiate in their chapel?'

(another Scottish woman with non-Catholic husband): 'It doesn't help anyone to insist on the law. My brother eventually agreed to please my mother to having a Registry Office marriage "put right". None of the family have any religious practice even so. Obeying legal prescriptions serves no purpose.'

(married man; recent convert with Anglican wife): 'Why upset people unnecessarily? They meet us; let us meet them part of the way, and have the wedding where they want it.'

With that consensus of ordinary folk, I reiterated my request to the bishop, aware that obtaining a ruling from Rome would be a lengthy business, even if I could overcome his reluctance to apply. It was still September; the wedding was fixed for January. October came and went – the first month. By the end of November I asked for news, and received the blunt response that there was plenty of time. The bishop had been taking the opinion of his Priests' Council, but I still didn't know if he had changed his mind. I decided to write again.

My dear Bishop,

Time, alas, is no longer on our side in the marriage case of James and Sarah. Naturally the Registrar has had to be informed about the date of the marriage in January; and he needed to know the place for the marriage; the couple have informed him – after consulting me to see if there was a decision yet – that arrangements are being made at the Baptist chapel in Rhosllanerchrugog. Now this may seem pretty outrageous to you. It is not because I believe bishops are fools. It is simply because I have explained in some detail to the couple what Christian marriage is, and what the requirements are for valid marriage under the law of the Catholic Church; and, in spite of all the discussion so far, it is fairly clear that their request for a dispensation in no way contravenes that which might be expected; it is simply rather unusual, to put it mildly. But because of the strong local ecumenical and community expectations, it is thoroughly in line with what we have been saying about one another as fellow-Christians; and the alternative would seriously scandalise, in the full sense, both the Baptist community and friends, and also my own parish council, and me.

I have told the couple that the Catholic Church's law requires the presence of the parish priest and two witnesses; we shall uphold the law. I shall be present and at least two other Catholics. The place of marriage falls under Canon 1109; this is subject to the ruling of the bishop of the diocese. The law says he may allow marriage elsewhere than the parish church for wholly Catholic marriages. It also states that marriages between a Catholic and a non-Catholic are to be celebrated outside the church. So while it has become customary (and maybe automatically lawful) to celebrate them in the parish church, we are not asking for any dispensation from this particular law, but only asking you to sanction a non-Catholic chapel in place of the sacristy. I quite understand that there is a contrary view that this is inopportune. I simply ask you to accept that on the basis not simply of my own personal opinion, but that of the local community, represented by my parish council and others, there is a strong view that this is what accords with Christian justice and charity in this case. The lack of British precedent has been adequately dealt with by the Anglican case recently; and it seems we are not to have the Synod's recommendations for a long time. You were good enough to ask the opinion of your Priests' Council; I believe that quite a majority thought the case was justifiable as open to an application to Rome for a dispensation; but as far as I can see, it is in fact only your decision that is required.

This is intended as a perfectly respectful request. If you finally refuse it, I shall of course have to accept it. But it is a matter of deep pastoral concern, and I am afraid I am unwilling to act as an intermediary of a policy which seems to contradict what else is being done in this parish. You are the bishop and entirely responsible for the decision. I don't think I have any case for strict disobedience; but I think I may reasonably decline to inform the couple, their family and my parish council of the decision. I am sure, especially after the general feeling for parish councils and full consultation so often expressed, that you would take over from me in this delegated authority I have from you, if this had to be the course of action. I have remembered this time to take a copy of this letter, because I wanted to be sure I have not said more than I should have done, or showed you any personal or official disrespect. This is a straightforward request from priest to bishop on behalf of some of the people over whom you have given me pastoral concern and charge.

Yours sincerely, Owen.

The bishop, in spite of his strong personal views, was good enough to apply to Rome. He was very humble to do this, and I was grateful. On 21 December, just two weeks before the wedding, Rome's dispensation arrived. The bishop forwarded to me also a copy of the letter he had received from the Holy See that morning. The bishop added, 'You will notice the prohibition in paragraph 2 (that you will not officiate in any way), but since you had already made up your mind, namely to be a member of the congregation, I take it that this paragraph will not affect you.'

The dispensation was granted because of a mitigating factor, namely that the Baptist girl's father was a deacon in the chapel. The bishop had asked for the marriage to be 'in the presence of the minister and the Catholic priest *(coram ministro et sacerdote catholico)* in the Baptist chapel. The dispensation was granted 'so that the marriage rite is carried out by the non-Catholic minister alone, and the Catholic priest is expressly forbidden to have any part in the matrimonial celebration' *(ut nuptialis peragitur ritus tantum coram ministro acatholico; et sacerdos catholicus expresse vetetur celebratii matrimonii partem habere).* The bishop was also to take care 'that it takes place without exterior pomp, to avoid the danger of scandal or popular notice' *(ut hoc fiat sine pompa exteriori, remoto periculo scandali vel admirationis populi).*

The officiating minister – as I have said, one of my friends – had already asked me to take part in the service: this was tricky in the light of the Roman veto. I put on my legalistic hat and avoided any part in the official form of matrimony – i.e. the receiving of the promises from the couple as an official witness, but I did in fact read a scriptural passage and say a prayer, as many congregation members might ordinarily do in the Baptist tradition. To have refused this would have been a cause of the scandal of uncharity towards the Baptist community, and of injustice to the groom and his entirely Irish family who had come across from Ireland for the wedding. They would not have felt at ease if I were not somehow associated publicly with the occasion. I was for them the assurance of the church's dispensation.

The event proved to be a help to local ecumenism: Roman officials could have no idea of the value of 'popular notice', even though I made no effort to encourage it. All the parties involved, including the Baptist minister and his congregation, my own parish pastoral council and the civil registrar, welcomed it. It was a 'first' for such a dispensation for a wedding in a nonconformist chapel. I still wonder if Rome really understood what it meant that the girl's father was a deacon *(diaconus);* they probably thought it involved some kind of 'ordination'. Anyway, their ignorance helped to smooth the way for the dispensation.

The Catholic remained faithful to his religion; his Baptist wife came to Mass with him frequently, and they brought their first child for baptism in the Catholic church, accompanied by her Baptist parents, who do not ordinarily accept infant baptism. That was a genuinely ecumenical gesture in its turn.

I don't think I came through this process with much credit. In my own way I was bullying the bishop, who no doubt had his own wider agenda, to sustain relationships with his brother bishops in England and Wales, not to mention his reputation in the corridors of the Vatican, where he would be answerable on his five-yearly *ad limina* visit to Rome. If I did not advert to these factors it was selfish of me, or at least revealed my limitations. Yet somehow I felt I was facing what I still believe to be a bit of ecclesiastical bureaucracy; and given the growing consciousness of an ecumenical imperative since the Vatican Council, my attitude was not so extraordinary, however ineptly I handled it.

Now it was time to write to all those who had shared their views with me; as a result I received some lovely messages of congratulation:

'Glad your tenacity was rewarded and you have established a precedent. Your bishop's openness is creditable too.' (Fr Vincent Rochford)

'So glad your marriage case ended so satisfactorily. *Deo gratias.*' (Fr Jock Dalrymple)

'It is very encouraging and helpful to have the evidence of what has been allowed here and there, and I'm very happy for all concerned.' (Fr Robert Murray)

From three other priests came these remarks:

'It strikes me as very satisfactory all round, and one up for the Parish Council. I am glad you were able to reach this solution without antagonising the bishop, and he has responded generously. I expect more will be gained when he talks about this at the hierarchy meetings.' 'I'm so pleased. You've loosened another brick' and 'It seems that the outcome was splendid, and no fur lost either. Well done; by your efforts a good thing has come out of an impossible one.'

It is perhaps not surprising that another tricky case was to arise not much later.

A second round
This time the Catholic young man, a regular parishioner, was engaged to a girl from a Methodist family, both living in the village. I knew her and her family quite well because she had been a member of the Brynfields Youth Club on our premises for a long time. He was well known to all of us as a regular altar server. In the summer I discovered that he had already arranged a marriage at the local Methodist church. He had ceased to come to Mass when the arrangements were made, because he felt obliged to follow the wishes of his fiancée's parents, and he mistakenly thought that this would excommunicate him, so he kept out of my way for a while.

The Methodist family actually had no wish to draw him

away from his religion; it was he who thought it would break all the rules, and the custom of using the bride's place of worship seemed reasonable. I managed to explain all this to both of them in due course, and undertook to apply for the special dispensation for them, not without considerable misgivings about another forthcoming negotiation with the bishop.

There was no paternal diaconate to produce as a factor this time! The lad 'returned to his religious duties' and came with his fiancée for three or four months of regular explanatory sessions with me. For some weeks there was difficulty in establishing that the promises to be made concerning the baptism and Catholic upbringing of the children were assured. With good reason the bishop had personal conversations with the couple, and also with the girl's father. The latter was adamant that these promises could not fairly be demanded of anyone, though he said that he would not interfere with whatever the couple decided to do after their marriage. The girl herself, especially after several of the explanations from me, agreed that it was not an unreasonable request, provided this did not mean that the children were to have nothing to do with her own faith and chapel. I assured her that this was not the correct implication.

It is also relevant to note that the local Methodist community is tiny – some two or three dozen only, without any great hold on its members; and the girl had been impressed by the relative vigour of our Catholic community and worship when she had attended.

It then transpired that the bishop was unable to send the application forward to Rome because there was lacking the special factor of a family member being 'a minister of religion'. It looked as though the bishops together had agreed only to support these special cases. Over the phone the bishop's secretary told me that, after a phone call to Westminster, no dispensation would be forthcoming. I made an effort therefore to have an agreement for a double ceremony: first in the Catholic church before me and the Registrar, followed by a Methodist service in its fullness.

The bishop insisted that it would be necessary for the couple to acknowledge that the first, i.e. the Catholic, rite was the real marriage, however private this might be. The couple were reluctantly ready to accept this as a solution, *faute de mieux*, but the girl's father was not keen, and in fact would probably have absented himself from the Catholic rite.

I had, privately, established that the Registrar was ready to meet a request to stand by the arrangement for him to be at the Methodist service, provided our rite took place on the same day, and preferably immediately before going to the chapel. Nevertheless it was the Methodist minister, a great friend of mine, who declined to have anything to do with such a solution. He dismissed it as legalistic nonsense. Fundamentally it meant that the Catholic authorities were not prepared to accept the validity of the Methodist rite. He felt it would be 'acting a lie' to present two already-married parties before himself and a congregation for a marriage rite which was empty of more than duplicative significance. He was not impressed by the bishop's attempt at helpfulness in saying that 'after all, nuns annually renewed their vows'.

The Catholic groom never intended to cancel the arrangements with the minister. He surmised: 'If, sad to say, the Roman authorities would not dispense, and I, as the priest, was not allowed to take part, so much the worse for the law.' We had been going into the legalistic details by now, and he knew that after a marriage in the Methodist church which was not 'valid' in the eyes of the church, he could apply for a 'convalidation' as soon as possible afterwards; and then the same documentation sufficed, and would not need any application to Rome!

I stressed the absurdity of this situation to the bishop's secretary, and the real scandal it would cause if, after all, the Catholic would not be permanently in bad standing after breaking the rules. It would also bring the law into contempt.

I even spelled it all out in local detail for Bishop Fox, who, as auxiliary bishop, was brought in to deal with me. His gentle courtesy was there as always, and he listened to my tale:

'Just think of it,' I said, 'the present position is that the lad is going to be married "outside the church" because the necessary dispensation about the place of the wedding cannot be granted by the bishop without going to Rome with it.

'So, immediately after the Methodist wedding, the couple need only drive, or walk, the 100 yards round the corner from the chapel to my front door, where they could stop and inform me of what had just occurred. I could then phone Bishop's House, and ask that, with all the necessary other paper assurances which he had before him, he should grant a "convalidation" without recourse to Rome, so that the danger of them "living in sin' would be instantly removed.' This, of course, was a *reductio ad absurdum*.

I think it was Bishop Fox who then realised that the real problem was not so much the place for the wedding as the canonical form that needed dispensing, i.e. the rite of exchanging vows. As I had uncovered in the Baptist case, Canon Law really disallowed a 'mixed marriage' to take place in our churches. In some more-populated Catholic areas, like Liverpool, the ceremony had to be in the sacristy – all part of the deterrence policy! But I was only asking for an adjustment from the sacristy ceremony to a nonconformist chapel. As for the 'canonical form', this meant that it should be *coram parocho* – which in my understanding of Latin meant, 'in the presence of the parish priest'. In this case nothing would be in jeopardy because I was of course going to be present in the Methodist church. Bishop Fox took this on board but judged that *coram parocho* (in the presence of the priest) really meant that the priest was not just present but the official administrator and recipient of the exchange of promises. If the Methodist minister was going to preside to do this in the service, this was technically not *coram parocho*.

This opened up a new possibility, as I saw it. Within an hour or two I was on the phone to the Methodist minister. 'Arthur, you know that you have kindly invited me to share in the Methodist service for the forthcoming wedding, and want me to have an active part. Would you have any objection if I actually put to them the words, "Wilt thou take each here present as thy lawful wedded husband/wife?"' 'No problem,' he said. 'That's brilliant,' I responded. So I was able at once to assure the bishop that in Canon Law terms I was the one who was 'doing the wedding', following the canonical form and requirement. There was therefore no need for Rome's permission. The bishop then wrote on the typed form the reason for granting the dispensation: *'periculum matrimonii coram ministro acatholico'*, the risk otherwise of a marriage before a non-Catholic minister.

I had learned the hard way not to get too het up about these items, and I regarded the whole ecclesiastical boxing match as rather laughable. Perhaps that is why this couple won through so easily this time: no appeal to church status of blood relations; just an ordinary 'mixed marriage' in a 'suitable place'.

I also decided to inform a number of priests who had helped me in the earlier case. I made a summary of the facts and added:

'I place this on record, because it might well be helpful in other similar cases. I surmise that many non-Catholic ministers might well concede the ministering of the exchange of promises, and thus facilitate a similar joint ceremony to the satisfaction of all. I add my personal impression that these problems seem to be largely of our own making; and I still doubt the correct interpretation of the canons which we made. I have no wish to give this undesirable publicity. My bishop in the earlier case forwarded the application to Rome contrary to his own wishes, after consulting his senate of priests and the deaneries. In this second case his ultimate co-operation has not overcome his real grief that I am, in his view, undermining the traditions of the church. I do not wish to grieve him any further. Owen.'

Again I had some interesting acknowledgements:

(from Fr John Fitzsimons, priest-sociologist in Liverpool): 'I was more than grateful for what you told me about the wedding business, because it gave me a way out for a wedding here which, by being held in an RC church, was not going to help anybody. So this morning, having gone to see the bishop about something else, I put it to him that I should do the wedding in the local Anglican church. No problem. Saw the Vicar with whom I'm very friendly, and it is all fixed up to everybody's greater happiness. So please go on having bright ideas!'

(from a South of England priest): 'It seems to me that we are somewhat confined till the rules change, and that changes take place by representation, discussion, etc. However, it is possible to argue that unless someone is willing to make a stand in a particular case, then we stay as we are. One should not under-rate the deep feelings of possible relatives in Ireland who would be scandalised by marriages in Catholic churches; we need to move slowly, and I have a large Irish immigrant population. I sometimes wonder whether the answer is not that the children can be brought up as Anglicans, Methodists as well as being Catholics.'

(from Fr Ted Mitchinson of YCW): 'I admire and envy you chaps who follow the logic and demands of your conscience. I feel quite with you on all this in heart and mind, but for some reason I can't make a thing of it with my bishop. Still, thanks for your pressure and a good number of others: a change in the end is bound to come.'

It was especially kind of Bishop Derek Worlock in Portsmouth to write. This was before I revived my acquaintance with him later in 1969 on my way out of parish work.

'Here is just a small comment on your circular, though obviously the situation will not be helped by its publication. We have of course endeavoured in these parts to find a solution along the lines which you mention in the case of the Methodist; but we seldom have problems over mixed marriages with Methodists. Usually our problems relate to Anglicans and here, together with the Anglican bishop, we have tried to find an answer. Unfortunately it is perfectly clear that no marriage can take place in the Church of England save in accordance with the rites of the Church of England. Thus it is not just a question of "place" but of dispensation from "form". I mention this because it would be a pity if people were to think that the solution could always be found along the lines you have mentioned. We even considered simultaneous utterance by the ministers of both parties but this really did seem to be mumbo-jumbo. It looks as though there may be some new regulations about mixed marriages before long. I get the impression that there is an increasing understanding regarding the "place" of a marriage but that there is not likely to be any move at all with regard to the question of promises.'

An amusing and typically short note came to me from Archbishop Roberts SJ, living at Mount Street, London. 'It was good of you to send me the cases. I wish it were possible to send you all mine!'

As another exercise in consultation, this had been valuable. I was determined not to act in isolation from the views of others, even though the decisions were to be my own responsibility as I took up the cudgels. I learned much from the varying perspectives on these problems from people much wiser than myself. All this is 'archive' material, albeit personal and maybe ecclesiastical tittle-tattle. Even so, for me it was all part of trying to be a pastor to people in a legalistic dilemma; and it was a further exercise in challenging conformity. The whole experience stood me in good stead in 1968 when a real *crise de conscience* arose, following the publication of *Humanae Vitae*, which I document in the next chapter.

CHAPTER SEVEN

On the Margins of Obedience:
Humanae Vitae and all that

'Real obedience includes the courage to be a troublesome subject. Not a grumbler, not one who is always complaining, who always knows better, who cannot fit in anywhere ... We should also have the will, and constantly strive to be amiable, friendly, agreeable subjects, meeting our superiors in a proper, manly and refined manner.' (Karl Rahner in *Meditations on Priestly Life*)

In between these two tantalising marriage cases came the publication of *Humanae Vitae*. I don't recall any of us taking much notice of 95% of it, which on later reflection it was possible to see as a positive view of married love. Because of its antecedents, all we wanted to know was whether the total ban on artificial means of contraception in marriage was to be lifted in any way. The advance news was that Pope Paul VI had given us an unconditional 'No'. The issue may seem to be totally passé; the details of the debate may now be unimportant, but as an exercise in consultation, sharing fear and anxieties, and in giving appropriate help to a parish congregation, it may still be worth tracing the procedure I decided upon.

Action
At the time of the encyclical's publication, but before actually receiving the text, I was so worried that I decided to send another circular letter to about eighty priests and some others. This is the text.

29th July 1968
Dear Colleague,
1. Before we have had the chance of reading the encyclical on birth control, it is obviously unfair and unwise to judge what we must do about it. Nevertheless continual phone-calls

today (about ten) have reminded me of our relative isolation. I dare to think it might help if I share a few of my thoughts with you, in the serious hope that you will do the same for me. I believe we must work urgently to get this in perspective, and save the huge pain which (whether rightly or wrongly) the decisions will already have caused from unnecessary consequences.

2. It very much sounds as though we have simply been given a repetition of the former disciplinary treatment, with the same justifying reasons; a repetition of the old formulae about natural law, about the dangers of sexual abuse, etc., with scarcely a reference to the attitudes, values and nuances of Vatican II. So far disappointing and puzzling; but very much in Pope Paul's recent pattern of thinking, as in the recent *Credo*.

I personally, for what it is worth, have never favoured advocating artificial methods of birth control. (I have to admit the population problems of the East are too remote for me.) I haven't direct experience ('God bless the dear man's holy innocence!') of sexual intercourse, but it always strikes me imaginatively as pretty inhibiting if you've got to adjust yourself with artificial devices, or take prophylactic pills, medical problems apart. I haven't yet met a couple who like doing this for its own sake.

I also believe strongly that we all need practical lessons in penance, self-control, cross-bearing, which are sometimes alarmingly absent from Christian teaching and practice.

Yet, avoiding (or even refusing) any *advocating* such methods of birth control is quite different from condemning them as necessarily sinful. I honestly believe that there are circumstances in which such things may here and now, in this particular instance or set of instances, be necessary for the sake of Christian marriage.

I do not believe that any man, or Pope, or even Council can tell us that any particular act or device or practice is *simpliciter* 'sinful', unless it is plainly so to the community conscience or directly revealed by God that it is so.

4. Accordingly I feel bound to say that my dilemmas about the way in which the magisterium of the church works are, on the face of it, gravely exacerbated now. I profoundly regretted the Pope reserving this matter to himself in the first

place. I am quite unable to see how he can bypass the majority
commission recommendations without producing new reasons.

I know that encyclical letters are not infallible, just like that. I
believe them to have high authority all the same. I believe I
am in grave danger if I set up my own opinion against an encyclical's teaching.

5. However, in the light of mounting opinions of theologians,
doctors, even of some express directives for confessional
practice by single or groups of bishops (what for instance
does Archbp. Beck do now?); but most of all in the light of
my own pastoral experience of listening to and counselling
many Catholic couples, is my dilemma simply a personal
opinion? My experience of those married people who have
upheld the discipline of the past is that they have done so, almost without exception, simply because they believed this to
be the teaching of the church – not because they could see
why it was the teaching of the church. I have been unable to
share their blind obedience, though I hope I have adequately
honoured their sincerity and docility.

For myself, I do not see how this is the teaching of the church,
though it is plainly the teaching of Paul VI. Is this private
opinion again?

6. If – a big 'if' till we have really studied the encyclical – if the
encyclical is entirely negative, something has gone radically
wrong. In this case we owe it to those in our pastoral care, as
we have done hitherto, to help dig out the nuggets of positive
teaching that may yet be covered up in the document, which
are certainly part of a fully Catholic understanding of married love. Insofar as we are in some sense only in our parishes
on commission from the bishop we owe it to him to say openly
what we can in conscience teach, and what we feel obliged to
be silent about. If he believes our teaching is incompatible
with our holding pastoral office under him, I for one am willing to take the consequences. To abandon, especially under
my own steam, a calling to pastoral work in the ministerial
priesthood is to me unthinkable anywhere along the line. I
have never seen how anyone can leave the priesthood, let
alone the church, for anything less than quite overwhelming
reasons. I can conceive of suspension or excommunication.
There are, alas, precedents.

7. I hate majority decisions. I dislike the acceptance of 'democratic' procedures in the church. I personally deplored the voting system at the Council. I have always favoured the Quaker way of discovering truth in the 'feeling of the meeting'. It was not therefore the simple fact of numbers in the 'majority-commission' report that made it morally binding on the Pope, as it seemed to me; but the fact that this was supreme evidence of the 'feeling of the meeting', or, as we say, of the developing mind of the church.

So far as I have heard extracts, the new encyclical is not for me the mind of the church. It is another deplorable disciplinary ruling. What is it for you? When we have had time to do our homework – but not too long, this is desperately urgent – may we be in touch again? And meantime, what are you going to say to your people?

Yours sincerely,

Owen Hardwicke

PS: Simply as a matter of interest, among my phone-callers today have been a distinguished Catholic musician, a training college lecturer, a rural PP, a Liverpool (on his silver jubilee) curate, and the joint message of sympathy and promise of prayers from the local Anglican Vicar, and Methodist Minister – senior men with whom I work at all times. ('In my own marriage experience,' said the latter, 'I had to work this thing out years ago. I couldn't have managed my marriage without methods of birth control.' What happened to the natural law here?)

The replies to this were, naturally, slow in coming. Meanwhile there was a Sunday to face. I slipped down to Cardiff to see my father in hospital, and managed to get a pile of CTS translations of the encyclical in time. I distributed them round the seats in the church before Mass, and prepared a special sermon. I read through a personal Guidelines to issue at the end of Mass, and I planned three study sessions for that week.

I do not normally write out my sermons. It seemed to me important to do so this once anyway. I wanted to be quite sure I could tell the bishop exactly what I had said, in case he asked me. And I kept plenty of spare copies of my Guidelines.The sermon went like this on Sunday 4 August 1968:

At the end of the Encyclical on Birth Control, the Holy Father makes an appeal to priests:

(28) 'Beloved priest sons, by vocation you are the counsellors and spiritual guides of individual persons and of families. We now turn to you with confidence. Your first task … is to expound the church's teaching on marriage without ambiguity. Be the first to give in the exercise of your ministry, the example of loyal internal and external obedience to the teaching authority of the church …'

It is with profound sorrow and regret that, deeply as I always hope to expound the church's teaching on marriage, or on anything else, without ambiguity, I am unable to tell you that the Pope's Encyclical Letter is a definitive and final word. It is an important contribution towards establishing the church's teaching; no-one can lightly set aside the words of the Pope. I would not, and do not, counsel you to any form of disobedience, but it is my clear conviction – a purely personal one, though supported by many significant voices – that this ruling of the Holy Father is not the whole story.

There are many, many things in the Letter which will remind everyone of the high ideals of Christian marriage. It is a thoroughly compassionate Letter. Anyone who says otherwise cannot have read it without prejudice. I was moved to realise with what deep anxiety he spoke in the hope of clarifying an issue which has been tantalising so many people. But in the event it does not seem to me that his contribution has advanced the situation at all. He has firmly repeated the former teaching and discipline without a single new reason to meet the conscientious difficulties of so many Christians. He has set aside, without saying why, the considered advice of the majority of his theologians on the Commission set up to examine the question, he has ignored the well-known views of the Cardinals of Vienna, Utrecht and Malines, of many other bishops throughout the world, and of the World Congress of the Laity which met in Rome last year.

I readily admit he has great courage; he does not believe it is an easy saying; he knows it will cause great upset; and he says that the gospel is always a sign of contradiction. He is a man in great personal distress now; for he has prayed and wrestled with the problem for several years. But so have millions of married Christians; and their conclusion is different. That does not make them right. But the Pope himself says that the matter is open to solution through the right understanding of the natural law – it is not specifically a matter of Christian revelation. This means that the actual conclusions are as good as the reasons given to support them, which he sincerely believes should be clear to all upright and unprejudiced minds.

If they are conclusions which seem to you to accord with reason; if you are able to accept this discipline as divinely ordained, I shall do nothing to disturb your belief. You will plainly be in the majority at present. My words are now addressed to those who cannot see in this a new contribution to the subject, which remains unsolved in clear terms. Obviously, however, I am in a great dilemma, and this is not the time or place to go deeply into it. I simply wish to remain a priest in the service of the church. I hope this will be possible. My responsibility is not first to the Pope or my bishop but to Christ; but I receive my commission to be your parish priest through the bishop. He has every right to decide that if I persist in this view, I cannot have his commission. It is unlikely that any of us who feel like this will be put on the carpet for some time – maybe not at all.

And if I am over-dramatising the event (quite possibly; you know me well enough), it is in the hope of giving you some sense of urgency about it all. I beg you to read the Encyclical Letter carefully – not an easy task in the usual papal language not too well translated – and state your belief openly in the light of it.

Many of you will be able to stand firm to the belief and discipline of Pope Paul; you might be able to give me reasons why I should do the same. Or you may be able to give further witness to another view of the matter which I believe has still not been properly weighed in the balance of the debate.

Let me say this, before turning to my summary of the situation; I have never at any time in the past, nor will I in the future, recommend any form of artificial birth-prevention. But that is very different from being obliged to say that such are always necessarily sinful procedures. I cannot in conscience say (as it looks as though I am expected to say) that artificial birth-control in all circumstances, for every person and at all times, is unnatural and sinful. I can tell you that this is what Pope Paul says, and you must bear this weightily in mind when you exercise your own conscience in the matter.

All I can do now is to make a comment on one of the crucial issues that this raises. If (and it's a big 'if'), if the Pope were wrong, if the magisterium of the church which is being apparently voiced through him here were mistaken, does this empty the magisterium of its real purpose? If it were the case that this claimed to be an infallible pronouncement, and it were proved wrong, there would be an impossible situation. One would simply have to cease to be a member of the church. But I really believe this, from Christ's promise, to be quite impossible.

But the magisterium has many times reversed its decisions – those that were authoritative but not infallible. I have only time to tell you of one – a rather famous case.

Up to the 16th century, it was the commonly accepted understanding of the world that the earth was the centre of the universe. This was part of the Ptolemaic astronomy, which was then called in question by Copernicus. He taught that the sun was the centre of things, that the earth went round the sun, and the great astronomer Galileo began to say so. He alleged that the scriptures might say otherwise (or rather assume otherwise) but they were not intended to teach us science and philosophy. The Congregation of the Holy Office summoned him and told him to abandon this opinion; he was not to deal with it any more on pain of imprisonment. Galileo acquiesced. This was on the order of another Pope Paul – Paul V. The books of Copernicus and Diego and others were to be prohibited and condemned. Under the next Pope, Galileo apparently began teaching it again, and he was arraigned before the Holy Office in 1633. He was told that if he said that the sun is the centre of the world rather than the earth, etc. – 'all this is absurd, false in philosophy and erroneous in faith; it is formally heretical as being expressly contrary to holy scripture'.

Here was the highest doctrinal authority in the church of that time, with the authority of first Pope Paul V and then of Pope Urban VIII, saying that you had to believe the world was immovable, and the centre of the universe. Of course it wasn't an infallible pronouncement; it was genuinely and sincerely held that this contradicted scripture. The decree suspending such teaching was reversed in 1757 by which time the philosophy of Newton had come to be accepted in the church. And as we know clearly today, we are officially taught that the scriptures are not there to teach us science or philosophy; they are to be understood in an entirely different way.

There was a time when it was condemned for anyone to lend his money for profit; now the church establishment herself has great investments. There was a time (only 1864) when Pope Pius IX condemned the proposition that a man had the freedom to embrace the religion which he believed to be true; the Vatican II Council has explicitly said the opposite.

There was a time when there were two Popes at once, each excommunicating the other and his followers for all they were worth; and on both sides were holy men and women, some of whom were later canonised as saints.

God's truth is not so easily come by; and maybe in some cases, we can only continue to make it out as best we can. The magisterium of the church is not a book where all the answers can be looked up with certainty. It is a guide, and one that will vary its guidance from time to time, round the nucleus of certainties that Christ himself revealed to his apostles. Sometimes the guidance will not prove to be of much help; more often than not it has done the church great service. The ways in which the magisterium of the church should operate in the present age of the church are under discussion; ultimately I believe that this will be the value of the present decision of the Holy Father; it will really make us look at the nature of the authority of the church. Meantime we must all, yes all, hold to that which we know to be true. I conclude with the words of the lay editor of *The Tablet*:

'Loyalty to the faith and to the whole principle of authority now consists in this: to speak out about this disillusion of ours, not to be silenced by fear. We who are of the household, and can think of no other, have the right to question, complain and protest, when conscience impels. We have the right, and we have the duty – out of love for the brethren. Who can separate us from the love of God and one another?' I hope I will not make it more difficult for you here.

Listening to a homily, a speech, or a lecture is of little use unless it is mulled over and discussed. (I wish we priests remembered that, and stopped wondering why we have so little effect from the pulpit.) So I issued a hand-out, together with copies of the Encyclical, as a prelude to three discussion meetings. I felt that many people needed something to activate their minds at once. It went like this:

A PERSONAL ATTEMPT TO GUIDE PARISHIONERS ABOUT THE BIRTH-CONTROL ISSUE

1. You may be among those who believe that Pope Paul's Encyclical Letter settles the matter once and for all – that all artificial means of birth-prevention are sinful, and are therefore not allowed in any circumstances for Catholics. If so, you will have at present the overwhelming numerical support of bishops and priests throughout the world.

Do not forget, however, that what the Pope condemns is artificial birth-prevention, not birth control. The so-called 'safe-period' method of birth-control may still be necessary in many circumstances.

Please continue to bear in mind that millions of your fellow-Christians (including many Catholics) will not be able to accept this as the gospel of Christ.

2. You may be among those who find that this decision challenges their own conscientious convictions about the matter. If so:

a. Please remember the extreme difficulty for the Pope, in spite of his huge, compassionate efforts in this Encyclical, of really understanding a married person's situation. Remember also that he has been under heavy pressure to make up his mind one way or the other.

b. Be quite clear that an Encyclical Letter is not an infallible document just like that. It clearly has high authority. But a matter of discipline is not a matter of unconditional truth. There is quite a history in the church of emphatic decisions being sharply reversed in the light of further study and understanding. It is important to note that the Pope has based his decision on the same grounds as those on which previous directives were given.

c. The Second Vatican Council has given us a fuller understanding of the nature of the church. While the Pope as chief bishop is of enormous importance, he is not the sole teacher in the church. The whole college of bishops together are teachers; and there is also a certain authority in 'the belief of the faithful'.

d. No-one can be obliged to do what is impossible. No-one can be cut off from the communion of the church by being unable to accept a high ideal of disciplinary practice. As before there will still be many priests who will hold that the field is still clear for the same pastoral consideration of the many exceptional cases.

e. Your dismay at the Pope saying 'No' to everything, does not mean that you wanted him to say 'Yes' to everything. There are many couples who find periodic and even total abstaining from intercourse quite possible, without any damage to themselves or their marriage. We must surely maintain that the procreation of children is normally a vital part of Christian marriage.

f. We all owe it to the Holy Father to read and study the Encyclical Letter carefully. We all owe it to the church to make our minds known.

On the reverse side I scribbled a last-minute post-script.

Three Study Sessions on the Encyclical have been planned for this week (see Bulletin). One in Penycae, one in Johnstown, one in Ruabon. It is *most important* that you try to come to *one* of these. Do *you* know where you stand? Can you explain yourself to others who ask?

The following day I was writing round again a) to report on the first responses to my circular, and b) to enclose another priest's sermon about the issue, on the basis of which I can see I had developed my own. It comforted me greatly to know that I was not the only one to think this way.

Pastoral Letter from Bishop Petit and Bishop Fox
I was away from my parish on the Sundays of 18 and 25 August, and on the first of these dates Bishop Petit, and his auxiliary Bishop Fox, asked for a pastoral letter to be read.

Dear Reverend Fathers and dear Children in Christ,
The Vicar of Christ, Pope Paul, has written a letter in the regulation of birth, to all men of good will. Before the ink with which it was written was scarcely dry, and certainly before any close study of other documents such as the statements of the church assembled in the second Council of the Vatican or any other Encyclical Letter written by preceding Vicars of Christ, including Pope John XXIII, a storm of opposition in the press, on the radio and on the television screen has broken out, the like of which we have never seen before.

All kinds of abuse have been heaped on the head of the Vicar of Christ not only by men and women who are not Catholics but sadly enough by some Catholics, even by some priests. The Vicar of Christ has become, like his Master, our Blessed Lord himself, a sign of contradiction. Some, like part of Christ's audience when he taught the doctrine of the Holy Eucharist, have said, 'This is a hard saying and who shall hear it' and have threatened they will walk with him no more.

Indeed it may be a 'hard saying' for some, yet softened by the words of compassion of the Vicar of Christ, 'We do not intend to hide the sometimes serious difficulties inherent in the life of Christian married persons. For them, as for everyone else, "the gate is narrow and the way is hard that leads to life". But the hope of that life must enlighten their way, as with courage they strive to live with wisdom, justice and piety in this present time, knowing that the figure of this world passes away.'

There are quite a number of people who are telling the world why the Vicar of Christ should not have written this encyclical letter, so let us ask why he wrote it and by what authority he wrote it. Let us take the first question first. Pope Paul wrote this letter because as he himself says, 'with recent evolution of society, changes have taken place that give rise to new questions which the church could not ignore.' In other words the Vicar of Christ, precisely because he is the Vicar of Christ, had to carry out his duty as the Shepherd of shepherds and teach the flock of Christ, the people of God.

Let us be perfectly clear in our minds on one point. This letter to the flock of Christ and to all men, is not the expression of a personal opinion of a bishop who happens to be the Pope. This letter is the authoritative teaching of the Vicar of Christ which demands our loyal inward assent even though this assent may be difficult and hard.

As Catholics we are bound to believe that the church was founded by Christ our Lord. The church is the Mystical Body of Christ. It is a perfect and imperishable society whose object is to continue the redemptive work of Christ through its teaching, its government and its priesthood. Our Lord Jesus Christ gave the supreme power of jurisdiction over the church to St Peter to be handed to all the successors of St

Peter as Bishop of Rome. Like St Peter, Pope Paul is the Vicar of Christ with all the duty of feeding, that is teaching, the lambs, the yearlings and the fully grown up sheep of the flock of his Master, Christ. 'Thou art Peter, the rock, and upon this rock I will build my church and the gates of hell shall not prevail against it, and to thee I will give the keys of the gates of heaven. Whatsoever thou shalt bind on earth shall be bound also in heaven. Whatsoever thou shalt loose on earth shall be loosed also in heaven.'

Truly the gates of hell are now trying to prevail as they have before, as they will again. Why did St John Fisher and St Thomas More die except for the truth that the Pope is the Vicar of Christ with all the full, supreme, universal power to teach, rule and sanctify the people of God? As the second Vatican Council proclaimed, 'in virtue of his office as Vicar of Christ and Pastor of the whole church the Pope possesses full, supreme, universal power over the church and he is always able to exercise it without impediment.' This is the doctrine handed down to us from the beginning and which we must defend in its fullness and for which we must be prepared to die, as our fathers did before us.

It is perfectly true that for some people to carry out the teaching of the Vicar of Christ on this matter of artificial birth control will mean self-denial, self-control, mortification. But this is only to repeat and re-echo the words of Christ himself. 'If any man will be my follower, let him deny himself, take up his cross and follow me.' There is no other way of being a Christian. Yet we must always remember that if we do carry the cross, it will carry us, because as our Lord said, 'My yoke is sweet and my burden light.' Marriage does not depend for its life-long happiness upon intercourse, but upon the selfless devotion of each partner to the other.

I close this letter with the words of the second Vatican Council: 'God, the Lord of life, committed to man the high responsibility of maintaining life – a responsibility to be carried out in a way worthy of men. So life must, from its very conception, be guarded with the greatest care. Abortion and infanticide are abominable crimes. Man's sexual make-up and the human procreative faculty are remarkably superior to those found in the lower grades of life; hence married sexual activity, ordered in accordance with full human dignity, is matter for grave reverence. Moral behaviour then, when it is a question of reconciling married love with the responsible transmitting of life, does not depend only on a sincere intention and the evaluating of motives, but must be judged by objective standards. These are drawn from the nature of the human person and of its acts, and have regard for the whole meaning of mutual self-giving and human procreation in the context of true love. This cannot be unless the virtue of married chastity is sincerely cultivated. For children of the church, taking their stand on these principles, it is not lawful to regulate procreation by embarking on ways which the church's teaching authority, in expounding the divine law, condemns.

Let it be clear to everybody that man's life and the business of transmitting it are not matters confined to this world or to be understood and measured solely by its standards. They always bear on man's eternal destiny.

We send you all our blessing.

+ John, Bishop of Menevia

+ Langton D. Fox, Auxiliary Bishop of Menevia

In the parish Bulletin I left the following message to accompany the reading.

The visiting priest will read you this Sunday a Pastoral Letter from our bishop and his auxiliary. I trust all parishioners will hear this respectfully as a letter from the chief pastor of our diocese, in the same way as we have tried to attend carefully to the words of the chief pastor of the whole church, Pope Paul, by circulating copies of his recent Encyclical Letter, and convening three sessions to study it.

Parishioners know my own hesitations about imposing anything on anyone, which is not absolutely clearly the teaching of the whole church. While it is quite clear that the Encyclical Letter is not an infallible statement (which means quite simply that it is open to the possibility of error, and can be corrected if necessary) – our bishops plainly believe that its high authority may not allow us to call it in question.

Our bishops are men of justice, and they will be the first to allow this official freedom if there is reasonable agreement in the church that the whole matter of birth-control is not after all a completely closed matter.

They are right in saying that much unfair abuse has been

poured on the Pope. But they do not say that every criticism of the Pope's teaching is necessarily without reason and foundation. You yourselves in this parish will know that the Holy Father has not been abused by some of his critics anyway. We must always bear weightily in mind what is said authoritatively within the church, whose whole teaching, as Pope Paul says, must be taught unambiguously by all priests. This I have tried to do.

What is more, no individual conscience is sufficient to justify departure from common teaching and practice. A public judgement can only reasonably be made by a conscience which is properly informed of the developments in the teaching of the church, and is aware of the mind of the church as expressed in the understanding of many others. As individuals we can only do the best we can; and none of us must lay claim to that infallibility which even the Roman authorities are insistent does not attach to this Encyclical Letter.

It deeply grieves me to give even the faintest impression of disloyalty to the church which it cost me much to join, and in which I fully intend to remain. I trust the bishops' cautions will be listened to, and my own guidance will not be misunderstood.

Should I have been making these comments? Should I have revealed so openly my doubts and difficulties with my parishioners? I am certain many people would have said then, and might say so today, that this only confuses the laity. Such a reply is related to a different model of church, of authority, of moral truth than I was able to uphold. I knew how shaken many parishioners were by the negatives of the Encyclical. I was genuinely trying to carry some of their pain and dismay, and hold them to the life of the church. My openness was a factor in favour of them holding on. One couple actually said that had I not made my statement on 4 August, they would have left our communion at once.

I kept the bishop informed of my outreach to other priests. I commented on the pastoral letter when I wrote to him on 17 August from my brother's London home:

My dear Bishop,
Since you have not acknowledged my recent letters, I take it at least that I am not immediately outlawed for my views. I understand that you said somewhere that you were anxious

to listen to what people had to say first of all. Fair enough; but I suppose that you will also convene a meeting in due course of all those who find immense difficulties in understanding the whole drift of the Encyclical. Maybe you will quash one day's subjects at the Pantasaph Conference, so that we can deal with this together? From my own correspondence in the last two weeks or so, I am acutely aware of the widespread sharing of difficulties.

I am also aware that I have no right to send on to you the opinions of Menevia men without their express permission. Only nine or ten have replied (out of about 45) in spite of my appeal for some word. Of these one was a plain 'Shut up'; that my whole reasoning was out of court; all the rest shared some, most or all of my own difficulties. As I travel about on holiday – five days so far – and from some 40 other letters, I am aware of enormous feeling which does not know quite how best to organise itself. So I am certain that the only thing is for the bishops to meet their diocesan priests in groups as soon as possible for much talking. I feel sure that the wielding of the heavy stick will only lead to greater trouble, and will not do justice to the depth of our concerns.

We had three study groups in the parish on the text, last week, and I was unable to solve the several questions that arose. Any appeal to simple authority did not help either; it was this that was questioned anyway.

I must say that (as respectfully as I can) your pastoral letter for this Sunday does not help in any way. I honestly believe that one or two passages are only true with certain qualifications; and the implications of some remarks are unfortunate and, I believe, unfair.

For instance: '… all kinds of abuse have been heaped on the head … even by some priests …' True, but the implication is that all criticism is necessarily abuse, and unlawful.

When our Lord allowed some to walk with him no more, it was as a result of a profound mystery which was presented to them as a continuing sign of his loving presence. I believe a papal ruling on a moral question is an entirely different category; I almost think the comparison blasphemous – sorry!

And to hold up the Holy Father as a sign of contradiction for the very reason that he is opposed, or at least challenged by learned and devout Catholics, is capable of a very different interpretation. Even the John Fisher example is unfair. True, he upheld papal authority – but over against the King's interference. John Fisher was a sign of contradiction in this respect against the whole bench of bishops otherwise. So far, I admit, there is no public sign of one diocesan bishop having difficulties with the Encyclical in Great Britain; but I don't think this situation will persist.

As Vatican II proclaimed, 'In virtue of his office as Vicar of Christ and Pastor of the whole church, the Pope possesses full, supreme, universal power over the church, and he is always able to exercise it without impediment. This is the doctrine handed down to us *from the beginning*.'

Please accept in deep respect for you and the Pope, an emphatic negative to this. I recognise that this is the point to which development of teaching has gone; a development which the collegiality of the bishops has not yet modified; but it was not so *from the beginning* and, unless we misunderstand the whole notion of development, not every development is to be accepted as legitimate, wise, or binding without chance of reversal.

I'm afraid that while you rightly avoid the use of the word 'infallible' throughout your pastoral letter, you give the strongest impression that the Encyclical is to be taken as virtually infallible and irreversible. This I cannot see, and profoundly regret.

I have two more weeks' holiday in which I am safe from any dangerous remarks; but I profoundly hope you will hear what is already being said by many priests and people, before judging whether or not I – or others like me – can reasonably hold commission under you in the diocese.

Yours sincerely, Owen

The bishop was good enough to reply at once.

When you have finished your holiday and returned to Ruabon we can meet and talk. In the highly-charged emotional atmosphere which has been created, writing or even talking at the moment cannot be as fruitful as one would wish. What I sincerely hope is that you will have a quiet and restful holiday, and not let matters get so much on top of you that they will affect your health.

Reaction

By the time I was back, our two bishops had sent a very helpful circular to all the clergy who were obviously in the front line to meet the distress of many married people. Their theme was to take up the words of the Encyclical, saying, 'In their difficulties, many married couples always find, in the words and in the heart of a priest, the echo of the voice and the core of the Redeemer.'

The bishops drew the following practical pastoral conclusions, which were directed as far as I could see against those who might now be heavy-handed with their people in the light of a hard-line decision by Pope Paul VI. They said:

'Therefore: 1. We must not fail to put the highest standard and encourage people to do their best to live up to it. Uphold the principle always. But consider each individual case carefully.

2. We must bear in mind factors which affect the morality of human acts and which can diminish responsibility and culpability. They are treated in all the Moral Theology manuals. They should be applied in this matter as in others.

3. We must remember that after the confusion of recent years, even the best will need time to form a firm conscience. Therefore we must be very slow to make a severe judgement and abstain from denunciations either from the pulpit or in private.

'Patience' and 'Goodness' mean that one should not invoke the full rigour of the law on those who are learning slowly and with difficulty not only how to keep it, but even that it ought to be kept.

With every good wish and blessing. Yours sincerely,

+ John, Bishop of Menevia

+ Langton D. Fox, Auxiliary Bishop of Menevia.

By the following week, on my return from holiday, I was at my typewriter and duplicator again to keep the communication open with at least seventeen of my fellow diocesan priests.

4th September 1968

Dear Friend,

This time a personal letter – not a circular; duplicated simply because there are more people I want to write to than I can manage individually.

I just thought that you might like to hear some of the responses to my earlier circulars; and perhaps also what I have gleaned during my three-weeks holiday which took me to Cardiff, Oxford, London, Birmingham, Edinburgh and Gloucester. Everywhere one found people, not merely anxious to discuss the crisis, but obviously relieved to discover that feeling was widespread and responsible concerning the insupportable aspects of the Encyclical Letter. Many people have the impression that criticism of the document is necessarily abusive (one false implication of our own bishops' pastoral, alas), unsound and simply rebellious. They are immensely encouraged to have personal evidence of the views of many distinguished priests, whose names have appeared nowhere in print.

It becomes increasingly clear that the real difficulty is not the particular conclusion (that every act must be open to the possibility of procreation; and that every form of artificial means of contraception is in every instance to be excluded as illicit) but the nature of the authority of the document, and the manner of the exercise of that authority. There are several I have met who accept the conclusion, though reluctantly, and yet reject the moral right of the Pope to speak here and now in this particular way.

It is also clear that there are almost as many difficulties felt by priests as there are dissidents. It is quite impossible to polarise people into two camps: either for or against the Pope, or for or against artificial contraception. But the consequence of this is that the debate is plainly wide open. More and more people seem to be saying, 'Read the Encyclical carefully; it comes from the highest teaching authority in the church; weigh up what it says, and then make your own judgement along with others.' The choice is not even that of papal authority versus private opinion; the Pope's decision is not that of a private person, but follows a weighty school of thought. No more is it personal opinion at the other end of things when it is a conscientious view widely held by very responsible persons, by a large section of the people of God in fact, and roundly supported by some very distinguished theologians.

In case you have not heard, may I help you with one or two other items of news; sorry if this is 'old hat'. Archbishop Beck has openly said the debate is still on; he has authorised his auxiliary to call in some 20 senior priests in Liverpool to pool their strongest views for him under the heading: 'The Pope has said, but ...' – and as many 'buts' as they can provide, before the British bishops meet on Sept 17th. He has also declared that no-one in his diocese will be suspended for anything he might say anywhere at any time on this issue.

And what says Bishop Butler? I could only discover a private view from a private letter during my holiday, though he graciously acknowledged receipt of my 'circulars', which I marked with the note: 'For information only'. But I have now heard of his, still private, but reliable views, and they are positively explosive. He is attending the meeting of the European bishops with Alfrink, Doepfner, Suenens, Koenig next week; and there is no question but that he regards the letter as a major blunder in the realm of authority. When one reads some of the backroom information from Fr Haring, one can appreciate the apparently clear pattern of pressurising that the Curia has used.

There is no sign of any more suspensions in the offing, even in Southwark; but it is not the case that Fr Paul Weir has been re-instated, as has been suggested. He is now living in a pres-bytery again with two sympathetic priests and has given an undertaking not to give publicity to his views; but he is still suspended from saying Mass, as well as from hearing confessions. Fr Cronin of Birmingham (today's *Times* gives his letter) has gone into some kind of voluntary resignation, be-cause it is plain that Archbishop Dwyer believes there can be no going back on the Encyclical's teaching.

And at the same time, more bishops have sent out the same sort of (exactly the same?) pastoral advice that we have re-cently had, which is compassionate and seems to some of us completely to undermine the rigidity of the Encyclical. And it is still not clear how one can give internal and external con-sent to a matter which is not incapable of correction. As Mgr Joseph Buckley (J.C.D. etc.) said: 'We have been told that the Encyclical Letter is not infallible; but no-one is willing to say that therefore it is fallible.' It would be difficult to see how its teaching can be imposed without any further recourse if this is so.

Our own bishop appears to be calling in those of us who have made known our inability to accept the whole Letter's teach-ing; one by one we are given some two hours (or more) of fatherly talk, and told to go away and say our prayers. He will not suspend anyone, by the looks of it; but he throws it back on to our individual consciences as to whether we can either hear confessions, given our views, or continue to be dissidents at all. I do not think he yet knows of the strength of the 'opposition' to the Letter elsewhere; though judging by replies from Menevia men, I must agree that numerically it is small here. However, out of 46 priests at the Liturgy Conference at Spode House today, no less than 43 found they could not accept the Letter's whole teaching. There was an amazing near unanimity among the priests from all over Britain, including seminary professors, senior PPs, and representatives of several orders or congregations. The resolution that went out to each of the British bishops was as follows:

> 'The seventh annual conference of Practical Liturgy met at Spode House to discuss the theme, Penance; Virtue & Sacrament. We were inevitably confronted with the pastoral situation created in the church by the Encyclical *Humanae Vitae*.
>
> The meeting felt unanimously that discussion of the Encyclical should be kept open in view of the fact that members of the church, both priests and laity, find themselves involved in considerable difficulties.
>
> We strongly believe that true solutions to these difficulties will only emerge in an atmosphere of openness and trust. We therefore earnestly plead with our bishops to reassure their priests that they may approach them to discuss with them their conscientious difficulties without fear of sanctions.'

All this, because there is much evidence, a. That priests are as inclined as anyone in the church to think that the Pope's juridical right to speak (unquestioned) obliges them to shut up altogether now on pain of disloyalty; and b. That many priests are keeping silent, and relying simply on a 'liberal' policy in the confessional being still allowed, rather than helping the bishops to contribute to the mind of the church – all out of fear of the chopper.

You may not like the activities of the 'Ad Hoc Society' of layfolk; but at least they have discovered quite widespread spontaneous groups of laity trying to keep the debate going;

they have over 1,000 personal offers of help for any priest who may be 'chopped'. And it is plain that it can no longer be held that this is a bunch of bourgeois intellectuals; it is the everyday type of working Catholic who is involved.

Yours sincerely,

Owen.

I then gave extracts from many of those who had already written back to me. By no means are the writers all of one mind, and certainly some of them flatly disagreed with me. The responses indicate how very much it was the issue of the nature and extent of teaching authority that predominate. The quotations will be of particular interest to those who knew the signatories; and I have taken care to ask permission of those who are still alive before including their names. Thirty years later some of them may have changed their minds. I have not.

Menevia priests:

1. '... with my background (for which I thank God) the desire for absolute unity of mind with the Pope is an overwhelming emotional and intellectual factor ... For my part I have been examining every possible means of seeing the reasons behind Pope Paul's pronouncement. I would, if I could, love to be convinced; but I cannot. In other words, I am reluctant to stand where I do; but I must ... Part of the apostolate is just enduring the strain as long as we can.'

2. 'I must confess that my own reaction to the Encyclical Letter was one of deep anger, and this has not been abated by reading the full document, nor by the various pleas for sympathy and understanding with the Pope in his "cruel dilemma". It is particularly exasperating that the Pope refers over and again to "the church this", and "the church that", when we know perfectly well that the one thing he has never allowed is for the church to be allowed to judge the matter as the People of God and the Body of Christ ... I had a talk with ... He says the Encyclical Letter is certainly neither infallible nor irreformable. He regards artificial birth control as a venial sin of disobedience, tapering off into no sin at all if reason good enough ...'

3. 'I have never advocated artificial birth control, but I wonder if at times it can be justified. Psychologically I would say it was preferable to "the Catholic method", i.e. coitus interruptus. The encyclical has not changed anything for me ...'

4. 'I personally am relieved by the Encyclical Letter. I think the church is saying "No, with reservations" and I shall hold onto those reservations ... The decision may be based on arguments which are old-fashioned, but if the decision itself was not in some way guaranteed by the Holy Spirit, I can see no reason for God giving his church a leader on earth.'

5. 'It was and is the most difficult pill I have ever had to swallow ... I cannot accept it as a rule directly from God Almighty. I can however accept it as a church's rule or discipline, which we should try to follow if it is possible, but in the impossible situations it cannot oblige under sin.'

6. 'I was sad and disappointed after reading it, but for me the matter is now finished, and I must accept it. If a pressure group was able to change the Encyclical, then indeed I would have a crisis of faith, as for me there would not be any certainty on any matter pertaining to religion. I sympathise with you, but in conscience I could not support you.'

7. 'Sorry Owen, but for me the Encyclical Letter is the mind of the church, not the private opinion of Pope Paul ... The assumption and accusation is that the Encyclical Letter denies freedom of conscience. What is conscience as distinct from licence? Or are we to accept that "freedom of conscience" is the basis of truth?'

8. 'I think that on the whole the Encyclical Letter with reference to the priest being the "echo and voice of the Redeemer" has at last acknowledged that sexual sin is not the only one, nor yet the worst. I have for many years been impatient with the traditional attitude towards sex generally. This appears to be an improvement ... I cannot see why the same intention being operative in both methods of birth control, that one should be licit, the other not, except that the church says so. One wonders how far this is but an expression of confirmation of authority as the chief purpose, particularly as no definition of the much disputed character of natural law was given.'

9. 'As far as I was concerned, I told the people I accepted without reservation or qualification what the Pope had said. I haven't felt the need to consult anybody; what the Pope said was perfectly clear. I find it difficult to see how priests can refuse him loyalty after the particularly loving way he appealed to us.'

10. 'I felt compelled finally to make my mind known to the bishop; stating simply that I cannot accept or teach that in every case without exception the use of contraceptives within marriage

is wrong morally ... It is the "poor" in the church that grieve me – how we can bind insupportable burdens and not lift a finger ...'

11. *A Liverpool priest:* 'I concluded my sermon by saying that, as opposed to what the Pope, some bishops and priests said, the question was still an open one, and that the principle of following an informed conscience was still applicable ... The reaction to the sermon was extremely favourable. I went to a UCM meeting; if what some of the bishops say about the loyalty of the people is true, then we are not a typical parish; these women just could not accept the Encyclical Letter.'

12. *Dom Peter Beazley OSB:* 'I think it is just possible that this crisis may mature the church rapidly, so that a. clerical paternalism will be diminished, b. papal infallibility will be soon in far more tolerable terms and never again as a personal charism guaranteed ... One of the things that disturbs me about the Encyclical Letter and Heenan's line is to convict married people of sin and urge them to the sacraments as repentant sinners. Doesn't this suggest that the church is to live out a lie?'

13. *Fr Tom Corbishley SJ:* 'Certainly I have no doubt that the Encyclical Letter must be regarded simply as a personal view of Paul VI; I have no doubt that, if not in his lifetime (or mine), at least in the foreseeable future it will be amended.'

14. *Fr Michael Richards:* '... everything must be seen in the light of the whole of the church's faith ... The whole trouble is the canonical approach to morals.'

15. *Archbishop Roberts SJ:* 'Without flattery I have not seen anything which gives the substance of rational questions about the Encyclical Letter with such moderation as your letter; shall be interested to know the reaction of your bishop.'

16. *Fr John Fitsimons, Liverpool:* 'I have borrowed very largely from your handout and enclose what is being distributed here today: *bonum est diffusivum,* etc. At the same time I am preaching at every Mass about authority, change, not panicking, etc. One can only hope that the awful behaviour of Cowderoy will act as a warning to the other bishops of where they may land themselves ...'

17. *Fr Charles-Roux IC:* 'Your circular has arrived just in time for me to slip it into the files I am sending at this moment to the Holy See. The personal advice I am adding to the documents gathered here and there, is that the Encyclical Letter should be purely and simply withdrawn ...'

18. *Fr Henry St John OP:* 'The Pope has gone against the collegial view of papal-episcopal authority sanctioned by Vatican II, by bypassing the authority of his fellow bishops, and the new experimental structure, the episcopal synod, and withdrawing the problem to himself and his Curia. The result is that criticism is already far advanced, and should be prudently encouraged; I thought *The Tablet* leader excellent.'

19. *A Benedictine with pastoral experience:* 'It seems to me the Pope is out of touch with the deeper kind of theological thought made possible by study of the Bible and ratified by the Council. Hence he is hardly speaking as leader of the church. It's not so much the assertions, as the whole attitude, which goes very deep indeed.'

20. *Robert Murray SJ (Heythrop Scripture Professor):* '… when the whole system of the transmission of the faith is working rightly, there results on the part of the bishops and faithful a *singularis conspiratio* … Now (in the BC issue) this *conspiratio* is evidently not apparent. I conclude that the process is not working rightly, and that because the theological sources haven't come to proper expression; a. Tradition is contaminated by non-Christian sources and hasn't yet been clarified; b. the faithful haven't yet witnessed enough. Therefore the Pope alone cannot resolve the state of doubt, which is a fact, not a matter of opinion … Meanwhile, there must be responsible freedom and no witch-hunting, and some of us may suffer, but that's fair enough, to be with the people.'

21. *Fr Hubert Richards (Corpus Christi College):* 'It seems clear to me now that a stand on this matter can be taken from within the church. Fears have gone of needing to secede to do anything worthwhile. What the outcome will be God knows. I hope for some modification of this extraordinary monarchical hangover from Vatican I.'

22. *Fr John Dalrymple (Drygrange Spiritual Director):* 'I do not think the pill is always an inadmissible form of birth control (I am not so sure about some of the mechanical means). I am therefore in conflict with the Pope's statements (there are only statements; he gives no arguments). As the encyclical is not infallible, it will be some time till we can judge whether its teaching is the teaching of the church … I shall acquaint my bishop of my views on this before the seminary re-assembles.'

23. *Fr Nicholas Lash:* '… Moreover I remind people that, in

responding to the voice that tells them to keep the family intact or happy, or the kids fed, they are also obeying the teaching of Christ and his church. The choice they have is not between obeying the church or following their conscience, but of following their conscience in trying to obey what seem, because of the distorting nature of loudspeakers, to be conflicting demands of Christ's truth in his church ... All truth is God's truth; and this one truth of God which commands us, comes to us, as it were, through a host of different loudspeakers, each conveying different (partial) aspects of the one message, and not all without distortion.'

24. *Fr Michael Winter (Beda Professor already chopped from his job, since writing to me):* 'My own view is clear. On theological grounds I cannot agree to it. I have no intention of leaving the ranks or my teaching post at the Beda or anything like that. It is a matter of pure ethics and I am glad Heenan has had the sense to say that Christians are not to be denied sacraments for a matter of philosophy.'

25. *Fr Jim Crichton:* 'I agree we must set out what is in the Encyclical Letter and invite people to make up their own minds about it ... There can be no question about our leaving the church (it's our church anyway) or the ministry; though we may get pushed. As I see it, the letter is not infallible; but if it is not, then how can it bind my conscience? ... Can we go on if we do not declare our conscientious objections to the bishop? At the same time I am aware we are jeopardising our "safety" if we protest singly. My curate and I are very conscious of the younger priests and feel we must give them some support as soon as possible ...'

26. *Fr French-Mullen:* 'To my mind the Pope is literally alienated. He has cut himself off from a General Council where the Holy Spirit works in the plenitude of the apostolic college. He has cut himself off from the Holy Spirit as the truth is pursued by the scientific experts he selected for his Commission ... Although there is no reason for leaving the church, it widens the credibility gap between Christ and Curial bureaucracy/Roman absolute monarchy; and can one in conscience continue in the pastoral ministry upholding a ruling which is promulgated as God's will, but which one regards as twisted human reasoning? Is perhaps one's true witness to ask for temporary suspension and go out into the wilderness? Meantime it is most heartening

for mutual strength and enlightenment, if priests of like mind are in touch and can exchange ideas, findings, etc.'

27. *Abbot Wicksteed (Caldey):* 'My own position is roughly as follows: I have no doubt that the Pope had the right to speak out as he did, but at the same time, I am appalled that he did it. It ought to have been evident to him that the day is past when Popes can get away with unilateral pronouncements on grave matters of faith or morals, even though the Council has safe-guarded their right to make these ... It is not that I think that the Council would have arrived at a decision radically different from that of the Pope. For myself I believe that the Pope's deci-sion is right, at least in the present state of our knowledge. But it seems to me that he gives the wrong (or at least inadequate) rea-sons for it. I don't believe for a moment he can support it validly by an appeal to the old concept of the natural law. But I still be-lieve that contraception is contrary to nature. I believe this not primarily because it frustrates an act which is necessarily or-dered to procreation, but because it strikes at the very nature of human sexuality ... Control in sexual relationships demands as-ceticism, and that is a dirty word in the church of today. This, to my mind, is where things have gone wrong.'

28. *Fr Peter Bourne (Ware Professor):* 'The pastoral problem for me is to bring couples to that degree of acceptance of the Cross of Christ in their daily lives that they will develop such delicacy of conscience which will enable them to see grave matter and mortal/venial sins in the manner I've described. When we've at-tained that with the majority of the people, we've won ... and we'll all be in heaven! Meanwhile forget birth control; leave it to their consciences, and work like hell on their consciences. This will feed back into the magisterium, by the very fact of the new articulation of the married couples, the needed "authentication" of this doctrine. We will find that the Pope's Encyclical Letter is true beyond our wildest dreams.'

29. *Bishop Derek Worlock:* 'You will see in my pastoral letter how I have tried to open up the question of conscience and of responsible discussion and I am doing my best as far as I can to restore the peace and serenity which is needed in the church if we are to carry out the study and reflection by the whole church for which we act. At times this means withdrawing from the scene and at other times intervening, so I ask your prayers that in all this I have the understanding of those who are disturbed and even more the guidance of the Holy Spirit.'

30. *Fr John Garvey (Worcester PP):* 'Your letter came as a gleam of light and hope in the blackness of incredulity and near despair. It has helped me develop a more positive and constructive attitude, but the real problems have hardly begun yet. I feel I must not wait too long before declaring my position to the Archbishop … on the other hand it does not seem to help the church if priests approach their bishops singly.'

31. *Fr Conrad Pepler OP (Spode House Warden):* 'I think your line is far and away the best I have come across in the mass of things written in the last ten days. It is full of clarity but leaving the future open to advance which seems to me to be the great hope for many people.'

32. *Dom Allan Rimmer OSB (Leeds PP):* 'I am of course disturbed by the actual problem which has arisen, but much more so over the whole question of authority and what is the church … Don't "shut up" whatever you do. Keep at it.'

33. *Fr Fergus Kerr OP (Sub-Prior, Oxford):* 'I cannot simply invoke papal authority and require people to be obedient, because I don't know what kind of assent is appropriate to a document to this kind. The Encyclical Letter seems to raise the whole problem of the relationship between the Pope and the church; it is an ecclesiological problem, and if the *sensus communis* of the faithful breaks out, I think the publication will have important repercussions in this field.'

34. *Baroness van Drakestein (Grail President):* 'Enormous thanks for your material. I have found it most interesting and helpful, and I have been able to help some priests round here by sending them copies. I thought you would not mind. I think this is the help we must now give each other, to make a stand quietly and resolutely, and I am grateful to you for taking this initiative.'

35. *Fr David Roderick (Westminster Curate):* 'My reactions were the same as yours, and during the first week I was thoroughly worried. It's a great help to know I'm not the only one.'

36. *Fr Michael Crowdy (Cong Orat):* 'We must encourage people to live up to it, even if they or we think it may receive significant modifications in coming years. Otherwise everyone becomes his own Pope.'

37. *Rosemary Haughton:* 'I don't see what people like me can do except keep on saying: "You don't have to leave the church about this; on the contrary the church (which is not the Pope) needs love and support more than ever".'

38. *Professor Hilary Armstrong (Liverpool Greek Professor):* 'Thank you very much for the documents, which we think quite admirable. I hope your letter produces a good response.'

39. *J. Robertson (Deputy Editor of* Universe*):* 'How can the Church reverse its universal teaching and still remain infallible? … I am far from unaware of the reasons which seem to demand the widespread practice of contraception. And I confess I do not know how the two sides of the case can be reconciled. But I do realise that if the church does change its attitude, it will destroy its own authority, papal and conciliar … I am personally perplexed and confused on where the truth lies. But I have to admit that the moment there is a reversal in the church's teaching on contraception, that is the moment to ask all to practise the Christian virtue of humility and acknowledge that I cannot remain intellectually honest and retain any confidence in the church's teaching.'

40. *Mr Jack Bate (Diocesan solicitor):* 'I realise that as a result of Vatican II the bishops have been given a larger share in the government of the church, but we must remember that the Holy Father is still the head of the church on earth; he alone is Christ's Vicar on earth, he alone is our chief spiritual guide and pastor; we must be guided by him. Some people may not like his ruling any more than they like having to fast on fast days ... but such hardships are an excellent penance … Do you seriously consider for one moment that the Holy Spirit would fail to guide the mind of Christ's Vicar on earth in a spiritual matter of such moment?'

41. *Mr Bryan Keating (Cheltenham parishioner, helps edit parish magazine):* 'Your general letter and your "guidance to parishioners" were masterly in facing up to the problem. They merited as wide a readership as possible and have been circulated among my Catholic brethren here in Cheltenham, and I've no doubt something similar has happened elsewhere with other recipients.'

And many other letters and long conversations …

The Bishops' Statement
The whole conference of the bishops of England and Wales struggled hard to respond to the confusion and anger created by the Encyclical. In this same month of September they issued the following statement:

1. When Pope Paul issued the encyclical *Humanae Vitae* he
asked the bishops to see that his teaching was presented in its
true light 'that is, to show its positive and beneficent aspect'.
The encyclical, nevertheless, concerning as it does the source
of human life, was bound to be a test of faith. Some Catholics
were convinced that a change in the moral teaching and practice of the church was inevitable. Others were just as strongly
convinced that any change would be a betrayal of the faith.
In view of the controversy which the encyclical has aroused
the bishops of England and Wales call upon all Catholics to
conduct their discussions in a responsible and temperate
manner and in a mutually charitable spirit.
Discussion has so far centred mainly on the question of contraception. The impression is given that the Pope set out
merely to condemn artificial methods of birth control. This
he could have done in a single sentence. The encyclical
speaks at length of the dignity of marriage, the beauty of
married love and the obligation of responsible parenthood,
although it has not been sufficiently appreciated that the
encyclical was not intended to be a complete treatise on holy
matrimony. The press has not surprisingly concentrated on
the subject of contraception but the faithful and their pastors
must study the document as a whole. In it the Pope reaffirms
the sublime teaching of the Second Vatican Council's *Pastoral
Constitution on The Church in the World Today.* The encyclical
teaches us that marriage:

> 'is far from being the effect of chance or the result of blind
> evolution of natural forces. It is in reality the wise and
> provident institution of God the Creator, whose purpose
> was to establish in man his loving design. As a conse-
> quence, husband and wife through their mutual gift of
> themselves, which is specific and exclusive to them alone,
> develop that union of two persons in which they perfect
> one another, in order to co-operate with God in the gener-
> ation and education of new lives.
> Furthermore, the marriage of these who have been bap-
> tised is invested with the dignity of a sacramental sign of
> grace, for it represents the union of Christ and his church.'
> (8)

This triple partnership of husband, wife and God gives marriage its particular sacredness. It is the guarantee that God
will never fail to support and guide the married couple by his

grace. It is also the reason why the marriage act is not under the sole dominion of husband and wife. (10, 13)

2. Pope Paul wrote his encyclical only after years of study and prayer. In the heat of controversy some writers appear to have forgotten that the Pope is the Vicar of Christ. It is for him to issue encyclical letters whenever he thinks it is his duty to do so. This right and duty were reaffirmed by the Second Vatican Council. The *Dogmatic Constitution on the Church* declares: 'This religious submission of will and of mind must be shown in a special way to the authentic teaching authority of the Roman Pontiff, even when he is not speaking ex cathedra. That is, it must be shown in such a way, that his supreme magisterium is acknowledged with reverence, the judgments made by him are sincerely adhered to, according to his manifest mind and will. His mind and will in the matter may be known chiefly either from the character of the documents, from his frequent repetition of the same doctrine, or from his manner of speaking.' (25)

It is well known that the encyclical is the fruit not only of prayer but of years of consultation with bishops, theologians, doctors, scientists and, not least important, married men and women. The Commission set up by Pope John to examine the demographic problem was enlarged by Pope Paul and entrusted with the study of marriage and the family. No member of the Commission thought that the questions proposed to it could be resolved by a majority vote. Its task was to sift evidence and to present the Pope with its findings. It was always understood that the decision must be made by him alone as Christ's Vicar. The Pope has assured us that he weighed carefully and conscientiously all the evidence submitted to him both by the members of his Commission and by hundreds of others.

3. Some have questioned whether in fact Pope Paul rather than a section of his advisers is responsible for the teaching contained in the encyclical. Those most closely concerned with the Pontifical Commission easily recognise the Pope's own thoughts in this document. From the beginning the Pope regarded this decision as one which he personally must make. He delayed his statement until he was satisfied that he had heard and studied the arguments of every school of thought. Only then did he publish the decision which he had conscientiously made in the sight of God. 'We now intend,'

he says at the beginning of *Humanae Vitae*, 'by virtue of the mandate entrusted to us by Christ to give our reply to these grave questions.' (6)

4. The encyclical has provoked serious discussion on the whole exercise of the magisterium. It is being argued that in a matter so intimately affecting the lives of millions the burden of responsibility should not rest upon one man even though he is the Vicar of Christ. At the Council it was generally recognised that a question of such delicacy as contraception could not properly be debated in that vast assembly. Collegiality must be the subject of further study, but it cannot be invoked as a reason for refusing assent to the encyclical.

5. An encyclical is a statement of principle, not a detailed personal guide. Thus, for example, when speaking of responsible parenthood the encyclical says:

> 'the responsible exercise of parenthood implies that husband and wife recognise fully their own duties towards God, towards themselves, towards the family and towards society.' (10)

The Pope does not attempt to tell parents how many children they ought to have. This decision is one to be taken by the parents alone in the light of all the moral considerations laid down in the encyclical.

One of these considerations is that 'each exercise of the marriage act must remain in itself open to the transmission of life', although, as the Pope points out, in fact 'not every conjugal act is followed by a new life'. (11) Nevertheless it is against the plan of God to take positive steps to destroy the possibility of the transmission of life. The use of marriage during infertile periods, on the other hand, does not destroy the act's 'openness to the transmission of life'.

6. At one time not only Catholics but all Christians held contraception to be abhorrent. In recent years, however, doubts have been expressed about the church's interpretation of the moral law. The very fact that the Pope created a commission to review the question tended to confirm their doubts. It was soon widely believed that a change in the church's attitude would be announced. Understandably many wives and husbands, anticipating the promised statement of the Pope, have come to rely on contraception. In this they have acted conscientiously and often after seeking pastoral advice. They may

now be unable to see that, at least in their personal circumstances, the use of contraception is wrong. A particular difficulty faces those who after serious thought and prayer cannot as yet understand or be fully convinced of the doctrines as laid down. This is not surprising in view of the discussions of recent years which have resulted in the present controversy. For others the problem of putting the doctrine into practice in their lives seems insuperable because of ill-health or other serious obstacles, sometimes because of a conflict of duties. All should bear in mind the great weight which attaches to a pronouncement by the Holy Father. They should not close their mind but leave it open to the influence of the Holy Spirit, persevere in prayer and be ready to follow his guidance when it is given. They should pray for light to understand the doctrine taught by the encyclical. It is not unreasonable to ask all to practise the Christian virtue of humility and acknowledge the duty of every Catholic to listen with respect to the voice of the Vicar of Christ.

The Belgian Bishops have pointed out that acceptance of the encyclical:

> '... does not depend so much on the arguments proposed in the statement as on the religious motives to which the teaching authority, sacramentally instituted in the church, appeals.' (Belgian Hierarchy Statement No. 3)

7. The Holy Father realises what difficulties face married people. That is why in the encyclical he recalls the example of Our Lord who was gentle and patient. (cf. *Humanae Vitae* 29). He came not to condemn but to save. He was clear and firm in condemning evil but there is no end to his mercy and compassion. In the same spirit the encyclical makes no sweeping condemnations. There is no threat of damnation. Far from being excluded from the sacraments, those in difficulties are invited to receive them more frequently.

8. It cannot be denied that the encyclical has created a conflict in the minds of many Catholics. Partly by reason of the discussions on contraception since the Council, they ask themselves how they can accept the Pope's decision with sincerity. It must be stressed that the primacy of conscience is not in dispute. The Pope, bishops, clergy and faithful must all be true to conscience. But we are bound to do everything in our power to make sure that our conscience is truly informed.

Neither this encyclical nor any other document of the church takes away from us our right and duty to follow our conscience. But if we were to neglect the guidance of the church, morality could easily become merely subjective. That would be disastrous. It is well to remember the *Declaration on Religious Freedom* in the Second Vatican Council:

'In the formation of their consciences, the Christian faithful ought carefully to attend to the sacred and certain doctrine of the church. The church is, by the will of Christ, the teacher of the truth. It is her duty to give utterance to and authoritatively to teach that truth which is Christ himself and to declare and confirm by her authority those principles of the moral order which have their origin in human nature itself.' (14)

9. Theologians will seek clarification of the teaching in the encyclical. Much of the field of human sexuality remains to be explored. We must ourselves continue sponsoring such research with assistance to initiatives already taken and the pooling of experience already gained. The Pope himself exhorts doctors to persevere in their studies in order to benefit the married people who consult them. We need to learn to what extent secular science can contribute to a solution of marriage problems. We must also enquire what are the implications of the encyclical's reference to the use of therapeutic means. Those competent in these matters will continue their researches but the personal problems have to be faced by faithful couples genuinely wanting to do God's will but facing formidable obstacles. They know that their own living conditions may not quickly be adjusted to accommodate another child. The prospect of pregnancy for some women is a risk to health and perhaps to life. Such Catholics are concerned not with academic disputes but with stark human decisions. Let them remember that the church has the charity and understanding of Christ our Lord. An encyclical cannot consider all pastoral problems in detail but the church has a care for those of her children with special difficulties. However difficult their circumstances may appear, they should never think that they are separated from the love and grace of God.

'Let married couples, then, face up to the efforts needed, supported by the faith and hope which do not disappoint ... because God's love has been poured into our hearts through the Holy Spirit, who has been given to us; let them implore divine assistance by persevering prayer; above all, let them draw from the source of grace and charity in the eucharist. And if sin should still keep its hold over them, let them not be discouraged, but rather have recourse with humble perseverance to the mercy of God, which is poured forth in the Sacrament of Penance.' (25)

10. There is a close connection between problems of the family and wider social issues. We therefore take this occasion to remind our priests and people of our Christian obligation to take an active share in social work both at home and in the developing countries. Housing aid and relief of hunger provide a response to the Pope's appeal to all men of good will to work together to raise the standard of life throughout the world.

11. During this time of controversy we should all bear in mind that self-discipline and the way of the Cross are part of our Christian calling. The easy way is often not the Christian way. We appeal once more for mutual charity. We are confident that the Holy Spirit will guide the People of God to understand the truth of the principles laid down by the Pope in *Humanae Vitae.* In working out these principles, bishops, priests and laymen must co-operate in a Christian spirit.

'You are God's chosen people, holy and well beloved; the livery you wear must be tender compassion, kindness, humility, gentleness and patience; you must bear with one another's faults, be generous to each other, where somebody has given grounds for complaint; the Lord's generosity to you must be the model of yours. And, to crown all this, charity; that is the bond which makes us perfect.' (Col 3:12-14)

A Letter to The Times

This was a vast improvement on the initial reaction of the hierarchy, but it still shows hardly any understanding of the strength and the depth of the response and the significance of the issues involved. Many priests still felt that as those who had to deal day by day with the questions of our people, we needed to show how widely we shared their reservations. Peter de Rosa had circularised a huge number with the draft of a letter to be published in *The Times.* I was happy to be a signatory, but I recall, when returning a signed copy, that I said it should not be published with less than a couple of hundred signatures, or it would be dismissed as coming from a small group of dissidents. In the event only fifty-five names appeared because, I was told, *The Times* only had fifty-five actual signatures on their desk ready – though up to two hundred had expressed willingness.

Before its actual publication it was sent to all the bishops at the end of September with the following covering letter:

To the Hierarchy of England and Wales

May we first express regret at having to communicate with you through the medium of a roneoed letter. We had no time or facilities at our disposal to do otherwise. We simply wish to inform you personally of what we propose to do so that you do not depend on the press for such information.

A letter is to appear in *The Times* on Wednesday, October 2nd signed by fifty-five priests.

We intend to make it very plain that this is no rebellion against ecclesiastical authority. On the contrary, we strongly re-affirm our loyalty both to the Pope and our bishops.

The venture began out of sympathy towards some of our fellow priests who perhaps spoke out overhastily and were overhastily disciplined. We knew that many priests were likely to speak out since they hold views identical with those of priests already disciplined. We wished to channel these strong feelings into an undertaking both corporate and constructive.

We have delayed this letter for four weeks out of respect for the proposed Statement from the hierarchy. We did not want to distract attention from this Statement.

Our only hope is that all priests can remain in the active ministry and serve the church well.

May God bless us and keep us all,

From the Revv. Kenneth Allan, Nigel Collingwood and Peter de Rosa.

The text of the letter was then included. I reproduce it here with the full list of fifty-five signatures.

2nd October 1968

Letter to the Editor of *The Times*

Sir,

We regret the decision on birth control made by our holy father the Pope according to his conscience. We realise the possible grave dangers that can result from the indiscriminate use of artificial means of birth control. We deeply regret however that according to our consciences we cannot give loyal internal and external obedience to the view that all such means of control are in all circumstances wrong.

As priests we feel that our duty towards Catholic people impels us to bear witness to the truth as we see it.

Yours faithfully,

Kenneth Allan	Daniel Futter	David Payne
Nigel Collingwood	Peter Gilbert AA	Adrian Peeler
Peter de Rosa	Owen Hardwicke	John Perry
B.L. Anwyl	F.X. Harriott SJ	Gregory Phillips AA
Richard Aston	Paulinus Healy OP	Anthony Prior
A.W. Beer	Giles Hibbert OP	Anthony Pyle
Peter Beazley OSB	Stephen Hinde	John Rohan
Simon Blake OP	T. C. Hoekstra O Carm	P. P. Rudman
Anthony Burnham	Michael Ivers	Michael Sharratt
John Challenor	John Jordan	Benedict Sketchley AA
John D. Cheales OP	John Lane	J. T. Swann
Guy Braithwaite OP	Nicholas Lash	Terence Tanner
Laurence Bright OP	Herbert McCabe OP	Patrick Tierney
Michael Cresswell	Vincent McDermott	George Towler
Christopher David	John McNamara	Bernard Trevett
Ian Dommersen	Paul Moxon	Harry Wace
John Foster	Edward Neary	Paul Weir
Aquinas Furlong AA	Bernard O'Brien	Michael Winter

It so happened that it was published on the very day that the Menevia priests gathered at Pantasaph for their annual residential conference. The only Menevia names apart from mine were those of Christopher David and Titus Hoekstra, a Carmelite. But all eyes were on us as word soon got round that the letter had appeared.

Christopher, Titus and I were only upset at the headline, '55 priests defy Pope.' Immediately we sent off another letter under our three names, and this appeared two days later alongside a letter from seventy-six laymen expressing their anxieties.

4th October 1968

Sir,

As three of the fifty-five priest signatories to the letter in today's (2 Oct) *Times* concerning our attitude to the Pope's encyclical letter on birth control, may we say how much we regret your own editorial headline on the first page, '55 priests defy Pope'.

We are quite certain that our attitude is in no sense a defiance. It is precisely because we respect episcopal and papal authority that we feel obliged to state the point at which we are unable to follow the encyclical. We hope indeed that our difficulty, calmly and clearly expressed, will help authority to clarify the full teaching of the church.

C. David, O. Hardwicke, T. Hoekstra.

The following days were somewhat tense; lots of us were in touch with one another, and we awaited official reaction. I don't know to this day whether or not the published letter really helped many Catholics. I doubt if they were high among the numbers of *Times'* readers! But it soon got out to the ordinary parishioner.

On the Mat

The next step in the process was the following letter from the bishop's secretary:

23rd October 1968

Dear Reverend Father,

His Lordship Bishop Fox has asked me to let you have a copy of an *Ad Clerum* which His Eminence The Cardinal has issued. The press, radio and television services will no doubt be commenting on the Cardinal's letter after noon on Thursday and in view of some of the garbled versions which these media have dished up in the recent past on the issue in question, you will no doubt welcome the opportunity of reading the letter in full prior to the mass publicity.

Although the letter is being issued over the name of the Cardinal only, it is one which has been approved by all the bishops of England and Wales and its contents apply to all priests in England and Wales.

Yours sincerely,

J. Hannigan

Dear Reverend Father or Superior,

A few priests have publicly and explicitly rejected the encyclical *Humanae Vitae*. Others, though deeply troubled, could not bring themselves as priests to oppose the teaching of the Vicar of Christ. Towards those who have found difficulty in giving whole-hearted assent to the encyclical we must be gentle and tolerant. A great deal of time, thought and prayer may still be necessary before they are able to see the implications or, indeed, the beauty of Pope Paul's teaching on love in marriage.

Many were led to expect a different answer to the questions so widely discussed in recent years. In their disappointment some seem to have begun to doubt that the Holy Spirit guides the whole church and its chief pastor. Some priests, weighed down at the prospect of having to solve grave pastoral problems, seemed to forget that the same theological principles in assessing culpability apply in this as in any other moral question. It is the priest's duty in the Sacrament of Penance to judge with compassion while upholding the principles laid down by the Pope in *Humanae Vitae*.

All this is clear from a careful study of the encyclical and the Bishops' Statement. It is evident that no priest in the exercise of his ministry may repudiate the solemn teaching of the supreme authority of the church which gives him his mandate. The open refusal of a group of priests to accept the Pope's guidance has caused dismay to their fellow priests who, while being no less aware of pastoral problems, give loyal obedience to the Holy Father. The opposition of these priests to the Pope's teaching has bewildered and saddened loyal members of the laity.

The Bishops of England and Wales have no wish to inhibit reasonable discussion nor do they propose to make a return to priestly obedience unduly difficult for those who have denounced the encyclical. The bishops, however, are not unmindful of their responsibilities – 'to the whole flock wherein the Holy Ghost hath placed you bishops to rule the church of God' (Acts 20:28). It was therefore unanimously decided at a hierarchy meeting last week that each bishop would speak personally to those of his priests who maintain opposition to the encyclical. Now that the bishops have had time to see the dissident priests, it is opportune to publish the conditions laid down.

Priests are required in preaching, teaching, in the press, on
radio, television or public platforms, to refrain from opposing the teaching of the Pope in all matters of faith and morals.
If a priest is unwilling to give this undertaking, the bishop
will decide whether he can be allowed without scandal to
continue to act in the name of the church. Although he need
not be required to cease celebrating Mass, a priest may not
normally hold faculties to hear confessions without undertaking to declare faithfully the objective teaching of *Humanae
Vitae* in the confessional and when giving spiritual guidance.
A priest who is unwilling to accept these conditions will be
maintained by the diocese until he has been able to find suitable employment. This is, of course, in keeping with current
canonical practice. Stories of priests in want for the sake of
conscience should be accepted with the greatest reserve.

Religious Superiors have been invited to make similar pro-
posals to those of their members who have publicly rejected
the encyclical. It is the fervent hope of the bishops that all
their priests, religious and faithful, united in prayer, will
grow in love of God and his holy church.

Wishing you every blessing,

I am,

Yours devotedly,

+ JOHN CARD. HEENAN

Archbishop of Westminster.

I sensed that this tough line was something of a change from the
Conference of Bishops' earlier letter; maybe the Roman Curia
was putting pressure on the bishops. Word came that all of us
signatories were to be on the carpet with our own bishop to
answer two questions. I travelled all the way down to Llanelli to
see Bishop Fox, who was still auxiliary bishop and the parish
priest. We lunched very agreeably together with his two curates;
then I went into his study for the questions.

'Will you undertake always to present the church's teaching
in matters of faith and morals with integrity?'

'Most certainly,' I replied. 'The second question?'

'Will you faithfully present to your people the teaching of
Pope Paul VI in *Humanae Vitae*?'

'Certainly,' I said. 'I could hardly have done it more faithfully.
I had copies on all the people's chairs the Sunday after it came
out, and we have had three discussion evenings to explore
together what he says.'

'Mind', I added, 'I can't accept it myself as an adequate account of the issue.'

'But surely,' said Bishop Fox, 'you have to submit to the judgement of the supreme teacher of the church?'

'Is that one of the questions I have to answer?' I asked.

'Not immediately.'

'Then I'll go home now.'

The bishop was immensely courteous, and I got away without a flea in my ear, or even a severe talking to, which would have been understandable.

Then it was a matter of informing my friends what had happened. After all, some priests had already been strictly censured and even suspended in other dioceses.

The following is what I wrote:

My personal position is that I was summoned by Bishop Fox in the absence of Bishop Petit. I was able to tell him that I will not *oppose* the Pope's teaching, and that I had never done so. I will certainly declare faithfully the objective teaching of *Humanae Vitae*.

That is all that was required of me at the moment. I continue to affirm openly that I do not 'accept' the encyclical letter in its entirety. (Regrettably the Cardinal said on TV last night that priests were required to 'accept' it; that is not what we are asked to say.) I do not believe it is objectively true in certain respects. It is a partial view, very badly argued and presented on the basis of an understanding of papal authority over matters of dogmatic and moral truth which I am unable to accept as Catholic teaching. But I am not required to speak of this.

I am aware that in some sense my distinction between 'not opposing' and 'accepting' is theoretically thin, though practically valid. The tight-rope we walk between personal integrity as Catholics and obedience as priests is not easy. If we are to be dealt with by a juridical authority, I think we have the right to juridical interpretation of terms.

However, I can see that if the same disciplinary line is maintained, my position generally will become intolerable. The bishop might judge that it would give greater scandal round here to suspend me than it would to leave me; he is given that discretion. But if he felt he had to suspend me, as he has every right to do, then I am requesting Bishop's House that they inform me at once, and I will try to help by voluntarily asking for leave of absence. I would not resign my office as parish priest, let alone ask for temporary 'laicisation', but simply for temporary leave on compassionate grounds. This would relieve him of the burden of suspending anyone whom he would then have to find reasons for 'reinstating' when the coast is clear again, as I am quite certain it will be in the end. To put it crudely, we do not wish to further divide the members of the church into parties; and we must help the bishops to save face. This may sound grossly arrogant; but it is not intended this way.

Meantime I continually try to clarify my own attitude to *Humanae Vitae*, and I now append some thoughts which seem to me to be relevant. I dearly hope priests (especially) will keep in touch, no matter how much they disagree, so that the utter confusion caused by this encyclical may resolve into greater peace, harmony and truth. I shall continue to put before people what the encyclical says in all its clarity. It is my belief that it is those who modify its teaching who are undermining the situation. Anyone who finds any exception to the absolute exclusion of all artificial methods of birth control (apart from the degrees of subjective culpability, which are another matter) is, to my mind, failing to follow the objective teaching of the Holy Father, whose plain intention was to settle the whole matter once and for all in every case. I shall continue to say that this is not an adequate account of Catholic teaching.

Your comments will always be welcomed.

J. Owen Hardwicke

25th Oct. 1968 Ruabon

This is what I appended to the circular:

Personal Attitude to Humanae Vitae

Since this encyclical came from the chief bishop, I would dearly like to have presumed that I could accept its presentation, its arguments, and its conclusions on the new questions which have arisen about marriage in the modern world. I am deeply saddened that I can neither give unqualified assent to its formal objective truth in all respects, nor to its opportuneness; nor am I able to say that it represents an adequate account of Catholic teaching on these matters, as I understand them.

That I should find myself in this position is of no great importance, but for the fact that I am in agreement with a wealth of solid theological opinion, and a large body of agreement among married people and many others deeply and professionally involved. I am unable to dismiss my attitude as mere personal opinion and private judgement. I feel obliged not only to maintain a personal attitude, but as a priest to place this before people as another aspect of the subject which must for the good of souls and the good name of the church, also be heard.

Of course I am willing – and indeed I have done so from the start – to encourage people to hear the teaching of the Pope, with all this implies. But I am increasingly aware that our understanding of the 'authority of the Pope' is very unthought-out. As a result Catholics are apt to presume a 'virtually infallible' note for statements which are not so characterised by theologians. In frequent and continual discussion with my own parishioners, we have had to acknowledge that never before has the 'authority of the Pope' made an impact on us like this. We all honour him as our chief bishop; we are more than ready to see in him a very special sign of the unity of the visible church; we are proud to be 'in communion with the see of Peter'. But what he says normally makes no impression on us – for we have imbibed the faith from parents, teachers and parish clergy; we never felt the need to check whether this was what Peter said. And when (in 1950) he did speak with peculiar solemnity on the Assumption, we were unaware of any change at all in our attitudes or our faith. That was simply a declaration of the unchanging belief of the church.

In *Humanae Vitae*, however, we have not heard a general statement of principle, whose interpretation might well be left to bishops, clergy and people; we have not had, as the Papal Commission Report outlined in 'Pastoral Approaches', a clear ideal of Christian marriage in opposition to the selfishness and perverted use of marriage; we have had a ruling on a most intimate, personal and particularised matter, that allows of no exception in any circumstance. The Statement of the Bishops of England and Wales that emphasised the obvious difficulty for many in accepting this conclusion immediately, is certainly compassionate. Yet it does nothing to qualify the suggestion that the minds of the faithful are not in accord with God's plan unless and until they accept the teaching of the encyclical as unquestionably true. There is said to be room for discussion; but there is only one conclusion allowed; we are to discuss how we can come to accept, but not whether or not this is true. Even those who are reasonably confident in their responsible dissent from its teaching, are left with a burden of ecclesiastical guilt, which is based on the unquestioned assumption that the Holy Father would not have said this unless it were entirely true; that this is how we would expect the Holy Spirit's guidance to work. But we dare not in all truth confine the working of the Holy Spirit to guidance to the Holy Father (and the four theologians who dissented from all the others on the papal commission); nor identify the magisterium with the decision of the Holy Father. These people, whether priests or lay, must be helped to see that we do not receive truth from the Pope, nor yet from the bishops in Council, but directly from God in the community of the church. It must be continually emphasised that God speaks directly to each one of us in the context of the Christian community. We do not believe in the Real Presence, or the co-redemptive work of our Lady in our salvation in Christ, because of the teaching of the Pope or the bishops, but because we have received the gift of faith whereby we discern in the teaching of the bishops together with the Pope the word of God. The *consensus fidelium* is our first medium, then the co-ordinating teaching of the bishops in communion with the Pope, who sometimes is called upon to clarify the mind of the church for all men to see.

This has not been the pattern with the teaching of *Humanae Vitae*; indeed it was explicitly not allowed to be the pattern. The normal instinct of Christian people has indeed been against the use of artificial methods of birth control; but it is not clear that exceptional circumstances may not alter the matter. The attempt by some bishops and theologians to say, 'In some extreme cases there is perhaps a moral impossibility of following the norms' may be pastorally acceptable, but it plainly contradicts the intention of the Pope of settling the matter once and for all in every case. The considered teaching of the papal commission was that:

> if an arbitrarily contraceptive mentality is to be condemned, as has always been the church's view, an intervention to regulate conception in a spirit of true, reasonable and generous charity does not deserve to be, because if it were, other goods of marriage might be endangered. So what is always to be condemned is not the regulation of conception, but an egoistic married life, refusing a creative opening out of the family circle, and so refusing a truly human – and therefore truly Christian – married love. This is the anti-conception that is

against the Christian ideal of marriage. As for the means that
husband and wife can legitimately employ, it is their task to
decide these together, without drifting into arbitrary decisions, but always taking account of the objective criteria of
morality. These criteria are in the first place those that relate
to the totality of married life and sexuality.

To defend the legitimacy of such a view as part of Catholic
teaching – if indeed it is not already more adequate than the
teaching of the encyclical – it may sometimes be necessary to declare publicly, openly, and even in the mass media, that there
are other factors to which the Pope has not done justice. Most of
all it is necessary to say that his authority, to which he has an un-
doubted juridical right in the light even of Vatican II, is still not
sufficient to clarify to the smallest point of detail a personal and
domestic issue of this kind. He certainly could justify an altogether infallible declaration if and when the mind of the church
was clear on the matter. But unless he is claiming a special revelation – which I take to be contrary to Catholic teaching on the
Pope's function – he can only give the weight of his authority to
support a considered opinion – not purely private, but one held
by one school of thought.

In this matter, while I try to respect what he says because he
is the chief bishop, I believe the encyclical to be a disastrous
error, inadequate in its dealing with the new insights on marriage, unjustified in its absolute conclusions, and gravely damaging to the right understanding of the use of papal authority.
While normally I am content to leave the matter in the hands of
theologians to qualify and clarify, there are countless ordinary
Catholics who have been not only disappointed, but shaken in
faith by the pronouncement. There are many occasions when as
a parish priest I must be open in my judgement on the matter,
especially as this is a view held by responsible theologians and
others, in order to safeguard the objectivity of truth and moral
judgement, and the real significance of episcopal and papal authority.

I would not deliberately seek any more publicity in the press,
radio or TV than has already been given; but I cannot rule it out
for the future should it seem opportune. There are times when to
say nothing is as dishonest as it is risky to voice an inadequate
personal opinion. For the good of the church I judge dishonesty
a greater danger than the display of one's personal inadequacy.

Aftermath

Just for the record, of the 55 who signed the *Times* letter, more than 12 are now dead; about 20 resigned their ministry over the following years. I believe there are only about 18 of us left. As far as I can remember there were no more repercussions for me personally, but when I decided eight months later to resign, not from the priesthood but from parish work, it may have facilitated a sigh of relief in some quarters, and I soon discovered that many people locally thought I had been 'sacked' because of my dissidence.

I shall not rehearse any further the efforts I made for myself, my parishioners and others to see what Paul VI was really saying; but a terrible blow had been struck about the way papal authority could be exercised. In spite of the hopes of many of us, the lessons have still not been learned, and the treatment of many theologians gives cause for widespread scandal today. We have for the most part learned how to carry on with the real work of the church, to bear witness to the love and forgiveness of God through the death and resurrection of Jesus, without worrying too much about the Roman Curia.

In 1968 I was asked to take part in a half-hour television interview when Vincent Kane was looking at particular 'cross-roads' in my life – the first in a series. The programme was 'canned' to be viewed several weeks later. Vincent had asked me how I had somehow managed with such a questioning mind to settle down in an authoritarian church. I told him that however difficult it could make matters for me, so far I had never been obliged to do, think or say anything contrary to my personal conscience. Before the programme was broadcast, the encyclical *Humanae Vitae* came out, and I was one of the public dissidents. How could Vincent not have asked me a direct question about it? I was summoned to Cardiff for a closed-circuit viewing with Vincent and the producer, to see if we could insert another question and answer. But no: the conversation was so rounded, it was impossible. In the event, at the end of the showing, the live cameras came back to Vincent who explained that this question about a response to *Humanae Vitae* could not have been asked as the programme was made before its publication. 'But maybe,' he added, 'Owen has come to another "crossroads".'

As a matter of interest, I don't think I have had any direct question about the issue of artificial contraception in the last ten years. That could mean that Catholics have obediently followed

Paul VI's directives. Few people believe this. If it means that they think that authoritative teachings have no relevance, that would be very sad. When I have seen young couples before marriage I have made it my business to say that their planning of their family needed very careful and shared discussion. A total contraceptive mentality, to rule out children, does not seem to be compatible with the nature and purposes of marriage. Whatever particular decision has to be made must be made in conscience between them, and related to the present moment, not to all circumstances. As for the methods of contraception which are acceptable to Christian conscience I have no opinion; as a celibate I have no experience of married love and intimate family circumstance. In the teaching of the church there are guidelines but there are also disputed questions. With prayer and shared thinking they must act responsibly. But artificial birth control? Not my subject.

For the most part I don't hear the matter discussed much these days; and I do find it sad that the Holy Father so often has lumped 'contraception' and abortion *tout court* under the same denunciation.

There will have been a black mark against my name in the diocesan files. If it is that which has blocked any kind of task or status preferment, I am profoundly grateful. I have had the freedom to explore things without holding official responsibilities.

But I wasn't sacked – honestly!

Epilogue

'The church,' we are often reminded, 'is not a democracy.' If that means that we do not decide our beliefs by obtaining a majority vote from the faithful, I entirely agree. As someone rather unkindly said, 'We leave that practice to the bishops in Ecumenical Councils.' (I believe there were only two negative votes at Vatican I for the decree on papal infallibility; but fifty-seven of the bishops had gone home already, so as not to be listed among a dissenting minority.) But the generally accepted belief of the faithful is a serious factor in determining the faith of the whole church. I wonder if we have taken seriously the paragraph from *Lumen Gentium,* the Vatican II Decree on the Church.

'The body of the faithful as a whole, anointed as they are by the Holy One, cannot err in matters of belief. Thanks to a supernatural sense of the faith which characterises the people as a whole, it manifests this unerring quality when, from the bishops down to the last member of the laity, it shows universal agreement in matters and faith and morals.' (Para 12)

There have been times when the laity has been ahead of the college of bishops in the development of our understanding even of doctrinal matters. In an issue about moral behaviour such as contraceptive practice it was certainly important that married people, and those with relevant scientific knowledge, should be consulted as well as moral theologians; that was why Pope Paul VI enlarged the commission to consider the matter. To have their views over-ridden seemed more like a tyranny. 'On Consulting the Faithful' belongs to a healthier tradition than that. In the light of recent documents and rulings from Rome, it is evident that the struggle continues.

'It must still be said of the church teacher: *in medio ecclesiae aperuit os suum.* As individuals, neither bishops nor Pope, nor the whole people, are ever the church. Occasionally they represent the whole church authoritatively and juridically; but not even in the person of a Pope does there exist the fullness of what God wants in his church, of what is authorised, concentrated and assembled in the church. We have no duty to interpret *sentire cum ecclesia* in such a way that an historically or sociologically conditioned taste or lifestyle, or a particular way of seeing things is simply identified with the mind of the church.' (Karl Rahner in *Meditations on Priestly Life*)

'Of course, it's only objectively that you've got it all wrong.'

Part Four

Changing Roles and Expectations
1969–1974

Chapter Eight:
Beyond the Limits of a Diocese: Moving out, or just moving on?
Breaking away from parish work wasn't easy, and was certainly liable to misunderstanding. There was the usual mix of ecclesiastical and personal nuances to attend to before undertaking paid employment in residential care of ex-custodial young men in Southampton.

Chapter Nine:
On the Borders of Clergydom: minister without portfolio
While working out a philosophy of residential 'after-care', it made me reflect on the relationship between such work and being a priest.

Chapter Ten:
Within the Parameters of a Profession:
Challenging priestly roles and identity
This development became more important as I moved on into the Probation service in Slough for a temporary post before returning to university studies.

[Courtesy of *The Tablet*]

CHAPTER EIGHT

Beyond the Limits of a Diocese
Moving out, or just moving on?

'My son, do not take on a great amount of business: if you multiply your interests, you are bound to suffer for it. Hurry as fast as you can, you will never arrive, nor will you escape by running away. A man labours and toils and forges ahead, only to find himself outdistanced.' *(Ecclesiasticus 11:10)*

Having to work out with integrity a standpoint for effective and honest pastoral work was clearly a very tiring process. It points to a flawed personal characteristic of mine that, while distrustful of my immediate reaction to disputed issues without consulting widely, I did not share discussion of the very personal consequences of these with my priest colleagues, or spiritual director or even close friends. The *Humanae Vitae* controversy had certainly brought some kind of focus onto the central difficulty I had with conforming to the historic Catholic institution – at least in its contemporary format. I had been expecting something more radically different to emerge from the second Vatican Council. My liturgical, ecumenical and other pastoral 'experiments' – if they deserve such an appellation – seemed 'ahead' of my neighbours in the diocese. I was beginning to wonder more deeply about what I intended, as well as what was apparently expected of me, by serving as a priest. It was time to bring this uncertainty to some practical outcome so, after much prayerful thought, I wrote the following letter to Bishop Petit.

The parish anniversary of ten years since opening the new church has helped me to focus many long-held thoughts, and I must come to see you as soon as possible about them. Meantime, so that I do not spring it on you without time for some thoughtful reaction, may I venture to make a very personal request in this letter?
I have been quite extraordinarily happy here in Ruabon through these years. Even before the questionnaire you sent

to the clergy on our wishes and hopes for future work, I told you that I was beginning to wonder if it wouldn't be fairer to the people of Ruabon if they had a change. In the end I decided, as you know, that on balance I'd rather stay here than do anything else. However, I want now to ask for a reversal of this; but I want to add, in a way I must hasten to explain, that I am not asking for another appointment in the diocese at present. In fact I want to be released for the time being to do something very different elsewhere.

Before this is misunderstood, let me assure you that I am not intending to 'leave the church' – impossible anyway, as I see it – nor the priesthood; my ordination commitment was for life, and I want to remain a priest of the diocese of Menevia. But I want some 'sabbatical' years, free from fulltime ministry, to have another look and think; and meantime to be useful (I hope) as a priest, but without any fulltime office.

You have been more than kind to me, even when I have done things in ways you would not have chosen. I know that you have even been quite pleased with much of what I have managed to do. However, as you found it necessary to tell me over the Mixed Marriage and *Humanae Vitae* problems, you fear that I do not have 'a Catholic mind'. Naturally I dispute this, but you have more chance of being right than I. Since my views on so many aspects of church life grow stronger, I am aware they deviate even further from your understanding of things and, as time goes on, it would be even harder for you to express any confidence in me at all. The link between the priest and his bishop is perforce weak in our present patterns, but I believe that there should be some basic accord; and this is getting more tenuous. Mind – I wouldn't like you to think this is anything personal. It is far more because of general attitudes and policies in the church, and which you naturally feel you must adhere to as a bishop loyal to the Holy See. I quite appreciate this, even though I profoundly disagree here and there with the implications of this kind of loyalty. For instance, as I have already told you, it is my personal belief that *Humanae Vitae* was a fearful mistake. My estimate is that the body of most solid thinking concludes likewise. But the 'party line' (not meant too unkindly) is that the encyclical teaches true and adequate doctrine. I get sadder and sadder at the impression that is publicly given that there is no real or valid dispute anymore. That is the tenor of the sort of literature you send us from Bishop's House; and if I had found myself under some other bishops, I should simply have had the sack. The local variation in sanctions is pleasing but illogical. I am appalled that this situation persists. You will know, to your personal cost, how much I disagree with the canonical legislation of Mixed Marriages. Again I stand a clearer chance of being wrong than you do; but I find it increasingly hard to justify in particular instances; and I lack sincerity to 'put it over' to couples who come to me. Should I go on holding formal office in these circumstances? The ecumenical situation likewise causes me acute discomfort. I am certain that people are ready for huge advances, but I see the official structures as likely to inhibit rather than encourage any real development. Good will there is a-plenty; and much good theology about, as I see it. But it all comes to virtually nothing on the ground. Our local efforts over the years have made me impatient for advance without which our whole exercise becomes banal. I am inclined to think that it is the local churches who have the primary responsibility for initiating ecumenical progress, and the formal structures should simply investigate what is possible there, rather than issue occasional modest directives for action. But I can see that this is to set the present pattern of church discipline on its head.

The liturgy has advanced enormously, beyond points where many bishops said, 'Thus far and no further' (e.g. the Canon in vernacular). Yet now it looks as though we are to have only a 'fixed alternatives' policy, rather than a more elastic period to allow us to discover the liturgy, or liturgies, that we need and deserve. I'm as fed up as the extreme conservative with 'all these changes', even when I see the theological sense behind most of them. It is the whole approach to development that distresses me. Again and again we see that everything is forbidden until it becomes compulsory in a way that is ridiculous. Through all this, just by lying low and saying nothing, many priests get on with the job, as I have tried to do, riding rather lightly to some rubrical requirements, and occasionally 'jumping the gun'. So far, I am happy to say, I have never jumped the gun in any way that has not later been authorised officially. My guesses were not inspired; a careful study of what's going on gives clear enough pointers all the while. Sometimes it has been those who have taken unauthorised steps forward who have moved authorities to make the desired changes.

I pass over the financial methods and policies of the church; the over-emphasis (as I see it) on Catholic schools; the lack of serious encouragement for the laity to take their full place. I am simply out of sympathy with so many things that I am not a true representative of my bishop, of the British conference of bishops, and certainly not of the Roman pattern of authority. I can hardly justify holding office. This realisation has grown of late. In some ways I have overworked myself – my own fault – and inside I am very, very tired. I am weary of thinking things out on my own. I am only too well aware of the huge gaps and fearful failures in my pastoral work here. I have lost the heart to try new ways when they seem to run counter to the current policies of hierarchy. You will know that many priests in the diocese view my activities with disfavour. Your own Vicar General in the north, and my own Rural Dean are seriously suspicious of Ruabon, though neither has ever challenged me, or been anything other than their courteous selves. I have never kept my views dark; I have always tried to find out other people's views and have tried to share my own on several public issues by circular letter. Almost none of those who (one learns privately) disagree ever bother to acknowledge any letter of mine. Remember how I waxed indignant over *Veterum Sapientiae* on the use of Latin, and tried to persuade reasoned dismay to be expressed to you? The attempt angered some; but *Veterum Sapientiae* is a dead letter now anyway. I got worked up about the method of electing bishops, for Wales in particular, and this was thought by some to be inept. At least the topic is generally discussed these days. I was deeply distressed by *Humanae Vitae*; the widespread signs of agreement were an encouragement; but this was offset by the sad discovery that some priests didn't want their views to be known. They feared to speak openly. I know you don't like this public approach of mine; but at least I have never said anything, or withheld anything, behind your back. However I have evidently undermined the confidence of my fellow clergy. Perhaps partly for this reason I have failed you in not getting the Diocesan

Youth Centre off to a real existence. All I have here is a premises apt for many uses, with a library of 4,000 books, sleeping accommodation for twenty-eight people, many meeting rooms; but no success in getting anyone to come (and pay for) the running of a 'centre'. There isn't much excuse for preventing someone else to have a fresh go.

I am therefore asking you to accept my resignation as parish priest and as warden of the Diocesan Youth Centre, and to release me from service in the diocese for the time being. What am I going to do? I must certainly be no burden to you; and for the moment I am not sure how this is to be achieved. I have written to my Oxford College to enquire whether I am too old to be re-admitted to take a Dip Ed or something like that. There are other social studies which I could undertake elsewhere if I can settle grants. With the help of Mass stipends I should be able to get by. I am also probing some aspects of social work where I have some competence and experience, particularly in the area of 'social inadequates' who have absorbed much of my time and energy in Ruabon already. I do not equate the work of a priest with that of a social worker, but such work would at least keep me in touch with people, and probably enable me to help out in some priestly work also in some measure. I would also like to give further evidence that we are concerned with people other than 'our own'. Above all this, I need opportunity to work things out, outside the responsibility of a formal 'office', where my attitudes must rightly be tied only to the current discipline. I would hope that you won't find it too difficult to accept my resignation on all these grounds. I am hurrying to get this to you now, because I hear that the late summer 'clergy manoeuvres' are being planned. I have spoken of all this to no-one at all, and I hope that a simple notice that I have asked for release for the time being 'for special studies' or 'specialist work' would not be misconstrued in the diocese.

I shall find leaving Ruabon's people a cruel break. Here is a marvellous community, so alive and co-operative. There are some – I suppose this is everywhere the case – who are not enthusiastic about their parish priest; but I am not aware of any enemies. However, in spite of many efforts to involve the people fully, the whole venture has centred round me too personally – probably because I am the only priest most of them have ever had. The longer I stay the more they may be dependent; they need a change of leader even if quite a lot of them won't want it. Any scheme for a team-ministry, which I still believe is an advance that is overdue in this area, would still be better in others' hands. The only thing that I seriously hope is that you will find some way of drawing people into consultation about the kind of priest that is needed here. Anyone with no liking for ecumenical work, and for young people, would be a disaster: I am sure they would say this.

If you agree to release me I shall feel more free in following up enquiries about work elsewhere, but nothing need be said of it to anyone else till the coast is entirely clear in your estimation. After a year or two, maybe I could return to the diocese? By that time, either my understanding of the church will show some signs of having been vindicated, or I shall have discovered that I am quite mistaken in my attitudes, and will be able to step back into the priestly ranks without undue discomfort. My thinking has changed over and again in the twenty-five years I have been a Catholic. There is no reason to think that I have reached any fixed point yet – except the one reached (in my early adolescence) that Christ mattered more than anyone or anything; and the other (on becoming a Catholic) that the church was where I must be.

Please let me know when you want me to come to see you. I am out all day tomorrow, but would suit you as early as possible otherwise.

Yours sincerely, Owen

The bishop's reply was generous, and I set about trying to find a job. I think he was a little easier in his mind that it turned out to be in a Catholic-founded project with ex-prisoners, though he seemed to think I would just walk into the job in response to the advert. In fact of course I had to have my application vetted and I had to go for an interview in Southampton. This was how I came to contact Derek Worlock again whom I had known when he was the cardinal's secretary in Westminster. Now he was Bishop of Portsmouth. I stayed with him in Bishop's House when I went for the interview, and I kept him loosely informed of my movements for the next two years that I was within his diocesan territory. Derek was actually kind enough to understand when I said that I felt that the 'Spirit was being quenched' in the diocese I still belonged to, for that was how I felt about it;

not my spirit, but the Spirit that discerned the signs of the times. He said, 'If this job doesn't work out for you down here, you can join us in this diocese.' I don't think it is a mistaken memory that he added, 'We have several eccentrics already', and gave me one of his wry smiles.

I needed to produce some personal references – a novel experience, but with hindsight I'm not so sure that such references would not be quite a good idea when a priest is being slotted into a new diocesan task. I was delighted with the willingness of a Probation Officer to give me one. It was a bit glowing, and no doubt boosted my ego but it was certainly helpful. He said:

> I have known Rev Owen Hardwicke since my appointment as Probation Officer in Ruabon Division a little over two years ago. We have come to know each other extremely well due to a shared interest in various local youths. He figured frequently in the records of people supervised by my predecessor, and it had become an integral part of my casework that if I find a person who needs more constant support than I am able to provide, I introduce him to Owen Hardwicke. He has made no distinction between religious views or denomination, and through the medium of his youth club and by personal interest I have seen him do a lot of excellent work. On several occasions he has taken boys to live at Bryn Hall with him either on a short or long-term basis. In every such person there has been a change in attitude and under his care one probationer changed from an introverted self-conscious adolescent to a leader of the local youth and a confident young man. In short, I have found that whilst most local churches seem to shun the wrong-doer and difficult persons, Owen Hardwicke has actively encouraged them to come to him. He has won their respect and their devotion, and it is always to him they turn in trouble. He has also won my admiration, and I have been bewildered as to how he manages to do so much good work and yet find time for regular church duties, a variety of courses and committees. I can only conclude that he must be an excellent administrator. P. J. H.

Well, the work I had done didn't always seem so successful to me, but at least the reference made clear that people knew what I was aiming at; and I think it impressed the interview panel. I still needed to give some kind of assurance about how it was that a priest was available to undertake such a job. Was I a total misfit in my parish work, they might reasonably ask? It was easy enough to check that the bishop had given me permission to move out of the diocese, but what might my parishioners say about me? Since it was totally unknown that I was about to depart, I had to delay on this. The parishioner whom I eventually approached at first felt it a bit odd that he should write a reference for his parish priest, but he managed to touch on what he thought were relevant aspects of my work, as he saw them. I treasured this reference, which was personally very comforting when my parish was almost 'written off' by other priests later on. The reference included this:

'Probably his best work has been in the moulding of those less able and less well-informed than himself. He has patiently and relentlessly worked to awaken and inform the consciences of his parishioners to a greater understanding and purpose of their faith, so that they would act from a reasoned self-discipline rather than from imposed law. He has succeeded to a large extent in changing attitudes from "I've got to" to "I want to".

Excluding any feeling of personal loyalty or obligation to the parish of Fr Hardwicke, I know of no other parish where there is 100% participation in the Mass; where during the year each individual parishioner is now involved according to ability in the work of the church; where the smallest contribution of the less able has equal ranking to the major contribution of the more capable; where the barriers with and prejudices about other denominations have been steadily eroded without compromising basic Catholic principles. The St Michael's parishioner is no better or worse than any other parishioner, and the achievements directly reflect Fr Hardwicke's patient and informed guidance over the years. This could not be done had he not been seen to be acting with dedication, conviction, honesty of purpose and with complete integrity. This would be the collective testimony of the Catholic and wider Christian community in Ruabon, and it is testimony to which I am pleased without qualification to be able to add my own.' (J. J. H.)

That was better than any farewell gift, and, as I have said, stood me in good emotional stead, when darker days passed by. I shall now treasure the story retailed at the funeral of Cardinal Hume about an occasion when a friend had just been paid a very generous compliment. It was reported that the Cardinal said: 'Enjoy that; but don't inhale.' That strikes me as real wisdom.

But now came the moment when I had to inform the parishioners of my departure. This is not an easy moment for any priest. One is not just leaving a job, but moving one's home, and all the very personal links which have grown round one through the years – fifteen of them in my case. I didn't trust myself to extemporise. I prepared a Supplementary Bulletin to be issued after Sunday Mass on 29 June, as soon as I had read it out to the congregation. I tried to arrange that all the most active parishioners should come to the morning Mass rather than struggle on into the evening with the news. I had a temporarily homeless lad still living in the house. He was not a Catholic and I said to him on the Saturday night. 'David, I've never asked you before, and I'll never ask you again, but would you please come to tomorrow morning's Mass? I do have a special reason.' And so, at the end of the liturgy I read this out:

> 'I have an item of news for you which I do not find it easy to give. I have thought deeply over the fairest way of bringing it to you, and my decision was that, instead of telling individuals, or allowing any rumour to grow up, it would be better if I told you all at one go. I have tried to ensure that most of the members of the Parish Council are at this Mass this morning so that they can have the picture clearly.
>
> I am due to go on holiday on the night of Sunday July 13th – two weeks from now. My holiday lasts until August 2nd. However, I shall not be returning to Ruabon. I have resigned as parish priest, and as Warden of the Youth Centre, and the bishop has kindly released me from the diocese to undertake specialist work in the south of England, in the diocese of Portsmouth.
>
> I think this is the best parish in the country, and so it is just as well that I am not going to another parish to make any comparisons. I am, anyhow for the time being, leaving parish work altogether. I am to work with the Society of St Dismas, founded to care for ex-prisoners and ex-Borstal boys. I don't think I need to tell you that I have developed some experience with "difficult" young people, among many others who only have the ordinary run of adolescent problems. There is an increasing need for this work to be developed; and I believe passionately that the church must be part of it; so as a

priest I may be able to signify the care of the church in a special way. I have tried to do similar work to this here, but it cannot properly be combined with the office of parish priest. I shall not find it easy to leave Ruabon which has been my home for so long. I have worked with you for nearly fifteen years. I hope you will help me to leave people and feelings in decent array! The announcement is sudden and perhaps unexpected, for many other clergy moves have been rumoured; but not this one, I think. I am sure it is time for you to have a change of leadership. I have in some ways slightly run out of steam, and that is not good for the parish. On Friday, June 11th we are due to have the next meeting of the Council of the parish. My successor has welcomed the idea of coming to this, to meet the members and any parishioner who is anxious about the life and work of our parish. Two days later, after the evening Mass on June 13th I shall leave, and he will take over at once, though his formal induction by the bishop may take a little longer. I shall have time to see you all before I go, of course; but I trust you will excuse me coming to the church door to see you off today. I don't think I need to explain why.'

I went straight into the house and up to my little self-contained 'flat' and cried my eyes out. When I felt better, and came downstairs there was a huddle of young people from the village, mostly youth club members. 'You can't really be going,' they said in a kind of stunned unbelief.

News spread around the district quickly, and I later picked up the widespread idea that I had been sacked because of the *Humanae Vitae* dissent. Indeed one lovely ex-Liverpool parishioner told me this when she was helping in the club canteen the following week. 'No really,' I said, 'I'm going of my own free will.' 'Listen,' she said, 'I've been in the Catholic Church longer than you. I know there are more ways than one of a throttling a chicken.'

It was pleasing that the Wrexham Anglican Deanery magazine thought fit to put in an entry:

A Community Loss. The news of Owen Hardwicke's impending departure from Ruabon has brought considerable sadness not only to his own Roman Catholic community which he has served so diligently as their parish priest for fifteen years, but also to members of all the Christian churches in Ruabon who have profited from his leadership in ecumenical activities and to those not actively associated with any church to whom he has proved himself a good friend. If one might presume to assess his contribution to Christian witness in Ruabon, one might say that he has inspired us to share his vision of the church as a society which does not stand on its dignity, but, like the Lord and Master, is here to serve.

After my last Sunday morning Mass I was asked to speed along to the Anglican parish church to be there at the end of their service, where they were waiting to give me a very gracious and warm farewell.

That then was how parishioners, neighbours and friends saw me off with such overwhelmingly kind words. Yet what mattered to me as much as the personal love shown, was their estimate of the contribution I had at least tried to make to collaborative ministry, to ecumenical relations and an outreach to the unchurched. I was unsure how the bishop would have seen it. Ten days before I drove away, the following letter came:

My dear Owen,

In case I forget till it is after 13th, I feel I must drop you a farewell note of thanks for the very good work you have done in this diocese, and to tell you that I am sorry you are going. It may be of course that you will come back, perhaps not in my time, since you have not asked for excardination, nor I take it likely to do so in the forseeable future.

I have put no obstacle in your way of taking up this work for the down and outs, because I have realised for some considerable time past that that was the way you were tending. I do not believe, unless I am compelled by overwhelming circumstances, in preventing a priest from developing the work for which he feels a great attraction.

I won't prolong this letter; there is always a temptation to do so when it is typewritten. As I started it, so I end it, with an expression of personal thanks, not only for what you have done in the diocese but also for what you did for me personally when you were my secretary.

My blessing to you, + John, Bishop of Menevia

It later turned out to be of importance that I had kept this letter. In 1971, when I was doing further studies in Social Work at

University College, Cardiff, for one year, a married couple, whom I had known since 1956 as fellow-parishioners, asked me if I was free to join them at their home for a party of school leavers, so that I could say a house-Mass first. They soon phoned to say that, when asking the permission of the archbishop, he banned me from doing so. 'Didn't you know that he has been turned out of two dioceses already?' They didn't know. Nor did I. So I obtained a letter from Bishop Derek Worlock, still in Portsmouth (covering my years of work in Southampton and Ascot), in which he said, 'You may have been turned out of two dioceses; but do not include me.' Together with a copy of Bishop Petit's letter which I have just given, I sent this evidence to the archbishop. Alas, he did not even acknowledge my letter. We had the school-leavers' party, but omitted the Mass.

One of the perennial problems, which I at any rate have not managed successfully or well, is how to release oneself and other people from the bonds established at a very personal level when leaving a parish. If you have shared some of the most personal and intimate facets of people's lives, especially in troubles, you are not only their priest but their friend. In my case, I had to add the larger number of people with whom I had worked closely who were not church people at all. I was their friend, before ever I was a priest. Friendships, however incurred, cannot be written off just because one moves away. To drop all contact and simply say, 'I am not your priest anymore' strikes me as positively inhuman. I recognised that the bonds of affection between myself and so many people were what I was going to miss more than any loss they were going to feel. That's what follows from being a celibate with no home of one's own, and particularly if one has no close family members on hand.

To balance against this is the right and expectation of a new priest to have unambiguous opportunities of building a new base for his parish 'family'. If his predecessor is going to keep fostering his contacts, that could be embarrassing and unhelpful. It would be insufferable if anyone were to exercise any influence over his successor's policies; but can he jettison his close friends? It can be a delicate matter when a particular family want you, for instance, to preside at their wedding or funeral; and this is only diplomatically 'solved' by one's lack of availability through duties in a new parish.

The problem came home to me vividly when so many of the

Ruabon people asked to be kept in touch with me in my new sphere of work. They knew I was apprehensive about it and hoped to have reports from me. When I did have forty-eight hours off from the intensive task in Southampton, I occasionally drove, all 190 miles of it, back to Ruabon for an overnight stop with Paul's family. This was not exactly noised abroad. To a number of others I sent an occasional news-sheet.

On one occasion, when writing a letter to one of my successors, I crossed the line of discretion altogether, when I made a general suggestion about how to set about managing the village set-up he was encountering, in the light of my experience. This was not just indiscreet; it was unpardonable, and it provoked a very angry response. I deserved such a telling off; but it included such a radical dismissal of all that I had done, it caused me to face a severe self-assessment. If it was true, I said to myself, that all I had left behind in Ruabon was a parish with a steady decline in its Catholicism, and the self-glorification of a gigantic publicity man, then I had no right to be a priest at all. Looking back now, it says a good deal about the inner fragility of a priest on his own that a harsh criticism should be so unnerving. One would have hoped that I had learned how to cope with personal hurt, and to realise that some things said in anger are not meant with the full force of the words used. Clearly I had not learned that; and for the first and only time in my life I seriously weighed up whether or not I should resign my ministry. In my anxiety I wrote to three priests who knew me well, and one of my earlier lay residents at Bryn Hall. 'If these remarks are really true, would you tell me so?' Their replies were a mixture of good spiritual direction, or such a different estimate of my work that they reassured me; so I stayed. I'm glad I did, and that no animosity whatever remained afterwards about the incident.

Later on, when I was returning to parish work, I tried out one solution myself about how a change-over of priests might be managed. Three weeks before moving back into a parish, nearly twenty years after leaving such work, I joined my predecessor to concelebrate the Sunday Masses with him. When the time came for notices, he graciously invited me to say a word of personal introduction. I remember saying that I was looking forward to coming. 'But a priest is not in a parish for eight or nine years without making some special friends. I want you and him to know that, if at any time, you want him to return to celebrate a

baptism, a wedding or some anniversary, he will be most welcome to come back.'

I am, however, still left with one unresolved question. How
do the private and the public persona of a priest relate to one another? Is not successful ministry always mediated through a
personality, and should one even try to dissociate them so that
no close bonds are established at all? This item continues to relate
to the discussion, not so much about the nature of priesthood,
but about the way it is to be lived. I have found no adequate
answers yet.

CHAPTER NINE

On the Borderlines of Clergydom:
Minister without portfolio

It was really not at all surprising that the work to which I now felt drawn to make something of a speciality was that with young adults in trouble – so much of my time had been spent that way already. It didn't always feel like 'work', because I valued their influence in keeping my feet – even my theological feet – on the ground, in touch with ordinary life, sometimes at its roughest end. I had (as became the pattern,) overworked myself. I rarely took a day off in spite of good resolutions. Yet what was I to do with a 'day off'? The only thing I missed was a good symphony concert – yet Liverpool and Manchester were too far away, and otherwise Chester and Wrexham didn't have much available – or not on the few occasions when I was free enough to attend. So good uninterrupted time with a record player was what I wanted; or to sit and read – and no doubt doze off now and again. The diocesan recommendation (though I don't recall bishop, dean or anyone else checking up on its implementation) was for a weekly day off. For some priests in the cities that seemed to mean Mondays on the golf course, and I am no sportsman, nor was I particularly keen to spend time with other priests. We had been brought up to believe that 'socialising' in the parish was unwise: it might cause jealousy through apparent favouritism. So, while I visited every one frequently and certainly had good friends among the parishioners, that was no outlet. My father lived in Cardiff, a four-hour journey, so impossible to call on in one day.

It was young unemployed youth club members who sometimes made sure I had time off. Hearing that I was going to try to take Wednesday afternoon off, several of them would ring up at lunchtime. 'Come on, we're going out. What time will you call?' and we went for a car ride to Llangollen, or to the cinema in Chester, or to have a meal in a café. Among these lads (who were not 'parishioners' so didn't offend the code) were some who had special difficulties at home from time to time, and even came to stay for a few days in Bryn Hall to be out of harm's way. The Probation service actually brought one young man, David, when his grandfather, with whom he lived, died in the night, and he didn't fancy going to his aunt's. Incidentally, he was a miner and for many weeks I had to wake him at 4.15 am, give him breakfast and see him off, before going back to bed. I was very fond of him, even though he had little conversation, and spent his free time out with his friends, or in the club. There was one period when several people told me they had seen him around the district by day, when he was supposed to be at work. Sure enough, I uncovered him myself one day at about 7 am, after seeing him off at 4.45 am. He was sleeping in the back of my van in the garage. Poor lad, I think he was just depressed, not idle – but he had had to invent several different stories to cover his inability once or twice to pay anything towards his keep. I didn't 'tell him off': I simply said that I thought it wasn't fair for the parish to have to cough up for his keep, though he was still welcome to have a room. He never let me down again.

Eric was somebody very special. I don't ever remember him without a mischievous smile. A club member, he spent several of my days off with me. Life wasn't up to much at home, and he was another of those who had some residential days in the house. This did not particularly please one of my priest colleagues who joined me for a year or so. He didn't like having 'these young men' around, for whom I cooked and cared. My view was, especially if they had been told to 'get out' in a fit of family anger, that it did them, and their families, no harm to have a cooling off period. After a few days of my inadequate cooking, and having to do their own washing (no machines in those days) they would probably appreciate home a bit more when they returned. Under the law I could not have housed under-16s anyway, and I usually informed the police about the older ones, in case the parents started looking for them. It didn't do the parents much harm to have a little bit of worry at their being temporarily 'missing'.

Eric's circumstances were not so dire, but as a bright, intelligent but poorly schooled lad, he disliked unemployment. One day he got a residential waiter's job down the Llangollen valley. He quite liked it and was glad to be in work. On one of his days off, he came to see me, and I was on the verge of a bout of 'flu.

This was almost an annual affliction, brought on as much by the vulnerability of my tiredness as anything. It sometimes lasted 10–14 days, running unto pneumonia on one occasion. We didn't talk for long, but I said 'Give me a quick call on your way back to the station,' because I wanted to be sure he didn't miss the last train, and thereby lose his job. That was to be about 9.30 pm. Nine o'clock came and went; quarter and half past – no sign of him. A worrier by nature, I had an uneasy night. Next morning at 11.00 am, I was still sick in bed, he phoned me up. 'Yes, Eric, I'm glad, but why on earth didn't you call as I asked? I've been worried sick.' 'I did call: but your priest colleague simply refused to let me see you. He said you weren't to be disturbed.' I expect it was meant as an act of friendly protection, added to which would have been the impropriety of a lad visiting me in my bedroom. In contemporary circumstances, with all the abusive priest scandals, that might make sense, but Eric and I were good friends – the difference in age, lifestyle and education was of no importance at all.

For me it was one of the significant incidents in my life when Eric and another fixed up to emigrate to Australia under a 'Big Brother' scheme. He asked to spend his last evening in the UK with me and, knowing I was very keen to see *West Side Story*, he said we should go together. In the 'intermission' I made some comment, and I realised from his response that he'd already seen the film, and was there a second time for my sake – never mind it was his last day in Britain. I saw him off on the train the next morning and knew I would miss his cheerful presence. Within 2–3 years he was in touch with me again by letter and audio-tape. By accent he was now an 'Aussie', and was attending university and displaying joy at some of the literature he was devouring. He turned up several years later with his wife one Christmas Eve when I was living over a shop in Wrexham in the Lift Project. He was back again four summers ago, and stayed in my house in Wrexham for a while – this is more that twenty-five years on. His work is with 'inadequate' and marginalised people, a Citizen Advocacy scheme, and he is a man of high ideals – and still full of fun. I am so very proud of him, and hope to visit him in Australia before I die.

Move to Southampton

The Society of Dismas was founded in Southampton by a fine priest Fr Patrick Murphy-O'Connor, (brother to Archbishop Cormac) after his prison chaplaincy work, to provide some half-way accommodation for men coming out of prison. A second phase was a home for 'young offenders', those released from Borstals or Detention Centres for whom 'going home' was not a possibility. An advertisement said they were in search of a residential Warden at Aubyn's House. That was the job I told my bishop that I wished to apply for, and he let me go, whatever anxiety he may have felt that I was giving up my priestly ministry. I had to prove my suitability by interview. I had experience but no formal qualification. The management team was very thorough in checking me out, and it was by no means a foregone conclusion that as a priest I'd get the job. The great thing was that at about the same time the men's hostel took on a Franciscan priest, Fr Andrew McMahon, and I had another one as assistant warden for a time.

Our immediate boss was a local magistrate who administered the Society's work. To begin with he was effusively welcoming. For reasons I shall never understand this did not last, and he grew to dislike me heartily and to disapprove of the way I administered the house and dealt with the nine residents, between the ages of 19 and 25. This was the most difficult job I had ever undertaken. I was content with my little bedsit above the office, but being 'on duty' might mean sitting in the office, or fussing about the practicalities of the home for an eighteen-hour shift on occasions. At night, even though not 'on duty', I could hear the comings and goings and was often very uneasy. One or two of the residents had serious personality problems and it was not easy to win their trust. My predecessor had gone around with a bunch of keys and lots of rooms, especially the kitchen stores, were locked up. This seemed to me so like the custodial institutions the lads had just left, and unlike the openness of a normal home, that I was unwilling to live like that. Of course openness implies vulnerability and it was often abused, but how else do you persuade people to be responsible, unless things go wrong, are assessed and confronted, and lessons are learned? One or two tried hardline physical threats at me, and I had a few narrow escapes from violence. I attribute my escape to my totally non-violent response and an obvious willingness to be struck, if need be, without any readiness to respond. One lad one day picked up a kitchen knife in anger, more like a tantrum, to 'have a go' at another resident. I hastily dismissed the latter from the scene, and was involved in a heavy scuffle to disarm him, which ended up on the floor with my arms round him, as he sobbed away as much in response to being held physically as in frustration. I made it my business to make the beds myself on sheet-changing day: to discover bed-wetting was sometimes a useful indication of the state of depression or frustration – which I then had no need to ask about. They knew I knew, and the privacy of the knowledge helped to build trust. For one lad my tolerance was too good to be true, and he was heard muttering as he walked up the road one day, 'He can't really be genuine.' In the long run, Tom became one of my cheeriest friends.

About twelve years later I was running the Lift Project in Wrexham when TV came to record 'Songs of Praise' from the fine Anglican parish church, St Giles. I was just one of the congregation from all the local churches. But the producer chose to 'pan in' on me, dressed in my cassock, and to include one of those personal interviews. Tom, now married and living in Peterborough, saw the programme and sent a letter addressed to 'Fr Hardwicke, Wrexham' which found me. He was so thrilled to have spotted me. Within another couple of years I was giving a parish talk in Peterborough for Pax Christi, and, after informing him by letter, he met me at the station: 'This is just magic,' he said and hosted me for a meal with his family. I lost him again for another two years, but we are again in touch.

(After that same 'Songs of Praise', when the camera zoomed in finally on me singing heartily, a friend remarked: 'Fr Hardwicke, you may be a Catholic priest, but you sing like a Methodist!' I valued the compliment.)

In the hostel I shared all my meals with the residents, and I found that one of my best allies in building confidence with them was Sally Mills, the cook. She was an attractive married woman, whose relaxed un-matronly manner helped many of them to stand talking to her in the kitchen. She helped to provide me with a barometer on their tensions. Such people are the best natural 'social workers', all the better for not having learned it all with the benefit of schooling from books and short placements. She was sufficiently self-confident not to be afraid of even the toughest of them, and consequently she was never in danger – though my little office opened into the kitchen anyway, so that help would have been at hand. The lads could be a pain in the neck sometimes. There was a dreadful period when, mostly unemployed, they stayed up half the night playing cards, lounged around by day, became quarrelsome, and the language was foul. I looked forward to the 48 hours off that were arranged for myself and my assistant from time to time. On return from one of these breaks the dinner table scene was especially grim, and someone threw something across the room and broke a window. 'Right, that's it,' I said. 'I've had enough.' I was so rarely angry that it really startled them all. 'I can't live like this. I've just realised why I enjoyed my 48 hours off so much. I was treated to decent conversation without f...ing and blinding, and I was respected as a fellow human being instead of being called "you b.... Welsh git". If things don't change right now, I'm off.' And I stormed out of the dining room. I wasn't far away and I realised that they were 'in conference' immediately. Several hours later, two of them came to see me: 'We've made a list of rules for the house: will you look at them?' When I studied them, they were much more like an institution than a home – not surprising perhaps, given their backgrounds. The rules were a lot stricter than I would have dared to propose. 'OK,' I said, 'but you'll have to see that they are kept. We'll have house meetings to check.' And they really did improve. One day after dinner they called a special meeting to discuss their concern: 'Listen, there's too much b.... swearing in the house', and their worry was not so much the language itself, as using it within earshot of Sally.

The lads came and went fairly freely, even in late evening. I said one day, 'I'm not going to hang around to let you in at 2.00 am.' 'Then give us a key if we're going to be late.' Touché! Why not, if they were to be trained for trust? And this was hardly ever abused. They didn't have the money to be out late, and they had no local friends – the latter fact was one of the drawbacks of the hostel. However, one morning, when I went at 7.00 am to wake one of them for work, in a room with two beds in it, on each of the pillows were two heads – male and female. 'What's this?' I said pointing at them, to their startled and confused gaze, and I stumped out. Later I heard movements, but I took no notice. Mid-morning the two lads came to the office and sheepishly started: 'Look, Owen, we came to explain about last night. You

know, we had our clothes on.' I interrupted: 'I'm not interested
to hear any details. I just want to ask you, do you agree that
bringing girls into our home, and taking them to your rooms, let
alone into bed, is "not on"? Will you assure me that it won't happen again?' They readily agreed, and were obviously staggered
that I wasn't going to sack them from the home. They babbled
on, 'Really we didn't plan this; it's just that they'd missed their
bus home, and we thought ...' 'No more explanations or decep-
tions, please. Just remember what assurances you have given.' It
was a tolerance that amazed them, and it worked.

This was one event that was reported to the management
team and director, and added fuel to his disapproval of me.
Another upset came from a resident who, twice on the run, had
no money to pay his weekly rent – he was in employment, and
his story was that he'd lost his money on the way home. (He
probably had, but on the horses.) I was sympathetic but incredu-
lous: 'Look Ken, this simply won't do. Who do you think is paying for your food and accommodation?' and I made it plain such
excuses wouldn't wash any more. Again it was reported to the
management who indicated that such lads should be expelled.
By now I realised I had lost their confidence – or at least the administrator's – and that my approach differed from their wishes.

Already I was working towards shaping a project of my own,
where standing alongside such people replaced standing over
them. I had been reading as widely as I could, and picking up
clues from colleagues in similar work. There is no better way of
clearing up one's own ideas that explaining them to others. So
giving a lecture in March 1971 to a Guild of Social Workers was
a good opportunity to outline where I had reached in my thinking.

The lecture was about 'Controlling Young Offenders in a
Residential Setting', but was in my mind more widely about relating to people on the basis of trust and partnership. It had its
relevance for relationships within the church community. Here
are some extracts:

a) 'An honest appraisal of the rules that most frequently
occur in hostels would show the similarity of those that are
deemed to be necessary. They concern the time of locking up at
night, i.e. curfew; meal-time arrangements, tidiness of beds and
rooms. The similarity is due to their relation to the convenience
and wishes of the staff. They are no worse for that. But I believe

one can argue hypocritically for the benefit to the residents of these, and many more rules, when in fact one is simply trying to make life more tolerable for those with different standards in this artificial setting where people live somewhat on top of each other. No doubt the personal discipline attached to avoiding late hours, irregular meals and untidy habits is a great advantage; but singularly brilliant and useful citizens survive, to say the least, without these things, and we must not exaggerate their necessity. "Control" of these matters might well be for the sake of the staff, whose pattern of life it may already represent; but it is not the kind of control that will necessarily be helpful to the disturbed adolescents, many of whom have already experienced long years of disciplined institutional life without it making any real impact on their character. Indeed, simple acceptance of a further disciplined environment might be a sign of personal immobility, rather than of social improvement. We may only be encouraging the disease of institutionalism.

b) 'To some it may seem that I minimise the real problems of discipline. On the contrary, I am only too well aware that behaviour is often tiresome, wearing, noisy, and nervously exhausting to those who work on the staff. It is indeed artificially exaggerated in intensity. Whoever heard of a family with eight or nine young men concurrently passing through the same period of adolescent turbulence? Whoever heard of such a family group all with legal offences and emotional or other disturbances in their make-up? I have no illusions about the problems and strains for the staff; but I suggest that a regime with many rules can of itself produce additional problems, and inhibit the development of those we seek to help. The most (and it is already quite a lot) we can aim at, or hope for, is the free acceptance of interpersonal convenience. If indeed a staff member has to wait up late for a tardy dancer or boozer, the complaint should not have to be based on the infringement of any rule, but on the personal inconvenience caused. The staff too have personal rights which can, and sometimes should, be voiced in a way that represents the rights of others in society – but there is little likelihood of improvement being brought about on this score until the bond of trust and affection has been built up; and this may necessitate considerable inconvenience first of all.

c) 'Here we touch on the real springs of social control. For good reasons or bad, most of these "homeless" young offenders have already developed considerable distrust of other people; of adults in particular, but also of the whole established order of society. Their behaviour is often offensive, aggressive and tiresome; no "do-good" social worker should be let loose in this field without knowing the hurt and heartbreaks that are ahead – the sheer rudeness, unco-operative spirit and ingratitude are almost unbelievable at times. The words and deeds of the residents almost invite rejection – their chips-on-the-shoulder about others are fulfilled by the reactions they so frequently arouse in outraged people. Unconsciously they seem to seek the treatment of which they also bitterly complain. The more deeply disturbed young men will probably cover this with a considerable layer of good presentation, pleasant and affable manner, and they very easily fit into hostel life – only to create a more devastating impression when the mutual confidence is abruptly challenged by some outrageous incident.

'This is the behaviour which is in need of control, but which is simply untouched by rules of the house, except as additional and sadly irrelevant occasions for being difficult. This is the behaviour that is the sign of, and our only means of getting at, the underlying disturbance, which has probably been at the root of the offences. If we are to break the vicious spiral of offences, we have to break, if we can, the pattern of social distrust, and replace it with some experience of trust, affection and care that continues even in spite of bad behaviour; but there must be bad behaviour somewhere to bring this about. In other words, it is to be expected, and in a sociological sense to be welcomed, when there is a breach of acceptable behaviour, for in this way alone will we start to come to grips with the real person. To "control" in this context means first of all to "contain", then to prevent (if necessary, and if we can) the worst consequences of such behaviour, if it would otherwise lead to further social reprobation; and then to get the young man to face the issue on the basis of a relationship that equally declines to moralise or condone; indeed a relationship which is able to allow strong disapproval to be expressed without the faintest hint of a new rejection. Timing of this vital stage of the encounter must be made most carefully – it is of the essence of the social skill involved. One may have to wait days for the right moment to occur. The advantage of residential work is that one can do this.

d) 'No mention has been made till now of group meetings, but they seem to me to be strictly necessary in all hostel situations, if there is to be any developing sense of responsibility. The hostel is not of course simply a commercial enterprise but there is still a delicate interplay of rights and duties among residents and staff; they partly pay for services rendered whether we like it or not, from their board and lodging money, and all this can be used to great advantage in social education. It is only fair that the income and expenses of the house should be laid open to residents; they will, incidentally, then see that in terms of their own contributions they do in fact get a bargain, for the house will cost inevitably far more than the income they can jointly provide. I see no reason why even the salaries paid to the staff workers should not be known to them. Why are we apt to be spiky about this? Are we ashamed of what we get for our work? Does it embarrass us that because we work mainly for and with people we should be paid for our hire? Do we need to give them the impression that it is all done for the love of the thing? If we have any real dedication which goes beyond the mere wages, it will tell in the end. But we have no monopoly of the generous spirit; and if we are to try to represent the "outside" world in any sense, then we must earn our living like the others, even if we have to overcome (in whatever way we think necessary) the occasionally voiced opinion that we don't do a man's job at all. While we usually expect them to get up and go out to jobs in which they get little or no pleasure except on pay day, it sometimes irks them that house staff simply seem to hover about the house, and freely choose to do this out of several alternatives, and still get paid!

'The long term aim of the group meetings was more to encourage a mutual concern. Indeed, it became perhaps our chief aim to establish social control more by an attitude of consideration for other residents than of working out a simple legislative regime. Informally it is a process of social education. Young men, especially with these background difficulties, were alike usually in maintaining a great disregard for others. Selfishness, maybe, but often stemming from the right to survive in adverse family situations and environment. It could not be eradicated in any single way. Without moralising or legislation, the group meetings were opportunities for at least some encouragement towards tolerable standards.'

Objective values and standards of behaviour, insofar as they can be established anyway, are not recognised simply by our insistence on them, or by the application of sanctions for failure to uphold them. The things we are liable to get worked up about, as people who have made crucial decisions for ourselves already, were often not so important at this stage for young men whose past histories had been greatly disturbed. In our own hostel we had, of course, a practical belief in original sin, to the extent that all our efforts to understand the remote and proximate causes of aberrant behaviour did not exclude a normal human tendency to be bloody-minded now and again. But this sure belief also helped us to resist that feeling of infallibility which a superior-inferior relationship is always liable to create. We did not pretend ourselves to total maturity and emotional ease; only to a relatively successful balance most of the time. When things went wrong in the house, it could be as much our fault as that of the residents.

Control, therefore, was not one of the purposes of the house, but as a means to personal development, and a discovery of the place each person could achieve in life, however inadequate and irreparably bruised some of them might be. If we helped each resident to look at himself from the outside and not only from inner feelings, we had made some progress. This did not mean that their way would be smooth, or their future behaviour always acceptable.

In all this, my indebtedness to books was enormous. The gaps in my social understanding were being filled by the writings of Howard Jones (*Crime in a Changing Society*); and reliable guidance came to me from people like S. R. Slavson (*Re-educating the Delinquent*), David Downes (*The Delinquent Solution*), Harriet Wilson (*Delinquency & Child Neglect*), and Professor J. B. Mays (*The Young Pretenders*). But there was nothing like the day-to-day experience of moulding a high theology of the infinite dignity of the human person with a recognition of our shared insecurity and fallibility to keep me alert to the risk of either authoritarian behaviour or of the surrender of all standards.

I have already indicated that there were some engaging personalities among the residents. One nineteen year old, Fred, was talking to me about marriage. This anecdote, taken straight from life, has enlivened many a lecture I have given since those days. 'Well Fred,' I said, 'I don't suppose it matters whom you marry, but I think it would be a good idea to get someone with a similar sort of background.' 'Don't be ridiculous, Owen,' he replied instantly, 'where do you think I'm going to find a bird with twenty-seven convictions?' He deserved 'A' Level for wit, but I don't suppose he was awarded anything but punishment for being noticed doing dishonest or troublesome things.

We called it a 'half-way' house, to rehabilitate lads after custodial sentences. I used to visit and interview them in advance, and we received enormous support from probation officers. One of them, Bill Griffiths, produced several excellent written pieces on residential care. We had staff meetings with leaders of other similar projects in the area, Church Army, Salvation Army and others, and I got to know a lot more about the hazards of this kind of work. It certainly was not enough to know how to relate quickly to young men in their late teen or early twenties. I had a file on each, and that was important – But! It was my practice to read it through before going to see them in Borstal or Detention Centre, just to get a rough idea of the area of their convicted offences. Then I made my own assessment of them as people, had them for a trial weekend, and let them settle in for medium term stay. Only after a few weeks, when I had established a relationship of mutual respect and incipient liking, did I go back to read the file carefully, to see what was to be found in their family history and social circumstances that may have led to their offences. What mattered was not just the past, but the present: who they were now, not merely who they had been in the past. Of course I took into account where they had come from, but that did not determine how I treated them. I would never condone wickedness, but their dishonesties were hardly ever malicious. Sometimes I had to be very patient to discover what was really paining them underneath the macho surface. One lad, Alec, was a twenty year old, who didn't manage to get a job in Southampton for months. We got on well together; he seemed at ease, but on the second week of a job he had acquired, I went to wake him up at 6.30 am. I got on with other things and gave him no more thought, till I went back to his room several hours later. There he was, fast asleep. 'Alec, for goodness sake, don't you realise it is now 9.15 am?' He sat upright and said, 'Why bother me with your problems?' and lay down to sleep some more. It was eight months after his coming to the hostel, when I was driving him to visit his younger brother in what was still called 'an approved school' he told me his story, and made me realise why he couldn't handle a job with a complaining 'clerk of works'. That's a long time to wait, seeing that we got on so well: I had to learn patience.

The hostel was in a fine road of houses towards the rougher section of Southampton: some even called it 'junkie-land', and one of the longest registered heroin couples lived next door. This was in 1970, and the drug scene was by no means as diffuse as today. One or two lads may have used cannabis outside, or an occasional mix of pills, but it never constituted a problem. It was one of the 'rules' they had devised anyway and kept to. The area was modestly full of prostitutes too, but none of them caused us any special nuisance.

Ecclesiastical links
It was in the context of this demanding work that I was also try-ing to clarify the meaning of ordained ministry and how it was to be lived in the Catholic Church. My connection with the ecclesiastical structures was minimal, though I had established an informal link with Derek Worlock, as bishop. He wrote to me as follows as soon as I was appointed,

> Dear Owen,
> I have just had a letter from Leonard Godwin telling me offi-cially of your appointment as Warden of Aubyn's House.
> I want to send you this line of welcome and to express the hope that you will be very happy with us and to ask that if you think I can help in any way with the development of your work you will always let me know.

I recall sending him a little rhymed notice which said:

> It always seemed uncertain
> Surely God might be annoyed;
> Slave of the Church as parish priest
> My 'class' was self-employed.

> My role is now 'priest-worker'
> And the situation's odd.
> I'm not sure who employs me
> Is it Godwin, or just God?

I developed personal contact with Bernard Fisher, the priest-chaplain to university students. He was a great help especially in the early months when the work, the area, and my situation were all so strange. Less than half a mile up the road was the

College of Education staffed and managed largely by sisters of La Sainte Union Congregation. They were glad of some Sunday help with an additional Mass to which most of the community and some staff came as well as some students. That was a weekly anchor point for me, and very often I was able to join their own chaplain for a weekday Mass – but my hours of work did not allow this to be a totally regular practice.

This led me to re-think the whole idea of a priest always saying a daily Mass; indeed, there were many weeks when I only celebrated on Sunday. I had been trained for ordination very largely on the basis of a priest being thought of as a cultic figure: one was ordained for saying Mass and, come wind or weather, however many Masses had been celebrated in the place, you still said Mass, provided there was at least one person to assist. But this increasingly lost not just its charm, but its meaning. In the richer understanding of Mass, it is not only an act of community, but needs to be seen as an act of community. I recognised the development through the centuries of Mass each day rather than the 'Eighth Day' celebration of the resurrection only, but the 'privatising' of each priest's daily Mass somehow didn't ring true. I was happy to concelebrate with others, if there was a community occasion – though in time I came to see this as unnecessary. One only needs one priest to preside, apart from those very special occasions when one wants to express the unity of the *presbyterium* with one's bishop. I began to fear there was financial consideration for the priest in celebrating or concelebrating, and it made me look more closely at the practice, and underlying reasoning, of 'Mass stipends'.

As usual, I was asking more questions than I had answers for. It was a valuable opportunity not only to assess what the meaning of the church's 'normal' practices were, but to know whether or not I could embrace them with integrity. In parish life many things had simply to be done, because that is what was expected: custom canonised many things on which the window-opening of John XXIII now cast light. This meant that I was liable to walk sometimes on dangerous ground: it wasn't always easy to talk about these things in Catholic company. The fresh air of Vatican II was already more like a nasty draught for some people. The sad departure from active ministry of so many fine priests during the sixties was bound up with a huge re-assessment of eucharist, priesthood, and ministries. I am sure Bishop

Petit was under the impression I was going that way – to question our understanding of the church and priestly identity was to demonstrate an unacceptable insecurity.

Not long after I had settled into my work at St Aubyn's, he came down to Southampton. Meeting me with Bernard Fisher as we came out from Mass in the College, he frowned and commented adversely on my neat collar and tie dress: 'What's this?', and in an angry interview he wanted to know if I was calling the priesthood in question altogether. My 'defence', as I thought, was to show how there was growing a richer understanding of priesthood and I referred to several distinguished writers/theologians whose books I had been reading. I didn't want him to think I was inventing a lot of new ideas on my own. 'Oh, books, books, books!' he said contemptuously, and we parted rather coldly.

I wrote to him not long afterwards to say that we shouldn't leave a disagreement in the air like this: he was still my bishop. I added – in a way that he may have taken as an insult rather than a joke – that I didn't suppose my form of dress put people off the church any more than rings, buckled shoes and purple socks did. Alas, he didn't seem to want to revive our links, and I was referred to his auxiliary bishop, Langton Fox, at that time parish priest in Llanelli, for any diocesan item. In 1972 Bishop Petit died and, at his funeral in Wrecsam cathedral – which he had had refurbished with altar facing the people, and a Blessed Sacrament chapel – I found myself in tears. As in so many times when I was his secretary, I disagreed with him on many things, but I bore him no less than great respect. For him such respect should have included docility. I never disobeyed him, but clearly I failed to meet his hopes and wishes.

Looking in from the outside
There is a sense in which my work in a 'secular' job enabled me to look at the church, as an institution, from the outside. Without the defences – and some would say the obligations – provided by clerical dress, I had to try to earn respect as a human being. I came to see clerical dress as the uniform of privilege. Among Catholics anyway there was an automatic response of deference to what one said or did, however much it would be criticised away from one's company. That is why I dropped the usage 'Father' wherever possible. It could express a filial relationship –

it certainly had done so for many of the 400 boys and girls who moved through Brynfields Youth Club – but it could also establish a distance and artificiality. I fear it helped to sustain the frequent immaturity of many able lay people and even, in extreme cases, infantilised them. To this day it is difficult to persuade many Catholics not just of their infinite dignity in the sight of God, but of their right and duty to develop a personal response to the gospel. In all my subsequent parish work, I have never been unduly disturbed by some of the individualists who are faintly heterodox in some matters, but I am agonised by those whose response is 'Well, if the Pope says so ...' Too little do such people realise their importance in the Body of Christ. It is an attitude of clericalism which really alarms me today, and was for so long shared by priests and bishops themselves. One distinguished bishop, returning to a later session of the Vatican Council, was asked if some particular item was going to 'change'. 'Well, if the church decides it should, then we will obey.' In such a remark there was no apparent awareness that he, especially a bishop, was a significant member of the church that was going to do the deciding. In some instances, bishops were almost swept off their feet by the winds of the Spirit – their contribution was moved from being negatively passive, to being positive. Not many British bishops themselves seem to have made any significant contribution to the debate.

What, if any, relationship did this ecclesiastical turmoil have to the work with young people? A story, which it is not really mine to tell, came from Sr Annunciata, whose work with disturbed children and those in need of special care, I visited in Portsmouth. She told me that during the council, when Bishop Holland was Bishop of Portsmouth, he used to assemble a rally of children and young people in the cathedral when he returned from Rome, and told them all about 'the ecumenical Council'. After one of these assemblies, which went largely over the heads of the youngsters, one of her children was writing to another one who had gone into residential care elsewhere: 'Dear Tommy, we've been to Portsmouth cathedral again to listen to His Holiness the Bishop of Holland. He says he's been to Rome again, and the Catholics are winning.'

Who says 'triumphalism is dead'?

Before I felt obliged to offer to resign over my unwillingness to follow the prescriptions for residential care coming from the

director with the apparent support of the management committee, I had felt the need to question whether it was the best way of
helping some of the residents.

I have often noticed that what is very warming as one walks
through the streets of one's home town, is the little waves and
friendly glances from people one may only know faintly. Their
light personal acknowledgement is always a stroke of friendship
and affirms one's identity. That is what one misses in a strange
town or setting. Now these young men, already humiliated by
or angry about, the custodial sentence they had already served,
needed as much personal affirmation as they could be given. It
was hard enough to get a job with a 'record' to account for recent
unemployment. They were often without any notable sporting
or other skills to help them integrate locally, and they never got
a 'hello' from a former schoolmate, because Southampton was
not their home town. Of course, our hostel did provide a basic
accommodation security, but they needed a lot more than this to
settle back acceptably in a neighbourhood to which they belonged.

One lad in his mid-twenties, with quite a long record of
youthful offences, had managed to get to sea in the merchant
navy, and he returned to find me as 'Warden' when he lodged
nearby, and took up some of the contacts he had previously
made. He grew quite close to one large Catholic family in the
area which provided some very supportive links with those in
the hostel; there was even talk of him being informally 'adopted'
as an additional member of their family. Another lad, of very
similar background, also had been to sea. One day he called and
in a depressed mood said: 'I wish someone would adopt me.'
'Hang it all,' I said, 'you're 25; you don't need adopting, do
you?' 'It's just that I'd like to belong to someone.' How right he
was. There were no remaining family contacts; he had unresolved inner problems, though superficially confident. But to
whom did he belong? In 1974 when my own father died in his
80s, I was then fifty, and yet I remember asking myself just before his funeral: 'Goodness, whom do I belong to now?' Even the
existence, or faint awareness, of a parent helps that sense of
personal identity however little contact there may be.

Several of the residents had been fostered or adopted in early
years. When visiting a prison to interview one lad, I remember
discovering how widespread was the 'career' of so many of this

kind: fostering, residential care, maybe adoption (failed), then approved school, Borstal or detention centre to young person's prison. Stephen was an unusual lad, a very good cook, so able to get jobs – but he loved 'scheming'. He easily took adults in, and then abused his information. But he, at 22 years, wanted to find his mother, and I began enquiries: he had lost touch since infancy. About 15 months later I discovered she had died in a mental hospital about the very time I was starting to look for her. Anyway Stephen and I went to the cemetery where she was buried and checked her name in the register. That was enough to satisfy him; she had existed anyway. Another lad, Sonny, traced his mother to Manchester, and I had the strange privilege of introducing them over the phone. She wanted him to visit her. There was one poignant question: 'But if I come by train and you come to meet me, how will you recognise me?'

Once I had left Southampton, and in a year or two had settled back in Wrexham, there were not many I had any contact with. One or two came to visit me in the Lift Project, but we were reaching out for straws, since North Wales was an even stranger place for them than the south of England. Johnny came several times, however, and made some local friends. What he valued most of all was having the residential use of a tiny cottage I had bought as my hide-away in the country at Bryneglwys. There I kept a lot of my books and records and a music centre. The idea was to have a place I could escape to once a week for twenty-four hours, but my work often prevented that. It seemed dog-in-a-manger not to let others use it sometimes – though that of course ruled out my being able to find the privacy I needed so badly. Johnny came and stayed there about three, even six weeks on his own. The isolation seemed to suit him, and he played many of my classics-only long-play records. When eventually I went to collect him for his journey south again, we could not leave the cottage without having to listen 'just once more, Owen,' to the 'Arrival of the Queen of Sheba'. He had been genuinely uplifted by so much music.

During part of his stay there and in my later house in Wrexham, he wrote his life-story. A total orphan in Ireland he had been brought up by Christian Brothers. He spoke very badly of them and, in the climate of residential abuse which we have been uncovering recently, he could have provided quite a dossier of unpleasant evidence. He came to Britain at sixteen, with the assistance of money from the Archbishop of Dublin, and started a life of petty crime. For some years he effectively lived as a burglar, and it was only late in his twenties that he re-alised the fear and anger such behaviour causes others. 'I was the one who was afraid,' he said. There was no personal malice against the shopkeepers or householders, more a total uncon-cern. He had a right to live, and if you couldn't earn it, you took. One streak of real frustration was deep in his soul. Why did his mother abandon him in infancy? Who was she that she cared so little for her child?

Having written all this at great length over months and months, he let me read it. It was heart-rending stuff, and he had done this at the suggestion of someone that it might be publish-able. An 'expert' then read it through and was tactlessly unfeel-ing in criticising much of the presentation of the story. Johnny tore up the whole thing, and so suffered another personal wound. About once every twelve or twenty-four months, he emerges briefly into my life again. I shall always have a tender memory of Johnny.

Other memories are not always so tender, but quite cheering. One former resident used to ring me up, and with his usual obscene greeting: 'Hello, Owen: how's the f.....g vicar?' I was act-ually present at his wedding – only a brave girl would have taken him on, but there was something warm about his friendliness.

Before feeling obliged to resign from my Southampton job, I did what I could to explain my perspective on the work of the Society and registered my growing difference with the policies and procedures apparently expected of me, in a lengthy report.

Report to Management Committee
The Society of St Dismas was founded as a Christian response to a real need – the need of homeless ex-prisoners.

From the start, it has not been altogether clear how the need was to be adequately met. Provision of material support for these men, and giving encouragement to return to 'normal' soci-ety has not proved a simple matter. Along with other voluntary workers in this field, it has been found that human nature is not malleable to a single or simple plan of campaign; people are al-together too diverse for any panacea. While there are of course recognisable patterns of behaviour, no single trick of psychology or sociology can 'solve' any man's problems when coming out of 'detention'.

Increasingly it has been seen that the competence of those employed to work in this field must be a professional one. Yet no amount of technical knowledge can outweigh the importance of a wide human experience of people. The rehabilitation of ex-prisoners cannot be achieved by those who are simply 'caring' sort of people; science must be mixed with art in this kind of human relationship. But neither can rehabilitation be achieved by the imposition of a code of behaviour which we believe to be good for them. Prompt and disciplined rising from bed, cleanliness of person and clothes, regularity, conscientiousness at work may well be marks of the ideal citizen, but it is not necessarily the ideal for those we are dealing with, and cannot certainly be claimed as the gateway to salvation.

There are times when those of us who do this work, albeit as employees of the Society, feel that we are at variance with the ideals of the Management Committee, and we cannot improve this situation unless we meet and discuss frankly.

The second house, St Aubyn's, for the younger offender has been based perhaps too easily on the notion that these young men are 'ex-prisoners' in the same sense as the men with longer prison records. While no clear-cut line can be drawn, the young men are not yet to be classified as offenders against society, though they may all have fallen foul of the law. They are disturbed adolescents whose chances of growth beyond their present state to a reasonably balanced maturity are quite good. They need, as we see it, basically a huge respect for their individuality, and a readiness to absorb their exaggerations of behaviour, as they struggle to find – and even perhaps to establish for the first time – their own identity. Their behaviour patterns are as varied as the men's; but in addition they have often no consistency in the same person. They are not regularly idle, aggressive and selfish, but variously all three, as well as energetic, gentle and generous at other times. Our task is to share life with them in the house, and help them discover themselves. Believing in their essential dignity as human beings, we have to be determined optimists, aware that they respond best to high expectations, and react worst to a moralising and authoritarian attitude – for their previous experience of morals and authority from parents or institutions has not thus far been very helpful or encouraging. Of course, all human beings need discipline, but the only abiding value is in self-discipline, which never comes into being in a rigorist society. All human beings need values and ideals, but these never come to the fore when the adults pretend that they already have all the answers.

In both the Society's houses, our misty attempts at rehabilit-ation will obviously clash with those of others who think that regular meals, tidy personal habits, and a straight talk or two will put anyone to rights. However desirable – and this can any-way be queried – it is pragmatically certain that such a policy simply doesn't work.

The sad thing is that we sometimes have the impression that it is this latter policy which our Management Committee expects of us. We find ourselves occasionally trying, without much ef-fect, to conceal the fact that we don't even attempt this. We try to cover up for late risers, for work-shy individuals, for not-too-clean clothing, and occasional real carelessness with public property and furniture, instead of resting assured that this is simply the material we have to work with. It is disappointing that the Society which was founded to help those who are inadequate seems to be surprised when they turn out *in fact* to be inadequate.

It would be invidious if those who are employed to do the work attempted to dictate the policy or the plans of the Society; but we feel there is at present insufficient contact between social workers and sponsors. The Management Committee should surely meet the staff from time to time, and hear about their findings to ensure that mutual confidence which is necessary for a successful project. While it is not exactly we who should de-cide how the sponsors use their money, it is surely desirable that the staff are consulted on projects, which may affect the direc-tion of the work already undertaken.'

The Society of St Dismas, after a radical reorganisation (to which in some measure my resignation may have contributed) went on to flourish with the adult ex-prisoners. Some very imag-inative developmental facilities were set up under the constant imaginative thinking of Fr Andrew, John Bleaden and others. I am proud to have been associated with the Society, even though I plainly didn't measure up to the expectation of my employers.

Developing perspectives on priesthood

The work, the place, the lifestyle were developing my thoughts about priesthood, too. I have referred in Chapter 8 to the moment when I faced my personal adherence to my ordination as a priest. But even as I moved out of parish life in the summer of 1969, I note that I was reading such books as Joseph Blenkinsop's *Celibacy, Ministry, Church,* because I was disturbed by what I deemed an unfair book-review in *The Tablet.* I wrote a long letter which was published in the issue of 16 August, the final paragraph of which read like this:

> Personally, I find that my own continuing option for celibacy (which I have ever felt was made in freedom) has been helped by Blenkinsop's excellent exposition of its perhaps limited sign-function in the contemporary world. He has brought me up closer to the real issues with which many of us are grappling – the diversity of forms of ministry, and the nature of the Christian presence in the church and the world.
> J. Owen Hardwicke

As early as September – scarcely two months into the work – I sent a newsletter to friends and former parishioners. The final paragraphs went like this:

> Ministry and Priesthood: That this is a real Christian service to people, to those who have great need of devoted and con-centrated attention for the sake of themselves and society – of this I am certain. It is a properly Christian ministry. Of course such work does not call for an ordained priest, but then it doesn't call for a priest to be teaching children, to visit the sick, to lead discussion groups, to administer parish property and finance, to share the worries of young and old alike. Perhaps for too long all these functions have centred too nar-rowly on the priest in his parish. Even there, the priest only 'exercises his Orders' when offering Mass and hearing con-fessions. For many hundreds of years now he has necessarily been part of a bishop's team, and thus the leader of a local community of Christians, as parish priest or curate, guiding and encouraging others to live the Christian life to the full. He is still a priest when doing all these jobs, though it is only a tiny proportion of his time that is spent in doing things for which he required ordination.
> Many of us believe that the church is now entering a totally new phase of her history – in some ways not unlike the early

centuries of the church, when the various Christian ministries were shared more widely in the community, and with
less sharp distinction between priest and layman.

I hope I shall always continue to be a recognised person in
the church, fulfilling the ordination by the bishop which was
meant to be for life – to preach the gospel, to offer Mass for
the people of God, to reconcile people with God and one another through the sacraments. But to do this, it is not essential
to be in parish work. Hundreds of priests have almost never
done parish work. In the developing life of the church, I
would hope for many different ways to emerge of sharing
the ministry of Christ, and even for new ways to emerge of
exercising the sacrament of Orders. This work with ex-offenders, fascinating, tantalising, and nervously exhausting as it is,
will help me – and maybe you, with whom I have worked for
so long to discover the ways of Christ – to see these new approaches to the Christian life; for it must always be adapting
itself to the real needs of people. One thing is certain already,
wherever there is a need, there must Christian men and
women be. Maybe a priest can exercise another form of leadership here, by drawing others into the work, and also by
representing the church in a special way to others in the field
You know me well; you will sense some uncertainty in my
attitude. I hope we have all learned to be content to be uncer-
tain about many things. God has never solved human difficulties and questions without much searching and struggle
on man's part, for God sometimes appears not to answer
some of our questions at all. And it is no shame to see
through a glass darkly. I hope you will always pray for me,
as I will for you, as we go along, one step at a time.

My mind was getting a bit clearer a year later, and I note that I
was involved in the correspondence column of *The Tablet* again
on 3 October 1970, following an article on 'Priests for a New
Society'. Here is the letter:

From the Rev J Owen Hardwicke, Warden of Aubyn's
House, (Society of St Dismas)
Sir: The article 'Priests for a New Society' (*The Tablet*, 26
September) is full of muddles, it seems to me. 'Role', 'function', 'job', 'status' are all mixed up, when it is really a matter
of ministries. In the organised life of the church, there are
many ministries; some of these coincide with sacramental

'powers'; most of them do not.

It is customarily understood that priestly ordination is normally (probably strictly) necessary for presiding at the eucharist, for reconciling penitents, for anointing the sick; that episcopal-priestly ordination is necessary for confirming and ordaining others. It is usual for a bishop or priest to baptise; but others may, and often do. It is at present a distinct obstacle to being a minister of matrimony if you are ordained. Even sacramental ministries, then, are not simply tied up with ordination.

As for the ministry of preaching, you do not even have to be a deacon, as long as you have ecclesiastical sanction. The ministry of teaching is shared by many who have not as much as a certificate in catechetics, according to the discretion of school heads and governors. The ministries of healing the sick, comforting the suffering, consoling the mourner need no further authorisation than one's baptism. Prophecy is a ministry nobody really understands; a layman or a priest gets into trouble if he thinks he is called to it, even spasmodically. Prophecy cannot be easily organised; and we have treated organisation, bureaucracy, as the 'top ministry', and this has been for so long exercised almost exclusively by ordained men. Yes, 'administration' is a ministry; but it is high time it was shared by laymen and priests alike; it is anyway in fact the least of the gospel necessities.

In an attempt to deal with the alleged contradiction in being a 'part-time priest', the writers serve up again the classical formula: 'anyone marked with the priesthood would still be a priest whether organising a church bazaar ...' All I can make this to mean is this: 'a man who has received priestly ordination may actually spend much time in organising a bazaar ...' But how is he a 'priest' in doing this except by his baptism? He does it as a Christian, not as a priest. Unless the writers are really concerned with his social status, they should not pretend he organises a bazaar in a 'priestly' way; that is as bad as 'Catholic table-tennis' in segregated youth clubs. A man's role as ordained priest is precisely part-time. He is the man who is officially and solemnly authorised – which is what ordination largely means – to preside at Mass, to reconcile penitents, etc., and he is not doing this all the time.

Celibacy – and I am in favour of it – does not go with being a busy bureaucrat, as the writers suggest, but with being a specially significant person in the church; with being a monk, or a prophet perhaps, or an originator, or a person so devoted to the care of one's fellow human beings that there simply isn't room for a one-to-one relationship in marriage. But there are many witnesses to the fact that a married couple may jointly share this devotion. The model here is not the married Anglican clergy, except by frequent accident, but the Salvation Army officers, by stern prescription.

In their scheme of things, but for the wrong reasons, the writers contrast 'married men, marked with the priesthood, but nevertheless engaged in some secular employment or profession ...' with the 'elite corps of dedicated men' – the celibate clerical bureaucrats. Why? Because the former 'would cost the Christian community little or nothing to maintain'. The only question our writers have uncovered is simply, 'Who goes on the full-time payroll of the church?' – not a very fundamental one, surely.

I was a parish priest, busy about many things: visiting parishioners, signing passport forms, sorting out marriage problems, teaching children, planning house groups – thus fulfilling some of the roles expected of me by long custom, and, to some extent, by acquired social status. I was very happy at it; but for none of these things did I need priestly ordination. Of course (part-time) I also said Mass and heard confessions. I still do. Now I continue as ordained priest, a celibate but, by kind consent of my bishop, in specialised secular employment; new roles, no noticeable status, and emphatically not a cleric or ecclesiastical bureaucrat. Where would I fit in the writers' New Society? It looks as though I'm going to get things muddled for them even further.

J. Owen Hardwicke

CHAPTER TEN

Within the Parameters of a Profession: Challenging priestly roles and identity

I continued to keep in touch with former parishioners, and with many friends who were not likely to be readers of *The Tablet*. So my next circular letter to them echoed some of the exchanges I had been having with Bishop Fox.

'I have some fairly clear ideas about how eventually to use whatever skills I will have acquired, in a project detached from the statutory services. There are many people – including bishops perhaps – who are still unused to the idea of a priest pursuing a pastoral vocation outside the usual parish structures. My work in this field over fifteen years has never been aimed even primarily at Catholics – though an alarming proportion of offenders are nominally Catholics; it is, as I firmly believe, still a work for God's people.

I would like to pursue this work – which, with problems like drug-addiction, looks like being an increasing need – back in Wales. Not only am I lonesome for the hills and accents of home, but I have reason to think I could make better headway in community involvement (one of the keys to "solution" of the problems I am concerned with) where I already have friends and relatives. I intend to spend the next eighteen months investigating further the possibilities of this – the matter of "permissions" may be a bigger obstacle. In this period, when my whole style of like, and dress, has had to be 'secular' I have learned for myself some of the hazards of working without the usual protection of an accepted social status usually given to a priest. For good company it is difficult to beat a bunch of priests, but I have never much favoured the solely clerical club in which priests tend to gather. I have increasingly enjoyed the mixed company of religious and layfolk, the celibates and the married, in an unstructured concern for the gospel in this field. With young offenders in particular

one has to make a person-to-person relationship which cannot use the customary protocol sometimes expected of a man
of the cloth. It is not a case of pretending to be something one
is not – as though one was a priest in disguise; it is to exemplify the fact that in pastoral work of this kind a priest is not a
special kind of man. It seems to be bad history and poor theology that would say he is.

On this matter it always seems strange to me that many
priests spend their lives as teachers, scholars, curial office-
workers or fund-raisers, and virtually never do pastoral
work in the accepted sense; yet no-one seems to find this incompatible with their priesthood. Is it because by reason of
dress and manner they are still obviously clergymen?
Pastoral work, however, which is done not under the direct
jurisdiction of the bishop, occasionally causes doubts about
one's very orthodoxy!

This period has also given me a chance to see an ever wider
selection of non-church-going Catholics. I don't mean the ordinary nominal or lapsed Catholics. I find there is a growing
number of "third men"; often they have been very active
members of the Catholic community; they have certainly not
rejected Christ and the importance of the gospel for the
world; but they just get nothing from the current church set-
up. They may go rarely to Mass (and if they do, they certainly
receive communion), or they may not go at all; but it is not
simply a matter of liking or disliking the "changes" in the
liturgy; the whole ecclesiastical "clobber" has gone sour on
them. Where the new liturgy is badly done, it does not do
what it evidently is supposed to do – to build up the community in Christ. So they wonder "what's the use?" Where the
liturgy is well done, it often seems to be a sign of something
that doesn't really happen outside – it is a facade, because
people don't seem to care any more than those who are not
Christians at all.

I suspect that more and more Catholics (and other Christians)
will reject "the system" in the next five or ten years. At the
same time they seem very ready to find God wherever else
he is. There is an apostolate in preventing the simply negative, falsely guilty feelings in such people from stopping the
contribution they can make to the wider vision of God's
kingdom to which we are being led in these days. It may be

that some "unstructured" priests have some special service to render here.'

What was to come next? I realised that I needed now to develop a better academic study of the social psychology of people if I were to make any significant contribution to work with 'ex-offenders'. I had already constructed a first draft of a project which I would like to undertake back in the Wrexham area. I even met Bishop Fox in London one day to discuss my special 'ministry' with him. He was very attentive and heard the outline of my plans, and soon afterwards he became bishop of the diocese, on the resignation of Bishop Petit. While I was still applying for a place in a university course for the Diploma in Applied Social Studies, I soon felt able to write to him to give him an outline of the project I planned to set up in Wrexham when the one year course was over. His courteous but firm reply was that I was welcome to pursue any such project in any diocese, but not back in Wrexham.

Now, I had based my planned work on the basis of the fact that I knew already a whole range of social workers, probation officers and other significant people in Wrexham, let alone a long list of individuals and families with problems whom I had come across during my fifteen years in Wrexham and Ruabon 1954–69. It was absurd, as I saw it, to waste this basic knowledge and acquaintance with the social infrastructure and to have to acquire it all in a totally new area. Besides, as I told him, Wales is not only the place of my diocese, but my country! That was a barbed remark, because Bishop Fox was English, but I reckon I was still reacting to my rejection as a candidate for Cardiff diocese, when I was advised to 'try Westminster'. I may not be much of a Welshman, but I don't like being ushered out of Wales.

I explained my reactions to his suggestion and said that if he could give me a 'canonical' reason for not returning to my diocese for this work I would obey. I had noted his wishes, of course; but would he not try asking around for other people's views? With great fairness he did just that. I imagine, but cannot be sure, that he consulted his chapter of canons. His next letter said: 'Thank you for suggesting I might ask others. I have done so and I understand that they think that everything done by Owen Hardwicke is a matter of controversy.' So he stood by his expressed wish. I thanked him for his action, and said that this was not a canonical prohibition, so I would probably just come and would sit out his disapproval. This was not the response of a co-operative priest, but not technically 'disobedient' as I saw it.

There was a time lag anyway. I had acquired acceptance on to a one-year course at University College, Cardiff to start in September 1971, and while I applied for DHSS financial support (which I got at £12.50 a week) I needed work to support myself. The job with St Dismas Society in Southampton was, according to the league tables, poorly paid, but that was not how I saw it. I had never had a 'salary' in my life before this, and to be offered full board and lodging plus £850 a year (in 1969/70 remember) seemed like riches to me. With the help of contacts in the Probation Service, I found a temporary eight-months job – just the right length before the new studies – with the Probation service in Slough. I was to take a small caseload under their tutelage, while my main colleague was moving towards a new job inside the prison service.

I was treated with the utmost courtesy and kindness. Indeed, the mutual care of the Probation team for one another was a model of charity, outshining many presbyteries, I think. The magistrates' panel who interviewed me and gave me the job, apologised for the small remuneration, which was geared to my lack of formal qualification. 'I'm afraid you won't get paid much more than your typist.' It was about £1,200 per annum pro rata. It suited me fine, so I looked for accommodation. I didn't want to have to alert another bishop of my presence, so I was fortunate to find a room with the Franciscans of Ascot – still in Derek Worlock's Portsmouth Diocese – giving me a pleasant car journey through Windsor Great Park to work in Slough which was in the next diocese. I really enjoyed this set-up. It was good to have a personal base in a religious house, having one meal a day with them, with a chance to assist at a morning Mass at the nearby convent school before going to work. The friars made a very agreeable home base. Fr Simon, the Guardian, was welcoming. One of the brethren was training for work in social services. One elderly friar was a lively old chap with a passion for telling Tommy Cooper stories at the table. While they made me laugh heartily, it was to the faint displeasure of the others, who had no doubt heard them all a hundred times.

I noticed an advert for a Tommy Cooper matinee at the London Palladium, and booked some seats to take the old friar. I managed to get hold of one of my former Southampton residents, now working in a nearby hotel, so that he could come along and escort the priest into the theatre while I went to park the car in Soho Square. That took some time, and when I reached the theatre myself, the show had started, and I had to make my way to the front row seats, which I booked so that the old chap could hear everything. Tip-toeing down the aisle, I still attracted Tommy Cooper's attention, who said, 'Sorry, sir, I had to start because it was time to get going' – and embarrassed me no end to the chortling delight of the old friar.

I never had a real chance of meeting the community of nuns who ran the posh boarding school where I frequently said an early Mass. The superior did pay me a rather formal visit in the sacristy one day, and I discovered that the daughter of my schoolfriend Roger Newsom was just finishing there, and becoming one of the first girls to go to Eton. All I vividly remember about the worship was a solemn Benediction Service when the nuns' singing was like something out of *The Sound of Music*.

It would be improper of me to refer in any detail to those offenders who were my 'clients'. They were mostly petty offenders, though I had one bank robber, whom I visited in prison, who told me, almost in innocence, of the terror he experienced as the get-away driver. The fact that he was caught was entirely due to his continuing post-offence nerves. He had recently had his bike stolen and had reported the fact to the police. The day after the bank robbery a policeman called to tell him it had been found and to collect it, but he felt sure he was about to be arrested and 'went to pieces' in the presence of the police. He decided he must get away altogether for a while, and set off rather too fast in a car. Quite soon the traffic police were signalling him to stop, and again he imagined he was to be arrested and was almost incomprehensible when spoken to. Yet another coincidence of events eventually led him to declare his guilt, so he was not surprised or particularly distressed at his court sentence: 'I'll never do anything like that again,' he said to me 'my nerves can't take it.' I realised there may be motives beyond motives to deter criminal activity. Nerves, that was his trouble!

Quite soon after starting as a Probation Officer, the colleague I was supposed to be assisting had to be absent for a long period because of his wife's sickness: so instead of a short caseload of 6–10 people, I inherited over 60. That suited: I would have overworked the others otherwise. As is my habit, which includes persistent impatience, I worked hard and fast – well past the statutory hours. Accustomed as I was from parish work to home visiting, I far preferred to interview my 'clients' in their own homes in the evenings or at the weekends. Some of them I would take out for a run in the car, when the non-necessity of eye contact made it possible for them to reveal more of themselves than I would have quickly discovered in an office setting – a practice I later found very useful. I can no longer recommend it to anyone in the caring professions, because of the potential for false accusations. It is definitely marked 'imprudent' today. Each of the Probation team had one weekly 'reporting night' for those who could not get along by day. The secretarial staff got to know which was my reporting night, because hardly anyone came; I had already seen them at home. Being a free unmarried man, my time was much more at my disposal than it was for others, and I followed the informal attitude of 'adult friend' to establish a relationship which might bring about a greater maturity or sense of social responsibility among these very disorganised people.

'What sort of things did you talk about?' people have asked. Until I felt I knew what made them tick, I didn't get round to their offences, because the trauma and formality of a court appearance had rarely cultivated much respect for justice. So I told them what I did with my time as an opener. One sixteen year old discovered that I drove to the Albert Hall for some of the 'Prom' concerts. He said he'd seen *The Last Night* on TV last year. 'I wouldn't mind going to one of those.' 'How about tonight?' I said. So at 5.30 pm, I drove to his home to pick him up. He was nervous, his mother said, about having the right clothes. 'Tell him nobody cares at the Proms.' When we did arrive, we sat in the cheapest gallery seats in good time and watched the huge audience – largely of young people – arriving in the 'Prom' area. The orchestra came on and started to tune up, and the sense of excitement rose. 'This is great,' he said, before ever a note had been played, 'Can I come again?' and with a minimum of explanation from me (for among other items Tchaikovsky's *Rococo Variations*) he followed the music with great delight. Some of my colleagues raised their eyebrows when I told them where and with whom I had been the night before. 'Well, at least it kept him off the streets,' I suggested.

For the first time in my life I came close to cultural differences.

One Sikh young man was a client. He lived with his two married brothers, his father having died. It seemed that the eldest brother acted as 'patriarch' for them all. The wages were pooled with him to be shared out appropriately. There was a great dignity among them all, and a real shame for having incurred legal action. Another was a Muslim boy near the end of his probation period, and his sentence was to be discharged early, and when I phoned the good news on to his parents, his father requested a supportive letter to present to his own employers asking for transfer to a regular day-hours shift. 'You see,' he said, 'if my son is once again my responsibility after probation, then I must be at home in the evenings, when he is at home.' I welcomed his sense of responsibility and visited their very ordinary home. I was invited into a medium sized room, where the father and other sons all sat around the walls. We had a brief formal family conference, and mother and sisters were kept out of sight. 'Discipline is my task,' said the father.

I was still working on a structure for my project in Wrexham, and anxious to gather every good idea I could get hold of. I tried to visit specialist ventures in the London area, including a very worthwhile project with drug-takers and others in Covent Garden. It was being run at the time by Jon Snow, who was a friend of Pamela Phillimore. (She had been one of the two supportive members of the management team in Southampton.) I was impressed with Jon Snow, and found it interesting when he turned up trumps in the media world of television. We have only met once since those days, but I have admired his social conscience, and was not surprised to find him, twenty-five years later, chairing the huge assembly in London for the National Poverty Hearing, organised by Church Action on Poverty.

I found an occasional niche in Soho, where the Reverend Ken Leech had founded the 'Centrepoint' night shelter in the basement of the bombed church of St Anne. On a number of Friday nights after work in Slough, I would drive to London for a 'Prom' or other concert and still be in time for the opening up at 11.00 pm of the night shelter. Here as part of rotating teams we admitted young males for up to three or four consecutive nights; they had to be sober and not 'stoned', and if they had any drugs on them we asked for them to be handed in for our care for the night, to be handed back in the morning. This was a delicate matter but, when successful, helped to foster the trust we needed to share. We gave them something to eat, drawn from the left-overs handed in from local pubs, and made available bunk beds and blankets. If we were not crowded, one or two of us would drive to Euston Station to see if any recent arrivals (often from Scotland) were hanging about without anywhere to stay. During their 'registration' for the night, we quickly tried to find out if any follow-up was desirable. New arrivals into London might be given addresses for allowances, accommodation and even jobs, but mostly they just wanted somewhere to sleep. By 1.30 am there was little more to do till 7.00 am, so perhaps after sharing of information among the staff-team, we could rest a bit or, in my case, wander around the mostly deserted streets; it was after all Saturday morning now. We got them all up for some breakfast and away by 8.00 am and then I drove back to the friary in Ascot and had an extended siesta, and caught up with lost sleep ready for Sunday duties.

I valued this occasional task, learned a lot about dealing with casual characters, and admired the sense of unfussy service being offered by many varied, often 'professional' people – including at least one former Catholic priest. Such were often to be found in the caring professions, among social service, probation and assistant governors of prisons. What an absurd waste of good people by the church who failed to recognise their ministries any more!

One of the anxieties Bishop Fox had shared with me when he was still auxiliary bishop was my secular dress. He felt I was deceiving people by not wearing the uniform which was immediately recognised. But who was I? Owen Hardwicke or a reverend Catholic priest? Within the life of the church I had a recognised set of roles (rather limited – as I shall explore later on – if one only counts those for which ordination was a pre-requisite) but in the world at large I had no right to any expectation of status or authority unless I had earned it. While my dress did not declare my role, neither did I deny it whenever it was important. My clients had no reason to wish to relate to a Catholic priest; they accepted a 'probation officer'. However, as time went on, I would notice on the home visits who were Catholics. I said to a lad one day, on seeing a little statue of Our Lady, 'Are you a Catholic?' 'Yes,' said the lad, 'are you?' 'Yes,' I told him, 'I'm a priest actually' – and that then gave rise to some special friendly conversation, but I did not then ask to be called 'Father'.

From the experience I had gained, first as a child, sometimes going to court when my father was advocate, and mainly from my personal appearances with club members as a reference before the magistrates' committee in the Ruabon/Overton area, I was well accustomed to court procedure, and had no sense of nervousness when giving my reports to the bench.

Just as well that I wasn't called 'Father'. I recall one appearance during my parish work, with a lad who had been caught poaching. The over-solemn way in which the presiding magistrate – Lord Kenyon, I think – spoke of 'this disgraceful behaviour', struck me as comic. Anyway Gwyn, the offender, didn't have many words at his disposal. 'Do you have anyone here to speak for you?' 'Father's here,' he said. 'Your father, is he? – well then' – and we had to unravel that a bit as I stood up.

The clerk of the court may have been in his own administrative eyes an efficient man, but he was a bully. His insinuations when addressing the magistrates were in my view quite unfair. He ruled the court with his advice, and the magistrates often seemed to condone this. I made it my business, at the risk of alienating him, to respond to any questions by addressing not him, but the bench. It especially amused me when the chairman was a woman to respond to the Clerk's direct question with a firm look at him and saying, 'Well, Madam ...'. He was not a Catholic, though I believe he had a daughter who had entered a convent. Maybe something like that helped him to be patient with me, even though he never publicly acknowledged I was a priest. I didn't want or expect any deference, but I was determined to see reasonable justice done to my clients.

What I liked about the Probation Service was what I later missed in my brief experience of Social Services – the relative autonomy of the worker. Everything was ultimately shared with one's senior, but you didn't have to ask permission for initiatives to be taken; you got on with it, and of course recorded it day by day. There are I suppose risks in this, especially in the case of a new boy like me, but it facilitated more personal work.

One man, with a long sixteen years of imprisonment behind him from his earliest years, had settled with his wife, and she had a child; he was only on a light supervision with me, but we hit it off. Discovering that I was a Catholic priest, he asked me if I would be able to officiate for the baby's baptism. The local parish priest was very co-operative, and so all arrangements were made. Alas, two days before the celebration, he was rounded up by the police 'on suspicion' and remanded in custody. The baptism went ahead, and following the usual rite at the end, I blessed the mother of the child, and, then, waving an arm in the general direction of Wormwood Scrubs, blessed the father. He was released soon afterwards because there was simply no evidence against him. It is a frequent hazard of former long-term prisoners that they are the first people under suspicion for similar types of offences to those they had been sentenced for. This is understandable but it makes it difficult for anyone 'to make a new start'; the neighbours quickly note it if a police car calls at anyone's house. I'm glad to say he moved out of the area altogether later on, and I had the pleasure of visiting him in another city once, running a quite successful little shop.

I bungled at least one case by an error of judgement, yet I was put right swiftly, even though the mistake could have embarrassed the local team. I cannot speak too highly of the co-operation received all along. One potentially alarming fact was that no sooner had I been obliged to take over the enlarged caseload from my absent colleague, than the team was due for its Home Office inspection. I was 'examined' in my office by an extremely competent and experienced woman. She questioned me on several 'cases' in detail: 'how are you going to deal with this or that?', and to my inadequate replies she gave such positive advice that I reckon it was the best 'tutorial' I ever had. She soon spotted my tendency to want to put people's problems right for them, instead of helping them work out the sensible solutions – shades of pastoral mishandling here – another lesson I was glad to learn quickly.

In youth club days I used to spend hours, or even days, working out how to protect lads from some of the consequences of their stupidities. I wanted the satisfaction of being their 'rescuer', and sometimes I succeeded. When crippled with worry on their behalf, I had slowly learned that no-one can live other people's lives for them, and maybe just standing by them through their mistakes was the best means of helping them mature. As a probation officer I had a rather more official responsibility as an officer of the court to help protect the public. But in the long run, all offenders had to work out the good sense and rightness of upright behaviour, if only out of enlightened self interest. A decent, mature personal relationship with a probation officer could go a long way towards this. I noted many times that, in spite of the generally adverse attitude to prison, Borstal institution or detention centre, many of them were able to single out some warden, some prison officer, or even some individual policeman who had related well and helpfully to them.

What was the specifically Christian content of this work? I was greatly helped in thinking this out when I was asked to preach at the annual Conference of the National Association of Probation Officers in Llandudno in 1971. I tried to unfold the necessary non-judgementalism with a positive and gospel view of who we are – 'other Christs' in our service, but also identified with the sinner.

These eight or nine months in Slough were valuable. I was well-motivated for some more academic study of the field in which I was working. My 'standard of living' was modest but quite adequate. Slightly 'better off' than in residential work I spent more – and soon I was no 'better off'. I went to sixteen prom concerts in that summer. I could never have afforded that before – I bought a new suit (in 1972) which lasted me till my seventieth birthday in 1994. Later more penurious days were greatly assisted by some savings I had deliberately made each month. They accumulated enough for me to buy outright the little two down-two up cottage at Bryneglwys, to give me a home base when I got back to found the Lift Project in Wrexham. £2,500 is what I paid for that, so I am glad I already had very economical habits.

I wrote to my friends in a circular letter:

I was able to be of service liturgically with a fairly regular Sunday commitment at La Sainte Union College of Education, and I got to know many of the staff and students where I found a widespread interest in social problems, and in our particular apostolate in the Society of St Dismas, where our team of two Franciscan priests, two laymen and myself were at work. Sadly we had serious troubles in the management field, and it eventually became necessary to re-sign from our posts, and I was therefore unable to complete the two years I had originally intended to give to this work. Much has happened in Southampton since I left. The society has an impressive new management committee, and the new Administrator in the field was one of the laymen from our former team. There is, I also know, an enviable spirit of co-operation among the University, statutory and voluntary bodies at work in the field of aftercare and rehabilitation of prisoners and offenders for the Wessex area. It was always interesting to find ministers of other Christian bodies deeply involved in the work: a Salvation Army Officer as Probation Officer, a Methodist minister as organising secretary of one of the hostel trusts, Church Army officers, not to mention the two Franciscans who are still at work in allied fields. Driving back from a New Forest Conference to which I was invited to return recently, I had with me an Assistant Governor of Parkhurst Prison. On the way we passed a fearful car accident. Instinctively we stopped the car and ran together to the scene, announcing ourselves not as from the Prison and Probation services, but as Baptist minister and Catholic priest. I mention this by way of a practical example of the way in which we are not alone in re-thinking the functions of priests/ministers in the modern world. Maybe our strict ordination functions within the Christian committees to which we belong remain the same – essentially concerned with worship, including preaching the Word of God and presiding at the liturgy. But what else we do with our days may well be different from other times. There are often articles about this in *The Tablet* and other periodicals, and I have contributed a couple of letters on this theme. A longer article on it is to be published in *New Blackfriars* in October, and a summarised version will appear in the Spode review the same month. I have found room for much development of thought in these last two years.

For some people I know, unless one is dressed up in a black suit and Roman collar, and employed in fulltime work as one of the parish 'staff', parish priest or curate, then one is not a 'proper priest' at all. On the face of it this is understandable; but in the light of the various ministries which have been exercised by ordained priests through the ages, it is a curiously narrow view. And as for dress and style of life (e.g. being addressed as 'Father') current custom is only just over a century old. I have no doubt the church still needs parishes with fulltime parish priests – though it might often be better if they worked in teams and had some fulltime laymen alongside of them; but some of us should also pursue our special competence, whether as teachers, fund-raisers or social workers.

During this time I shall also recall happily the other events that could be fitted in. The retreat in Holy Week to the nuns at the Southampton College of Education, the lectures and talks to various groups, including the parish at Aberystwyth, the Wrexham Social Workers Conference, the Study Day for Diocesan UCM at Windsor, and tutoring at Youth Leadership courses at Portsmouth's Diocesan Pastoral Centre at Park Place, Wickham, where I found a place to dump my large library of books from Bryn Hall, (vowing unsuccessfully never to accumulate books again!). There was also a moving and interesting weekend conference with fifteen priests, (now laicised from their duties), and their wives in the Midlands; they were so full of zeal for the church. (This was the start of the Advent Group to whom I gave a paper on Ministry and Priesthood, which was later published in *New Blackfriars*.)

After two weeks' leave, I shall start in October as a student at University College Cardiff, for a one-year intensive course in Applied Social Studies. The course is designed for graduates, and they are graciously accepting my philosophy degree plus the experience of recent years as a substitute for the presumed degree in sociology. The two professors at Cardiff (Paul Halmos and Howard Jones) are both distinguished men; and one of the tutors is Miss Joan Miller, a Methodist deaconess, who at my interview exchanged some interesting views on the combination of a formal ministry with social work. My only other fellow applicant on that occasion was a young Baptist minister-teacher.

My father, now eighty-one years of age, is still going strong, at his lawyer's office three times a week. I shall of course be able to see him with some regularity for this coming year, which will be a pleasant change.

And then, when the course is over, what? Where's it all leading to? Will I return to ordinary parish work afterwards? I shall not conceal the fact that I still miss the wonderful, if hard, years in Ruabon as parish priest. I also make no secret that I would find it difficult, if not impossible to return to the requirements of a close structure of parish life now. Ruabon parish always was a bit odd, anyhow. What I liked about it was its openness to the whole local community. There are other and more traditional approaches to parish life which serve the gospel as well; but I would be unable to work in them. The bishop was very kind to tolerate my oddities for so long. By now, I have grown into more radical thinking about the ways in which the church should be expressing the message of joy, reconciliation and hope; and the office of parish priest as usually interpreted would not be a workable means for me.

To put it concisely, you could say that I am an ordained priest who has ceased to be a member of 'the clergy'. Even the 'traditional' theology says, 'Once a priest, always a priest'. I am no longer on the pay-roll of the church, but the work for which the church prepared me, and formally acknowledged by my ordination, is still at the service of the community. I have no doubt that we shall be discovering new and exciting forms of the ministry in the next twenty years. I have no wish to discontinue the one I undertook seventeen and a half years ago, even though I see it all very differently these days. It may seem 'modern' to some people for a priest to wear ordinary clothes, earn his own living, and share a community concern with laypeople (religious and priests as well) and right across the board of Christian and humanist concern. But just look at your history books again. I have found that the facts of my personal situation have opened up some people to share with me far more revolutionary ideas about the Christian life that the usual structures could tolerate or cope with. Deep concern, and great courage in trying new ways are widespread. People don't wait to be involved in 'Catholic' plans. On a recent Friday-night team in Soho at the project which is centred on the Anglican parish of St Anne's, eight out of the ten helpers were Catholics, including one priest, now resigned for marriage and Probation work. I have come across about eight formerly active priests who are Probation Officers. I have no idea how the bishops will deal with the celibacy problem. I am certain we are losing a corps of first-rate men by insisting on their giving up their ministry if they wish to marry. But married or not, they are full of care for the gospel, and many of them wouldn't come back to the present structures, even if allowed to. Over and over again, I find priests are just not content with administering the older ways of the parish, which sometimes (but not always) bypass the real problems of people, and close them off from sharing in Christian life – at least officially. And the more the bishops say 'No' to any developments, the more people regard the freedom of the gospel as higher than any decisions of the authorities, and they take the law into their own hands – an unhealthy but probably inevitable result.

Sometimes one has the impression that our eyes and ears are not sufficiently open to the Holy Spirit, but are under the influence of powerful people with set ideas; but I am sure there is an ocean of goodness at all levels in the church. We have no need to be afraid; we are bound to make mistakes whatever we do; and the worst mistake of all is to try to keep things just as they are under the illusion that this is how they always were. Meantime I have a great sympathy for those whose upbringing was in a different climate; I don't see why they should be forced into new ways. There is room in the church for all of us. And one day we'll meet together again and laugh at our over-anxieties.

So now it was farewell to England again, and back to Wales – indeed to my home city of Cardiff, where my father was still alive, and no doubt more puzzled than ever about the strange odyssey of this 48-year-old son. After Newnham, Marlborough, Oxford and Rome – more fulltime study?

Part Five

Passionate Concerns

Chapter Eleven:
Through the Struggles of Conscience: A pursuit of peacefulness
This is something of an interlude, as I returned to active involvement with 'the peace movements'. This drew me to explore again the first passionate concern of my life as a Christian, which led me to refuse military service. Now as a Catholic I had wider international opportunities of reflection and application through Pax Christi International. As a parish priest again I also had to focus on the obligation to explain moral teaching on the issues of war and peace.

Chapter Twelve:
To The Accompaniment of Music: Joy, consolation and inspiration
Here is a very different topic, but which has been no less a passionate concern, for without music I wonder how I could have experienced things so emotionally. I see this not just as a hobby, but as a factor in spiritual life also.

'What you've got to try to do is smile nicely at each alien invader.'

[Cartoon: Angelo Edwards]

CHAPTER ELEVEN

Through the Struggles of Conscience:
A pursuit of peacefulness

As a matter of chronology, my study year and subsequent return to Wrexham to found and operate the detached project with 'disorganised' young adults took me through the years 1971 to 1980; and from 1974 I was also a lecturer in Social Work at the N. E. Wales Institute. The little history of the Lift Project, and the insights I gained from helping in the education of social workers and probation officers, does not need to be retold here. It hardly affected the way in which I now understood ministry and priest-hood.

My return to my priestly 'home ground' in Wrexham, but in an entirely different capacity, led to some initially delicate manoeuvres with Bishop Langton Fox; but he was ultimately satisfied that, when I was called upon to help out liturgically in parishes or convents, I did a satisfactory job. My priest col-leagues for the most part ignored me, but without harsh intent; and a few of them, together with a number of religious sisters, supplied very supportive encouragement.

By the end of the 70s the reviving peace movements were making their mark. I had for long been a passive member of Pax Christi, the international Catholic peace movement (and before that of the British Pax society), but now I felt stirred to wake up my long-held conscientious convictions about the status of war in our times, and the madness of nuclear deterrence. While still teaching at Cartrefle College, I started showing the notorious formerly-banned *War Game* film to anyone who chose to come. It had a stirring effect in both the college and the town, and soon we had the formation of Wrexham Against Nuclear Armaments, which later became Wrexham CND. By 1982 I was Secretary of CND Cymru, and a part-time worker on disarmament with Pax Christi UK, travelling to London for a day or two at a time. It was for me a return to my earlier struggle with conscience and roused memories of those days.

Because the second World War broke out when I was fifteen, and I was a convinced Christian, it happened that the first major ethical decision I ever had to make was whether or not to accept the compulsory enlistment into the armed forces. I had taken part in the Officers Training Corps at Marlborough for two years without much thought. It was an unquestioned part of school life, though I disliked it very much. But the more thought I gave to it, the less happy I was as a Christian being called upon to kill for my country – which was my nuanced version of the usual call to be ready to die for my country. I had spent holidays in Germany in 1935 and 1936 and had some German friends. Were they now my enemies because their country was being led by a harsh and militaristic leader? In my last year at school I simply left the OTC, and before I set off for New College, Oxford, I registered as a conscientious objector, and applied to join the Quaker-based Friends Ambulance Unit. There were several consequences of making this decision, but remarkably few difficulties. I was acutely aware of the embarrassment my parents would experience in the presence of those with sons in the forces. That fact nearly made me abandon my decision, and I shall always be grateful that my father, while disagreeing with me, stood by me at my tribunal which had to be undergone.

During the one term I was allowed at New College before leaving for the FAU training, I found myself almost alone in not appearing in uniform at any time. Most of the undergraduates were obliged to combine their studies with some kind of military training in a more advanced sort of OTC. After three weeks it was not surprising that I was questioned about this. In one of those stereotypically public school accents, a Wykehamist said to me: 'I say, old boy, why is it that we never see you in uniform?' I replied, 'Well as a matter of fact I am a conscientious objector.' 'Oh my God,' he said, 'how fearfully brave of you.' And no-one ever mentioned it again!

It was many years before I realised just how crucial my rejection of military service had been for my personal development. As I have already mentioned in Chapter 7, in 1968 – more than 20 years after the war, and by this time I had become a Roman Catholic and a parish priest – I was asked by Vincent Kane (the long-standing presenter on Radio and TV) to join him for the first in a series of chat shows under the title of *Crossroads*. (Not the soap series, I hasten to add.) Vincent and I had been friends since 1946, when he was a schoolboy and a fellow parishioner of St Mary's, Canton, Cardiff. I travelled to Cardiff to stay the night with him and his wife, Mary, and we spent several late evening hours in conversation so that he could shape the unscripted interview for the next day.

The whole experience in the TV studio was a bit alarming, though Vincent managed to work through it all in a very relaxed manner. He had obviously decided that the main 'cross roads' in my life were that of becoming a Catholic, and becoming a priest, so the conversation turned mainly on this. What the experience did for me was to make me realise that the decision to opt for pacifism had provided a kind of model for much of the rest of my life. It made me challenge political orthodoxy in the light of a personal understanding of Christian faith. It broke me away from the public school ethos and onto a fairly lonely path for a while. It brought me into touch with Quakerism, which was a really significant development from my Anglican upbringing, and through an experience of wartime Europe, and into a fairly dedicated service which underlay many other important decisions of later life.

Now I'm not very keen on re-hearing any of my broadcasts, which in various forms must number well over a hundred. In this case an audio-tape was made of the interview for the sake of my father who was in hospital and unable to watch the TV programme. Even thirty years later I wouldn't want to alter anything substantial in how I answered Vincent's searching questions, though I could have made a better job of the presentation. The BBC had asked for some photos of myself at various stages of my life. On arrival at the studio I found that four of them had been blown up to a three-foot square size. There I was staring at myself from four angles of the studio, all a bit disconcerting. Vincent faced the camera and introduced the programme by wandering from one photo to another as he described roughly the points in my life that they visualised. In particular he highlighted the FAU group photo pointing out that I was sitting next to Gerald Gardiner, who had joined the FAU after me, though he was much older, and he became the Lord Chancellor in the post-war Wilson government. After relating briefly how my life had developed since those days, Vincent asked me which of the crucial decisions of my life had been the most difficult, and I said that it was the decision to refuse military service; but it had strengthened my readiness to step out of line as a result of a conscientious conviction. It stood me in good stead.

Certainly on becoming a Catholic, while still serving with the FAU in Germany, I didn't see much sign of Catholic pacifists. When the war ended and I was back at the university the issue took a slightly back seat in the order of my priorities. However I did soon uncover a number of Catholics returning from the war who had been morally shaken by the atomic bombing of Japan; it made some of them call into question the whole apparent justification of war. I recall helping to organise a public seminar at the university chaplaincy to be led by Mgr Francis Davis of Oscott College. To my surprise about forty undergraduates turned up for the event and Mgr Davis found himself facing a near consensus against war altogether. Contrary I think to his personal standpoint, he found himself having to outline the 'just war theory' showing the church held that some wars could involve the legitimate participation of Christians. Soon afterwards I uncovered the lesser-known alternative tradition of the Catholic Church – the one that came before 'just war' ideas – the tradition of active nonviolence, which emerges in time of war as pacifism. Those of us who hold to this tradition are still perhaps not numerous, but together with those in what are called the 'historic peace churches', e.g. the Quakers, the Mennonites and others, we are by no means without influence in the violent world of our time. People are now discussing 'How to rid the world of the institution of war'. The massive consequences for the environment, and the scale of wars all over the world, are bringing more and more people into thinking positively about the pursuit and the culture of peace. Those who still cannot take on pacifism as a realistic option have inaugurated studies of 'defensive defence'.

I rather dislike the word 'pacifism' because it usually implies only the negative of taking no part in war, whereas the philosophy of nonviolence involves programmes of personal and social action, together with spiritual discipline, which stretches back into family and neighbourhood disputes, the use of mediation and arbitration, and proactive initiatives in troubled times and places. It is no longer a cause of surprise that Catholic writers, including those in the USA, come out with passages like the following:

'The arrest of Jesus is unforgettable because in the midst of it he teaches Peter that his disciples must not draw their swords. In disarming Peter, Jesus disarms every Christian. At least that was the intent. We would have lived in a vastly different world if Christianity had given itself wholeheartedly to the banishment of all weapons from the beginning, with no exceptions allowed. If it was not right to save Jesus from a horrible death, how could it be right to employ violence to protect the church? Christianity's most glorious centuries and most impressive saints were non-violent. Christianity could have made such a difference in teaching the human family nonviolence. Because it did not, and does not, we weep for the loss of the innocent and the kiss of betrayal.' (*Anthony Padovano* in *National Catholic Reporter*, March 1997)

However, it is simply not enough to say 'Thou shalt not kill', as though that settles the issues. There are real life problems out there, starting with the questions which ask, 'What would you do if ...? I have led sessions, especially for intelligent sixth-formers, many times when I have felt obliged to start with the dilemma I faced in 1942. I had to go before a 'tribunal' to test the validity of my conscientious objection. Somewhere the questioning went like this: 'If a Nazi burst into the room to rape your sister, what would you do?' My actual response could have been 'I haven't got a sister,' but facetiousness was not recommended. However war is not in the first instance about personal encounters of this kind. War is largely impersonal. It is the careful organisation of violence on a huge scale, directed as much to destroying the morale of whole peoples as to destroy military targets. I wanted to examine the origins, the nature, reality and consequences of war. While the question must not be evaded altogether, an invented scenario of that kind should not be the starting point.

It is a generalisation which needs a little qualification, but not altogether untrue, that for about three centuries after Christ's death and resurrection it was deemed incompatible with being a Christian to take up arms. There is of course no precise command of Jesus, 'Thou shalt not take part in war'. Yet his respect for the dignity of every person, including the sinful, and his constant message of love and forgiveness could scarcely be interpreted in any other way. The first Christians were very often marginalised people, outcasts from Jewish orthodoxy, and often the poor and the slaves of the Roman empire. All the apostles had a rough time of it, becoming the victims of suspicion, hatred and persecution. There was already a promise from Jesus that this was likely to happen 'for the servant is not above his master'. There is an immediate riposte of course that Jesus did not evidently forbid the carrying of a sword, however that is to be explained. The Quaker tradition reminds us of one of the stories about William Penn who, newly converted, was anxious that he still wore a sword according to social custom. Should he now discard it? 'Wear it as long as thou canst,' said George Fox. This beautifully encapsulates the refusal to answer for another's conscience. 'If sword-carrying is incompatible with discipleship, then be a person of integrity' is what he is saying. Like Jesus, Fox gave no precise answer to such a direct question but pointed to the issue behind the question.

It is probably true as an additional factor for Christians in the time of the Roman empire that being a soldier might have involved taking an idolatrous oath. There is however one clear piece of evidence from the story of Martin the soldier – honoured in due course as St Martin of Tours – who, after baptism as a Christian, declined to receive the emperor's gifts, saying he ought to leave his military career. 'As a Christian I cannot fight.' His feast day ironically falls on 11 November.

How then did this tradition change? Was 'pacifism' part of the Christian way of life? There could be no change from Christ's precept, 'love your enemies and pray for those who spitefully use you', but that could be seen in the first instance as a direction for individuals. What if – as surely happened when tribes and kingdoms banded together in fury, legitimate or otherwise, with one another – the Christian's own family, neighbourhood or his nation-state, were attacked by armed violence? However ideal, was it right or just to let one's attackers have it all their own way? It would seem that defensive fighting – and this was for the most part still a person to person affair – was legitimate. Soon it occurred that attack was seen as the best form of defence; and so the moral dilemmas arose.

The Christian presumption against war and violence remained, even though organised nonviolence had not been developed as an alternative strategy. Christian teachers, from St Augustine onwards through the Middle Ages, devised a set of criteria which became known as the 'just war theory'. More correctly it should be described as the limited justification for Christian participation in war. This is not the place to expound it in any detail, but coming late into the Catholic tradition I was alarmed to find how few Catholics seemed to know about it, or to apply it with any vigour if they did. I am unable to make this tradition my own, but apart from a practice of total nonviolence, this is the only set of guidelines we have. That is why it needs to be more widely understood.

Briefly to say, to be willing to take part in a war a Christian needs justifying reasons under two headings: 'Ius ad bellum' which considers the moral legitimacy of the particular war, and 'Ius in bello' which focuses on the methods to be used. 'Ius ad bellum' covers Just Cause, Right Intention, Lawful Authority, Last Resort, Proportional Effect, Moral Certainty of Success. Plainly no Christian should even consider involvement in a war where there is obviously no just cause. The intention must not simply be anger or vindictiveness, but the aim of restoring a just peace. There must be legitimate political authorisation, and even then only when every other tactic has been tried to settle whatever is in dispute. Finally some thought has to be given to the likely effects, so that the slaughter and destruction is not on a scale that will outweigh the bad effects of non-resistance.

'Ius in bello' is concerned with the way in which a war is fought, which applies the criterion of proportionality to individual campaigns and tactics, but also – the most important principle of all, that of discrimination, whereby those who are non-combatants may not be made the direct intended victims of war strategies. Combatants may of course be more than those in the armed services, because people like munition workers are directly involved in the war effort. Lines cannot easily be drawn in some areas. However no-one would deny that the elderly, the sick, the handicapped and the children may not be the direct target of military action. To defy this is not only to contravene the principle of ius in bello but (as we now express it in the light of the Geneva and other conventions) to commit a war crime.

It always seemed to me, once this principle was outlined, that modern total war fails altogether under the traditional criteria. Saturation bombing surely contravened them, and if one adds the totally indiscriminate nature of weapons of mass destruction – biological, chemical or nuclear – the case is even stronger. Breaching the conditions for legitimate ways of waging war might not be sufficient to remove any possibility of ius ad bellum;

but the practical impossibility of applying them once war has begun makes them a shaky guide to moral action.

The criterion of a 'just cause' depends on official presentation. Every side in every war declares it has a just cause. The desire to halt the military aggression of Nazi Germany was obviously *prima facie* a just cause. That however was not obvious to the majority of Christians in Germany; they were brought up to believe in the legitimacy of 'defending the fatherland'. With extremely rare exceptions, the Christian leaders have always supported the justice of their own nation's 'cause'. To narrow it down a bit, we have the totally absurd situation of devout Catholics on both sides receiving Holy Communion and then going out with the blessing of their bishops to kill the devout Catholics on the other side. That remains as true for the Falklands/Malvinas war as it was of World War II. Something is radically wrong somewhere. Maybe if Christians really believed in applying the principles of 'just war' they would not get beyond the problem of 'just cause'.

'Right intention' also gets blurred when we demand 'unconditional surrender'. 'Lawful authority' might make us look at the fact that decisions about going to war are left in the hands of a small number of people even in a parliamentary system like our own. Since the existence of the United Nations Organisation, one wonders who has the authority to go to war any more except in immediate self-defence; yet the recent Balkans war saw a notorious breach of this. 'Last resort' cannot be established simply by setting a critical ultimatum – 'If you do this, then we go to war'. There really has to be exploration and implementation of alternatives. In the Gulf War, 'desert shield', ostensibly wholly defensive, was soon allowed to become 'desert storm' by a dishonest slide past the severe sanction policy which, somewhat unusually perhaps, seemed to be having some effect. The background story of Iraq, and British earlier support to Saddam Hussein when it suited us, as well as the history of the borders of that state, need to be taken into account when examining the justification for war. No-one would deny the illegitimacy of the seizure of Kuwait, but there is a singular inconsistency in the international consideration of Israel and the occupation of the West Bank.

I cannot resist including an anecdote here from 1991, when I attended the Synod of Bishops on Europe as representative of

Pax Christi International. Invited along with eight other English-speaking people to have dinner with Pope John Paul one evening, we had a truly memorable occasion. As we moved along to his chapel for some prayer after the meal, I was walking by his side. 'Thank you for opposing the Gulf War,' I said. 'I did too.' That implied in my usual cheeky way, that this must have made us right!

Of course a great deal of moral wrangling has continued since the invention, use and widespread deployment of nuclear weapons. There is absolutely no doubt that to use them is a war crime, because it breaches the principle of discrimination – and this is not only across space but across time, because the effects of nuclear pollution cross generations. There are still people suffering in Japan from the first atomic weapons used there. However the casuists have kept the argument going by proposing the strategy of 'nuclear deterrence'. The argument is that the possession and the possible threat to use such weapons is morally justifiable if it sustains 'peace'. The hypocrisy of this stance emerges when one notes how only certain states may legitimately manufacture, possess and deploy them in a potentially threatening manner. The World Court judgement of July 1996 ruled against the legitimacy of nuclear weapons (threat or use), but allowed one narrow condition, viz, 'in an extreme circumstance of self-defence in which the survival of a state would be at stake'. But such a condition is of course restricted to the nuclear states who continue to delay any serious moves to honour the conditions of Article VI of the Non-proliferation Treaty which commit them to reduce these weapons on the way to complete disarmament. To this day it completely baffles me how some distinguished Christians continue to justify the possession of nuclear weapons.

My real objection to the 'just war theory' is that it is a device of philosophy only, and the Christian faith is more than this. The Christian has a vision of the goodness of God's creation and the care we should consequently bestow on it; and then the special dignity of every human person, and the necessity of showing understanding, love and forgiveness. It seems to me that the 'just war' arguments avoid a serious reflection on this vision, and steer us away from serious contemplation of the possibilities of understanding, mediation, arbitration, and the constant need for managing conflict.

There had been opportunities of curbing the growing Nazi militarism which were thrown away, especially in the collapse of the World Disarmament Conference if 1932–3. The story of this is vividly told by Noel-Baker, in a book published in 1979, from his own Foreign Office experience. It was one of the privileges of my involvement in the peace movement of the 80s to attend public and private meetings with him and Lord Fenner Brockway, when both of them were in their nineties.

But why was it possible for thousands of British (French and others of course) ordinary people to set out day by day to kill ordinary German people with whom they had no quarrel, except that they did so in obedience to their government, as did the Germans? In the midst of it all, some six million Jews perished in the terrible camps without any effort being made to bomb the gas ovens. The German people had been silenced into apathy or blindness. The British did not highlight the evil that was known to be increasing. We had made no notable protest at the pre-war Kristal-nacht incident when people, Christians especially, should have risen up in massive non-violent demonstration across Europe. We have learnt since those days of the effectiveness of some non-violent protest – e.g. for the overthrow of the Marcos regime in the Philippines. The end of Soviet domination and Stalinist communism was also managed almost without any violence. Active nonviolence is not only a practical possibility when planned and prepared for, I think it has gospel values at its heart. It proclaims the necessity of discipline and willing vulnerability, and never challenges the dignity of its opponents, however wrong-headed their policies may be. It needs forethought and training, and above all, a broad consensus behind it. We should be thinking about this as much as about disarmament. Education for peace involves both channels of action.

Was this what we were doing in the Friends Ambulance Unit? Not explicitly. When we moved beyond our training into active service alongside the army, we took on board quite a few mental compromises. We wore British army khaki for a start – even though we were not exactly 'against' German grey. We accepted all the hardware we needed, the ambulances and trucks, all other equipment, as well as our food and lodging (which sometimes dislodged the lawful occupants) from the hands of the army. In north-western Europe, where I was, we worked with Civil Affairs Units, which later became part of 'military government' when the fighting ended. We got into some odd situations. In Holland we were once called in to a village from which the German army had retreated, to help uncover the several hundred civilians who had taken shelter in the basement of their town hall, over which the Germans had blown up the building before they left. The British army had camped outside, with only an hourly motor-cycle patrol to check that the Germans had not returned. In one break from our task I was walking along a dyke with Richard Wainwright (who became Liberal MP for Colne Valley after the war). Two Dutch Resistance young men came and asked us to arrest some German soldiers they thought they had cornered in a basement. 'Sorry, we don't go in for this war business,' we said; but agreed to inform the next military patrol. Where was the logic or the compromise in this? Anyway it turned out that they must have been misinterpreting the noise of rats, not German soldiers.

Much of the thinking on active nonviolence is due to the amazing example of Mahatma Gandhi. I believe it took a period of two years to train his followers into the right spiritual discipline for the salt march, so vividly displayed in the well-known film. 'Offer no resistance' is a gospel admonition so courageously implemented by people who were mostly Hindus. His dramatic fasts were not so much moral blackmail as a readiness to take on himself the pain and weakness of countless victims of injustice. His actions were provocative, as those of any prophet; they roused people to anger, but they highlighted situations which morally demanded confrontation. Martin Luther King acted similarly for the civil rights of black people in USA. The main demonstrations in which I have happily taken part against nuclear weapons in the 80s with the Campaign for Nuclear Disarmament are little more than token gestures in comparison with those who have become vulnerable to the power of a hostile state. We have a long way to go in confronting the powers of this world which lie behind the manufacture of the trade in arms, the manipulation of natural resources and human labour, the wanton destruction and waste of so much of our environment; but we have to start somewhere.

Meister Eckhart wrote: 'It behoves a man in all he does to turn his will in God's direction, and keeping God in view to forge ahead without a qualm, not wondering "Am I right or am I doing something wrong". If the painter had to plan out every brush stroke before he made the first, he would not paint at all. And if, going to some place, we had first to settle how to put the front foot down, we should never get there. Follow your principles and keep straight on: you will come to the right place; that is the way.'

I suppose that many people might accept the ultimate wisdom of nonviolence yet still believe that in a wicked world we cannot do without violence altogether. Very often the pacifist is challenged by the question about whether we disapprove of a police force, because such a force uses violence sometimes, but for good purposes. (Incidentally I have a notion that Roman soldiering was largely a policing function, before ever it was for fighting wars. Maybe that is how there were Christians among their ranks.) Here I would offer a distinction which I originally heard being made by Donald Nicholl. Donald had been one of my Oxford Catholic contemporaries, coming back from the services, as I returned from a different form of war service. His friendship, together with that of Dorothy, his wife, has been a significant influence in my life. I felt privileged to have a part to play in the moving funeral Mass in the Keele University chapel when Fr Gerard Hughes presided, and Adrian Hastings, another Oxford contemporary, gave the address. Donald helped me to look at the use of the words 'force' and 'violence'. Force, that is, physical force, is morally neutral. There are occasions when it must be used, for instance to restrain a drunken or drugged or mad person from committing some offence; how else can we restrain an angry child or young person? But violence is using the force that violates. It is by its own definition morally unacceptable. So we may use physical force to stop someone hitting himself or someone else. But we may not do so by striking him in a way that violates his dignity or his physical integrity. You shouldn't try to separate two fighters by joining in the violence, but by throwing yourself between them with force – and probably suffering violence yourself as you separate the assailants. You might have to pressure an aggressive drunk to the ground, but that is different from violating his dignity by punching him in the face, or kicking him in the ribs. In all honesty I don't know exactly what I would do in detail, but I trust that if I am self-disciplined in the exercise of love, understanding and forgiveness, I will be the better able to absorb whatever violence is committed against myself as I try to prevent continuing violence against others.

This of course takes me back to the original question posed at the tribunal, and which deserves a considered answer. What then would I do if a Nazi burst in to rape my sister? I would insist on my obligation in love and justice towards my sister. If I did not give her some practical assurance of my wish to defend her, I would fail in love. Force might well be necessary, but as a Christian I would of course be unarmed, and it would be absurd to offer an aggressive defence; it would be bravado to no purpose. But I need to challenge the scenario. Why should I presume that the German soldier who bursts in, probably as much out of fear of the unknown as with an aggressive intent, is an evil Nazi who is going to attempt rape? Isn't that kind of presumption the result of warlike activity? What if he were to discover no-one showing any hostility, and even a friendly exchange: 'There is nothing to be afraid of here. I expect it isn't much fun being a soldier at war. Are you hungry or thirsty?' This may seem fanciful, but is it any more so than reading violence and rape into his arrival in my home? Isn't it his duty to be ready for opposition and to present an aggressive stance while he feels unsafe? I do indeed have obligations towards my sister (if I had one), but so do I have obligations in fearless love towards a potential enemy. Of course the tribunal's scenario may be proved correct. I should then have to accept the death that comes to millions of unarmed civilians in wartime.

For some people the pacifist is simply not living in the real world at all. If the real world perpetuates violence between states, or stands in perpetual military readiness for such violence, with all the suffering, destruction or wastage that is inevitable, then it isn't the kind of world one wants to live in. I have it as a prior conviction that love is ultimately more powerful than hate, and that suffering violence innocently is more fruitful than responding with more violence. When you think of it, it was the very moment that the ultimate violence of crucifixion was wreaked on Jesus that he was able to call for forgiveness for those who killed him. And at that very moment the centurion was able to say, 'Indeed this man was the Son of God.'

Of course pacifists do not expect to be treated as heroes. My dear mother simply could not fathom at the end of the war how I could have joined 'the most military church there is'. 'The word is "church militant", mother,' I said, 'not military' – but I know what she meant and I felt somewhat ashamed. She had always shown complete loyalty towards me in my wartime stance, as had my father, who stood by me as a witness at my tribunal. But I recognise how difficult it must have been when meeting parents of sons in the services; my brother had already been invalided out of the army, and I was a 'conchie'. As my life in the FAU moved into work alongside the army it made it a little easier for them. I recall my mother's visit to me when I was in training at Burntwood Hospital, near Lichfield. It grieved her somewhat that, after all the expensive education I had been given, I appeared to be involved in rather menial tasks as hospital porter or nursing assistant. That was not how I saw it. In any event it was the corollary of being willing to do any menial task, living on the hospital premises, that we were given the chance of a range of medical experiences alongside student nurses. I worked variously in the X-Ray department, the wards, and even 'scrubbed up' with the surgeons on some occasions, when staff were short.

The wounded troops returning from the North African campaign were none too complimentary towards us on arrival; but as always a good relationship was struck up between us when they got to know us. Indeed, the whole hospital experience when, after twelve months residence, one knew all the doctors, nurses, domestic staff and patients, was an extraordinary one. We related to one another, as human beings should, acknowledging that we had differing convictions which we had to live up to. Throughout the war, members of the FAU were unpaid. We received free board and lodging wherever we were, and there was, I think, a little personal allowance for those without any means. My generous parents let me have an allowance from their resources, and I didn't need much because I was, and have ever remained, a non-smoker and absolute teetotaller. I probably spent what money I had on books, so that I could read to myself along my own vaguely eccentric journey.

One story about attitudes towards us came from the immediate post-armistice period in 1946, when I had taken over from Richard Wainwright as effectively the 'personnel officer' for our various sections in the British zone of Germany. I was stationed at Vlotho-an-der Weser, quite a small village but with a reasonably sized hotel, sufficient to cope with dining facilities for all the headquarters members of the various British voluntary societies – Red Cross, Salvation Army, CoBSRA, etc. We lived in

various houses in the village, and our offices were across the
road from the hotel. Colonel (rtd) Agnew, who led the Red
Cross contingent, was also the accepted leader of the whole set-
up. 'Now I want you all to be smartly in your offices this afternoon,' he said to us one day, 'because we are going to have a
visit from Field-Marshal Montgomery.' 'Good grief,' we thought
and said, 'he won't want to see us conchies surely.' 'Yes, all of
you, be in your offices,' the colonel insisted. So Michael
Rowntree, Deryck Moore and one or two others including myself duly awaited the Field Marshal. After a long wait, the
colonel knocked our door and brought in our distinguished military visitor. 'Now Field Marshal,' said the Colonel,' all these
men here are conscientious objectors, but they're as brave as
lions.' And we all had a formal handshake.

As a matter of fact I don't remember much opportunity for
bravery, though some of our men got into tight corners, and
were even taken as 'prisoners of war'. In some ways we were
glad to share some of the limited experiences of vulnerability
and discomfort which go with 'active service'. We were pretty
ignorant about what to expect. I recall one day in Holland, near
the front line at the time of the battle of Best. I was sitting round
a table with a Dutch civilian doctor and others. There was a sudden whooshing sound, and the others disappeared under the
table. It seems we were under shell fire, and though a last
minute ducking might not have made much difference if we received a direct hit, it was certainly more prudent than staying
upright as I did. I soon learned more sensible procedures. For
weeks on end I slept on a stretcher in the back of the ambulance I
drove. One got used to it, but I promised myself that when I got
back to the comfort of a real bed, I would always be thankful. At
the end of many tiring days since then, I have remembered this
as I clamber in between the sheets.

At one period my particular section had provided an ambulance service for the city of Antwerp since the German army had
either destroyed or purloined all the city's facilities when they
retreated. This was the time when V2 rockets were being used.
They were land-based and shot into the air as little 'pilotless
planes', returning to earth with their deadly explosives. Since
we were in the 'lowlands' military observers were able to spot
the ascent of each rocket. So as we sat on alert at the various fire
stations, we received – as the population generally did not, prob-

ably because it would have been of little help – a thirty second warning. We sat under the table till we heard the explosion, and then waited to be called to pick up the dead or the injured, if the bombs had fallen in our area. I found the off-duty hours in our billets more frightening than being on duty. But then I had also been very frightened in the east end of London when the V1s and V2s were bombarding us. And before I left for my war service I can still recall the horror of the air-raids over Cardiff, when I usually moved into a cupboard under the stairs at night. My father was often out on duty with the Observer Corps, and my brother sometimes on fire-watch duty. He was certainly at home with me on the night a land-mine floated down by parachute onto the site of Llandaff Cathedral, about a half mile from our house. Civilian life in these circumstances was as fearful and dangerous as much of war service life. At the end of the whole war, some 45% of those who died were civilians.

I have one light-hearted memory of my days in Hamburg on ambulance duties. An ENSA team arrived for the entertainment of the troops. Among the distinguished actors who came were Sybil Thorndike and Margaret Leighton. They were to perform *Arms and the Man, Peer Gynt* and other pieces. Knowing that Sybil was a pacifist, we invited her and Margaret to lunch with us in our billet. It was a most entertaining conversation. Several years later, by which time she was a 'Dame', I visited her in her dressing-room at the Cardiff theatre, and we laughed again over our memories.

Memories of wartime by now are pretty jumbled. I do remember that, especially at night-time, I felt a deep longing for the war to be over. The grim reality of it was a powerful incentive to clarify one's priorities. My little saga of experiences shaped my determination to hold to convictions and follow my understanding of truth wherever it would lead me. The decision not to take part in war began as my attempt to apply what I understood to be the gospel to life as I knew it. On my boyhood holidays in Germany, especially in 1936 when Hitler's men had defied the Versailles Treaty by marching into the Rhineland where we stayed, I had a first taste of the militaristic regime that was intensifying its power. But back at home in 1939 no-one would ever tell me that I should have to set off to kill my friend Wolfgang Otlinghaus. That was perhaps simplistic, but the challenges that followed that decision and conviction were ultimately to lead me into the Catholic Church and to discover the largely ignored tradition of nonviolence. I continued, when other things did not crowd the topic out, to study and pursue it until it seemed to be of immediate relevance in the 70s and 80s.

After leaving my lecturing job in 1981 I became active locally and in the N. Wales area, helping to build up peace groups, and as CND Cymru became numerous enough I was employed as part-time secretary, working from my house that had now become a 'Peace Studies Centre', and making closer links with Pax Christi UK. I took over as General Secretary when the CND job finished, and then began to commute weekly to London. My eighteen months in this post were not too successful following the outstanding work of Valerie Flessati, but when I left I was fortunate enough to be elected to the International Council. This brought me into contact with some of the finest people from across Europe and the wider world. The three-fold tasks of Pax Christi for international peace and reconciliation are Prayer, Study and Action. Hours and even days were spent in heavy-going international commissions and working groups, but none of them were mere talking-shops. For some time I remained a member of the British CND International committee, and the next ten years found me often travelling in some representative capacity to Moscow and Leningrad, to the UN in New York and Geneva, to Rome, Dublin and Budapest, to Assisi, Vicenza, Berlin, Munich and Vienna. The Russian journeys in 1982 and 1985 were truly memorable, and have left me a with a load of anecdotes of long conversations in the Kremlin, and with the Central Committee of the Communist Party in the Brezhnev days, and something of a contretemps with the KGB in Gorbachev's time. One unusual journey came just before I returned to parish work in 1988 when I travelled to Kazakhstan for the symbolic destruction of some SS20s after the Reagan/Gorbachev agreement to get rid of this range of weapon. My subsequent journeys to Belgium, Italy and once-again to Russia were somehow fitted in with holiday absences from the parish. I gave a report to parishioners on my return and it is fair to say that this helped to widen their horizons beyond the confines of parish thinking.

At the time of the Gulf war I spent several weeks explaining the just war criteria to help moral judgements. I made no secret of the fact that I could find no justification for the military action, and, among other things, I joined Tony Benn on a public platform in Liverpool to say so. My contribution to BBC's *Thought for the Day* was insufficiently patriotic and was censored out in advance. In preparing and reading a short statement in the parish at the outbreak of hostilities, I simply said that I would say no more on the subject publicly, but would willingly discuss it with any parishioner who had conscientious doubts about what was happening politically and militarily. Everyone was very tolerant, not least the several ex-military men. As often they turn out to be thoroughly pacific in their views. The role of pastor in moral guidance became very vivid to me. I offered no infallible or unconditional negatives, but made clear that there were two traditions in the church which had to be borne in mind.

A review article which I wrote for the *Clergy Review* in 1986, now somewhat shortened, may serve as an appendix to this chapter.

APPENDIX TO CHAPTER ELEVEN

The Healing Power of Peace and Nonviolence: The theme of Bernard Häring

'Of course we all want peace.' 'The Church continually prays for peace.' With such truisms in their minds, many Christians have been able to pursue their lives without realising how fearfully inadequate is their grasp of the meaning of the 'peace of God'. Peace is too easily identified with calm, quiet passivity. 'Sit down now quietly,' we say to the children, 'and give us a bit of peace.'

It is thought of as acceptance of, and almost resignation to, the complexities and problems of the world; and in the face of these, we should be up and about, and especially when our much vaunted western democratic values are under threat. To be peaceful then is to be treacherous, weak, lacking in courage and manliness. For centuries Christians have rallied to their various national flags (often on both sides of the war) for open warfare. We have extolled the virtues of the military man, and have even filled some of our ancient churches with the emblems of their struggles, victories and braveries. Once a war is upon us, there is scarcely any place for approved dissent from support for the war effort. Some of us recall with dismay the prohibition by

Cardinal Griffin on priests belonging to PAX – a British forerunner of Pax Christi – in the thirties, in spite of the fact they only sought to apply traditional just war teaching to the issues of war and peace in our time. The outstanding example of Franz Jagerstatter, an Austrian farmer, who found in conscience that he could not fight a just war for the Nazis, is only now being appreciated. His family, his parish priest, his bishop all told him he should fight. In spite of his isolation, his understanding of Catholic teaching impelled him to refuse. He was executed in 1943.

The majority of Christians certainly believed there was a 'just cause' in fighting Hitler's forces; but just wars have to be fought with justice and mercy according to clear principles of proportion and discrimination. Alone among the Anglican bishops, Dr Bell of Chichester condemned the saturation bombing of Dresden, Hamburg and elsewhere, and found himself isolated in the House of Lords. I have not seen any evidence of what Catholic bishops of the day said, but the much quoted paragraph from *Gaudium et Spes* clarified the issue unequivocally long after the events:

> All warfare which tends to the destruction of entire cities or wide areas with their inhabitants is a crime against God, and man, to be firmly and unhesitatingly condemned.

Yet even so, when there is more widespread consensus on the immorality of the actual use of weapons of mass destruction, a distinguished Catholic, Leonard Cheshire, continued to say that in Hiroshima and Nagasaki the end justified the means – those acts of mass destruction were a regrettable necessity. No-one apparently challenges the orthodoxy of this moral attitude. It is perhaps understandable that many Catholics are wearied by the logic-chopping of the moralists, and the arguments that continue in some quarters for the possible use of 'smaller' and discriminate nuclear weapons, and the hypothetical legitimacy of attacking a purely military target – especially a fleet at sea. Others were confused by the words of Pope John Paul at Coventry condemning all (not just nuclear) war as a means of settling conflicts, while British Christians were in no way discouraged at that very time from going to war against Argentinians whose bishops similarly supported the legitimacy of their cause.

It is high time we heard from a distinguished moral theologian, of the stature of Bernard Häring, who feels able to say:

At this crossroad of human history, a failure to give very serious consideration to a nonviolent alternative undermines the credibility of our faith in the Redeemer of the world. I understand we have to accept respectfully the given pluralism, but, as I see it, we have to work firmly at this critical time to rid ourselves of the 'just war' theory, especially while it remains so distorted in the minds and writing of many Catholics.

The US Catholic bishops in their remarkable Pastoral Letter of 1983, *The Challenge of Peace*, reminded us that there are two traditions in the church – the just war theology, and the earlier total nonviolent tradition.Yet in spite of the fact that the latter practice of nonviolence lasted for the first 300 years of the church, there are still Catholics, including many priests, who regard pacifism as little less than treachery, cowardice and the grossest negativism.Those of us, like myself, who have been life-long pacifists, will feel a trifle less isolated as Bernard Häring expounds the scriptural and theological basis for the proclamation and pursuit of pacifism – though he wisely and helpfully speaks of the healing power of peace and nonviolence, instead of 'pacifism'. His book is relatively brief, but gives considerable depth to the subject, and is still within the grasp of non-professional theologians.

To show how seriously Häring deals with the subject, here is how, towards the end of his book, he summarises the church's ideal stance:

The Lord has entrusted to his church a mission to heal and to reveal the healing power of peace and nonviolence, as an integral part of her mission for salvation and wholeness. The wholeness of the church herself depends to a great extent on her fidelity to the gospel of peace in her own life and ministry to the world. In the fulfilment of her role, action and prayer must always be joined so that she may never forget that peace and the strength to choose nonviolence are undeserved gifts of God given to those who seek in all things the honour of God, Father of all ... The peace mission concerns the whole church, the people of God and its pastors. What is most needed on all sides is concrete prophetic realisation.

That generalised statement is then followed up with these words:

A central task of the pastors of the church is the integral and
credible proclamation of the gospel of peace, including,
above all, healing nonviolence in the perspective of the all-
embracing redemption. At this juncture in history to neglect
the message and practice of nonviolence could easily make
the church and her teaching seem irrelevant.

and again,

... the evangelisation of today's world is possible and sound
only if the gospel of peace is made transparent and becomes
the yeast in all dimensions of the proclamation of salvation
and pastoral care.

... The gospel of peace and the signs of the times constitute
the greatest challenge and opportunity for moral theology
and missiology. By giving a central role to the gospel and
mission of peace and nonviolence, they rid themselves of any
possible insinuation of irrelevance in today's peaceless
world. They can reach out to a huge sensitive audience.

What Bernard Häring does is not to repeat all over again the
just war criteria, and reopen the complexities of that debate, but
to look at the other tradition, the older tradition, of total nonviolence. His message is not only for those who still defend nuclear
deterrence, but for members of the peace movements also:

Is it not also a sign of widespread anomaly and blindness
when even good people believe and firmly assert that the
present system of "deterrence" (of Mutual Assured
Destruction) is acceptable or even an obligatory means of assuring liberty and peace? Some call it "a last resort" under
certain conditions, yet they tend to justify it even when all
those conditions which they say are indispensable for its ac-
ceptability are ignored.

Even considerable parts of the increasing peace movements
all over the world remain in the narrow circle of protest
against nuclear armament instead of giving full attention to
the gospel of peace and nonviolent spirituality and action.
Many of these good people are still victims of the collective
blindness that cannot perceive the healing power of nonviolence. Have we, moral theologians and churchmen, fulfilled
our role of healing and revealing in this decisive field?

Moral Code or Spiritual Challenge

My own view is that we all need reminding over and again that the gospel message was never intended as another 'morality'. An examination of the whole just war theology, important as it may have been in church history, shows that it draws very little, if at all, on gospel principles. It can and should be argued by moralists that there is nothing theological about ensuring Just Cause, Lawful Authority, Last Resort, Right Intention and Proportionate Evaluation for the *'Jus ad Bellum'*. There is nothing especially Christian about Proportionate Means and Discriminate Methods for *'Jus in Bello'*. I was happy to hear both Bishop Montefiore of Birmingham, and Anthony Kenny (formerly Warden of Balliol College) assert this clearly in their lectures at St James's, Piccadilly. The gospel is a spiritual challenge, a prophetic stance; it confronts the values and ways of the world, finds them wanting, and offers a demanding, sacrificial alternative.

In practice – whatever its original intention – the just war theology has provided the justification of war, and what Häring is saying is that what we need now is not another philosophical analysis of deterrence or war practice, but a return to the challenge of nonviolence.

Some people seem to imagine that those who proclaim nonviolence as a demand of the gospel are going to indulge in a naïve fundamentalist appeal to some isolated text, saying or event in the scriptures, as though 'Put up thy sword' did not have to be evaluated alongside 'two swords? that is enough' or 'I come not to send peace but a sword'. There are no such simplistic solutions to establish codes of conduct. Häring expresses the 'clear insight that the point of departure for a theology of peace is not just particular words of Jesus, but his whole life, his actions and his death'. He examines how Jesus saw his mission in the light of Old Testament theology, which were his scriptures, and especially the Servant of Yahweh themes of Deutero-Isaiah. He also takes line by line the vision of the Beatitudes, and shows how our love of enemies becomes the very test of our gratitude for God's gift of peace and reconciliation to us as sinners. That is the whole motivation of forgiveness – for the work of reconciliation which is outlined further by St Paul.

The Practice of Nonviolence

Not practical at all? We have sorely neglected those who have practised loving and healing nonviolence, albeit on smaller scales than national confrontation. Häring looks with admiration at the development by Gandhi of the philosophy (spiritual not moral) of Satyagraha and Ahimsa – Truth-Force and Non-Violence. There is a growing belief among Christians that it more truly reflects the Christian vocation than any arguments for even the restricted use of violence. More are turning away from nuclear pacifism – to which they long ago concluded we were obliged under just war criteria – to total pacifism. There is no knock-down quotation from the Popes to demonstrate their total support for this yet, but Pope Paul VI at the UN in 1965 said:

> If you want to be brothers, let the weapons fall from your hands. You cannot love with weapons in your hands. Long before they mete out death and destruction those terrible arms supplied by modern science foment bad feelings and cause nightmares, distrust and dark designs. They call for enormous expenditures and hold up projects of human solidarity and of great usefulness. It suffices to remember that the blood of millions of men and women, that numberless and unheard-of sufferings, useless slaughter and frightful ruin, are the sanctions of the past which unite you with an oath which must change the future history of the world: No more war; war never again! Peace; it is peace which must guide the destinies of peoples and of all humankind.

Gandhi developed his thinking and practice before ever the totally new atomic weapons were on the scene. His conclusion about the latter,was:

> Now we know the naked truth about war. War knows no law except might. The moral to be legitimately drawn from the supreme tragedy of the bomb is that it will not be destroyed by counter-bombs, even as violence cannot be destroyed by counter-violence.

His disciple, Martin Luther King, while practising nonviolent methods to achieve greater justice for black people, said:

> I refuse to accept the cynical notion that nation after nation must spiral down a militaristic stairway into the hell of nuclear destruction. I believe that unarmed truth and unconditional love will have the final word in reality.

Gandhi was eminently practical. He saw the need to prepare people for the practice of nonviolence, which starts with a discipline of the spirit:

Three quarters of the miseries and misunderstandings in the world will disappear if we step into the shoes of our adversaries and understand their standpoint.

He knew that it would involve one in civil disobedience, and was careful to watch for a self-righteous attitude, or the development of a technique only:

Non-cooperation is not a movement of brag or bluster or bluff. It is a test of our sincerity. It requires solid and silent self-sacrifice.

Whatever our leading theologians in the church have or have not said about this, it is notable that Pope John Paul stood by Gandhi's grave on his Indian visit and expressed his 'profound conviction that the peace and justice of which contemporary society has such great need will only be achieved along the path which was at the core of Mahatma Gandhi's teaching: the supremacy of the spirit and nonviolence.'

Bernard Häring has recognised the need for education and training. Transition to the work of healing nonviolence will not happen overnight. He believes the moment has come for this totally new approach to be undertaken – an approach which might even appeal to those who do not share our beliefs. He thinks these bridges can be built. It is gratifying to find reference to those who have made a start:

I see one of the promising starting-points in the numerous active and creative groups of Pax Christi. They are indispensable champions of the spirituality and promoters of the project of nonviolent defence, as well as competent communicators for public opinion.

Cardinal Koenig, at that time the international President of Pax Christi, pointed out that paragraph 78 of *Gaudium et Spes* had praised those who renounce all violence:

That message from the Council expresses the essence of the salvation of Jesus Christ, and recommends the peaceful power of the nonviolence of God – yet has only been marginally propounded in the last twenty years of our history.

Some Pax Christi members may not find much welcome in many parishes. There are places where discussion of some issues is encouraged but those who go out, even after prayer and discernment, to practise nonviolent and symbolic gestures against the mounting militarism and nuclear arsenals in Great Britain are often written off as the equivalent of dissidents. When we work to try to understand those who are classified and stereotyped as enemies in the Soviet Union we are quickly dismissed as 'lefties'. Outside the church the Pax Christi booklet, *Looking at the Russians – a Christian Perspective,* has sold well. I fear that many Catholics would share the view of the *Daily Mail* which listed myself with three others, after a journey to Moscow for talks in 1982, as 'dupes of the Soviet Union'.

Bernard Häring is calling us through the work of reconciliation to a fundamental option for healing nonviolence. He gives us a vivid quotation from Rudolf Pesch:

'Are we afraid that the solution offered by God, the very way of Jesus, might not be true? Are we nurturing distrust towards God, towards Jesus Christ? Are we really believers?'

CHAPTER TWELVE

To the Accompaniment of Music:
Joy, consolation and inspiration

'Whether the angels play only Bach praising God I am not quite sure. I am sure however that en famille they play Mozart.'

(Karl Barth)

Although I seriously call in question the psychological wisdom of sending children of seven away to boarding school, I didn't have too painful a time at Brightlands school at Newnham, Gloucestershire. I certainly picked up some valuable cultural clues. The school had its origins when two men, Messrs Robathan and Bryce-Smith, who had been joint heads of Llandaff Cathedral school, near my home, decided to set up their own private fee-paying residential school. It was that link with Llandaff, and more generally with Cardiff, that made the school such a re-source for many parents of the Cardiff 'professional classes'. Even from the same road where I was born, Dr Harvard Davies sent his son, Robert, later to become Professor of Medical Practice, so one wasn't among strangers. Academically it was a good school. It wasn't exactly home from home, but a fairly relaxed regime. We benefited as much from the teachers as people as from the content of their classes.

Even before I had left the Llandaff kindergarten (we don't hear that word today, I think) I had started to learn Latin. (That was Elm Tree House, where Roald Dahl had also been a pupil, a contemporary of my older brother Glyn.) Now at the age of nine or ten I started Greek, and I was fascinated. Language became a matter of importance from then on. Among the staff members, the one who did the most for me was Miss Olwen Picton Jones, who was with us to teach music. Apart from versing us in the standard hymnody used in our daily worship, she had an enthusiasm for music which was infectious. Sunday evenings, when we had several hours of free time, were often filled by sit-ting with her at the piano while she played through a wide repertoire of classical music. I began to know Beethoven's Sonatas right away. I wrote to her annually for many years, and the news of her death was phoned to me by her niece in March 1999. I had only visited her once since 1938! She was staunchly supported by Bryce-Smith through his own musical interests. He arranged for those who wished to do so, to go to Gloucester Town Hall each term for an orchestral concert under the baton of Herbert Sumsion, the organist of Gloucester Cathedral. We were prepared for those concerts by listening over and over to records of the main works. Sometimes we were given some insight into sonata form, etc. As soon as I got to know Beethoven's Fifth Symphony I saved up to buy a recording myself. It took up no less than twelve sides of the old shellac 12′ records, and somehow one followed the flow in spite of turning over the records sides every five or six minutes. That was the special joy of the concerts – it was all joined up! Then came Brahms' second symphony, Mozart's A major piano concerto, Haydn's 'London' symphony. These are ever engraved into my memory. Listening to them on my gramophone (not then a 'record-player' or 'music centre') at home was always a sacred occasion.

I still don't know how one describes what is happening when a well-known work is being attended to but I know I couldn't bear to have anyone disturb me – not even the rustling of a newspaper. I had to be on my own and secure in that solitude if I was to derive full satisfaction. Music was not 'wallpaper' while doing other things. I was deeply in contact with something, or someone, as the music played. I bought the orchestral miniature scores and a little stick for conducting (I still have it) as the music played. It was my way of absorbing the full impact of the music, and, even without a score, I often 'conduct' on my own today – though it is more of an arms and body dance. This has always been a very private matter, of course. I would hate to be watched. One day, when on duty in the office of the Southampton hostel, but also listening to the Third programme (not yet Radio Three). I was busy 'conducting' Elgar's first symphony. Two of the resident lads were peeping through the door to the kitchen! They never let me forget it.

So it was a matter of reverence with which I approached 'the classics'; and I wanted to grasp the complete works, not just the 'purple passages' which today perhaps (e.g. on Classic FM) is a way of introducing people to the range of music. But I always feel this is cheating. My mother was naturally musical and would accompany me to some concerts in school holidays, till I ventured into more 'difficult' music. She wanted 'a good tune', as did my less musical father. (Maybe 'less musical' but the whole family liked to sing and harmonise songs on our car journeys.) My brother was a dab hand at the ukulele, and swiftly mastered the necessary chords for accompanying popular songs, and those he later came to write himself. On the piano he could do absolutely anything in the key of F. Symphony concerts were not his particular taste, though he appreciated rich romantic music like Rachmaninov. His later study was a thorough one of the music especially of Gershwin, about whom he knew as much as any professional.

In 1938 a really crucial event in my musical evolution occurred. My mother and I went to a concert of contemporary music at the Queen's Hall, Upper Regent Street – the original home of the Proms, soon to be destroyed in the war. One work was by a young composer of whom I'd never heard, the twenty-five-year-old Benjamin Britten. It was *The Ballad of Heroes*, to a poem of Randall Swingler, dedicated to those who fell in the Spanish civil war. It was written for tenor solo and orchestra, and when Walter Widdop, the soloist, had taken his bow with the other performers, the young B.B. came on to much applause. The interval followed, and then Widdop and Britten came and sat next to us for the rest of the concert. I asked him for his autograph on the programme (I still have it) and from then on I listened to every new work that came from his pen. He became my 'favourite composer' for purely personal reasons, but this little encounter opened my ears to other contemporaries – Walton, Tippett and others. This widened my horizons enormously, even though I didn't easily come to terms with very dissonant music. When fifteen I once wrote a worried letter after hearing a Bloch Quintet, asking for help, which was published in the *Musical Times*. They gave me helpful advice.

Twenty-five years later, now a parish priest in Ruabon, I was still learning the breadth of music. I had been reading Alec Robertson's autobiography, entitled *More Than Music*. As a leading member of the BBC's music department I greatly admired his broadcasts. In the light of his moving description in the book of setting aside his ordained ministry in the Catholic Church for health reasons, I wrote to thank him for a story well told. I also added my anecdote about meeting Benjamin Britten. To my delight he replied, and told me that he had on his desk the score of Britten's *War Requiem,* due to receive its first performance at Coventry Cathedral soon. 'This is profound and should be lasting,' he said, and I made a careful note of that. He also added a bit of sound advice to me: 'Take care not to overwork.' I should have thought about that many times. It was perhaps the only way I could cope with what I thought were the demands on a parish priest concerned with the whole community of people in my area, not just the Catholics. I falsely imagined that I was indispensable till someone pointed out to me that the graveyard was full of indispensable people. Probably it was one of the false ways one makes up for the emotional gaps left by celibacy. A better way would have been to take more time off to listen to more music. I did have a Manichean tendency to think it was wrong just to sit still and absorb music, when there were so many things that obviously needed doing.

This had not been helped in the early years of my priesthood by working for an unmusical bishop. In the three and a half years I served as his secretary, I only had about three 'days off', as I tried to combine so many jobs with being secretary, including the parish work to which I was later appointed. This was not episcopal tyranny, but my over-enthusiasm. I don't think the bishop noticed. He worked hard himself. For my summer holidays I booked in at the Three Choirs Festival, where I was going to attend two, or even three, concerts each day. When I told him, he gave a smile as well as a dismissive grunt, 'Huh! Sensual orgy!' But then his special recreation was going to a circus. At least annually he teamed up with the Bishop of Gibraltar to attend one – not my cup of tea. One night, not long after midnight, I was driving him home from a dinner with the Knights of St Columba to which he was a devoted ecclesiastical adviser. It had been held in Belle Vue, Manchester, and I was in none too easy a mood at the end of a (for me) dull evening, aware that even after the sixty mile drive back to Wrexham I had a short night ahead, so that I could be up to offer the 7.00 am Mass at a nearby convent, as was my wont. I was quasi-chaplain there also. The car headlights picked up an enormous poster advertising a forthcoming circus. The bishop said, 'Do you like circuses, Owen?' I guessed what might be coming – a suggestion that we came to one together. 'No,' I said, rather baldly. 'My God, haven't you any low tastes?' he retorted. Touché! After Alec Robertson's signal alert about the Britten *War Requiem,* I was determined to listen to its live broadcast of the first performance. That very day I had been in London for some meeting or other and had stayed the previous night with my brother and his wife in Putney. I set off to drive back to Ruabon to be in time for the broadcast, but as this was to be part of the opening celebrations of the new cathedral in Coventry, I turned off the motorway at mid-day to pay a quick visit. To my dismay the cathedral was closed for a couple of hours, while the Requiem was being rehearsed, so I walked round the city. I happened to pass the Festival ticket of-fice, and on enquiry found I could get a seat for the performance. I gladly paid up for this, and I shall always be thankful I did. All the musical world seemed to have assembled, and I had a chance of a chat with Imogen Holst, not seen for many years, and with Donald Swann who had been with me in the FAU. (On one occasion he acted as the accompanist for a little nurses' choir I had organised at Christmas.) Of course I bought records of the *War Requiem* as soon as it was available, and I was present for the first concert-hall performance in the Albert Hall.

My rather frequent London journeys for the Catholic Youth Association – up to twelve each year – facilitated concert-going. As soon as the meetings were over I'd go to a concert and catch the night train back in time for morning Mass in Ruabon. Otherwise it was a matter of arranging summer holidays to co-incide with music festivals. I managed these at least twice at Edinburgh, at Luzern and the Netherlands as well as the Three Choirs Festival.

My tastes were expanding slowly. I was determined, for in-stance, to have a go at Schoenberg. I bought records of some of his more 'difficult' music. I played them over and over again while I typed letters, etc. After a while I sat down to listen prop-erly, and I found that I had already got used to the language, and they no longer seemed unreachable. In a similar way I over-came my cultural prejudice against Wagner for his anti-semi-tism. I had earlier memories of the Monday nights of Henry Woods' Proms, which were given over largely to Wagner ex-cerpts; they had not attracted me. Now however the Third Programme took to broadcasting one act at a time of his massive operas. Suddenly I would be overwhelmed by the majesty of the writing, and I'd have to stop what I was doing and wallow. I had even ignored *Die Meistersinger* till one evening I heard bits of it as I moved between the house and the Youth Club. When the master-song came round in the third act, I sat down, my eyes wet with emotion. Now music for me is not of course always the cause of religious emotion. Sometimes it seems almost diabolical (e.g. bits of Strauss's *Elektra* or *Salome,* or Schoenberg's *Erwartung*). Sometimes I am quite frightened by Ravel's *Bolero.* But in the context of prayer and liturgical services it can elevate my spirit more than words on their own. I love Gregorian chant, but that depends on it being sung well. It is romantic nonsense for most parishes to bewail its passing; it was often poorly chosen and badly sung. I still think the *De Angelis* Kyrie is very dreary; and some of the long Alleluias and Graduals leave me cold. I sincerely hope some places, especially monastic communities, keep it alive.

Music in the Catholic Church was in pretty poor shape when I first experienced it. Participation by the whole congregation was minimal, and not many of the little choirs were very inspiring. The Anglican tradition of psalmody in parishes was on average of much better quality than anything Catholics sang. Hymns were kept for the mainly vernacular evening service of Benediction. Some had good reason to be old favourites of the people, but nineteenth-century words were sometimes a bit flowery. We only slowly moved to sharing the settings of the English Hymnal till our own anthologies came to be very similar to those of Anglicans. With the arrival on our desks of the Constitution on the Liturgy – the first document to emerge from Vatican II – a whole fresh look was given in principle to liturgical celebration. Unfortunately it was often very badly conveyed to the people by priests who had been brought up with a totally different understanding of liturgy and their own role in it. Very few were given any chance of a sabbatical break to study liturgy again. It has sometimes meant that vernacular hymns are substituted for the former antiphonal chants, and we have largely developed a 'hymn sandwich' approach to parish Masses. There are huge resources, formal and informal, to help people grow in their understanding of the Mass and therefore of the propriety or otherwise of certain kinds of music at the most significant moments. There is a plethora of some really inspiring music in use and it has been wonderful to see the skilled and knowledgeable parish musicians working for real improvement. In my own

diocese a really notable series of training days has recently benefited everyone.

Music has a power to draw people into prayer, and one only
has to look at the astounding effect of the use of Taizé chants, not
only at the community's home in Burgundy, but across the
world and the denominations, to exemplify this. That is not
everyone's experience and it does not do to pressurise people
into singing when they have no voice or liking for it, but some
Catholics' resistance has been determined by a wholly inadequate grasp of the difference between personal and public
worship.

For myself it is true that 'to sing is to pray twice'. Even the
most uninteresting words can be elevated by a shared chant. I
reflected on this during my extended stay on Caldey Island
when worshipping seven times a day with the Cistercian
monks. I tried to share the whole of the monastic horarium
while there. I noticed how much more prayerfully I joined in the
simple chanted psalms of Lauds, the day hours, Vespers and
Compline, than in those of the night Vigils, because the latter
were only recited on a single note. It may partly be from the fact
that a fair number of the 'aggressive' psalms are recited at Vigils,
and I truly find them very difficult to empathise with. I simply
have no experience of enemies such as the psalmist complains
about, and even though historically the saints and martyrs of the
church have had fervent enemies, ready to persecute and kill
them, the Christian response is still meant to be that of love, and
of prayer for their forgiveness. The psalmist continually calls on
God to curse and even obliterate the enemy, and seems to take
delight in doing so.

Some might put my failing attention at night Vigils down to
the fact that one had just got out of bed at 3.30 am. This however
was not so hard as I had expected, as I contentedly had retired at
8.30 pm; in the winter months it was at least dark at that time,
and I have a great gift of sleep. Quite how I would have managed in the summer I am not so sure. But why one earth do the
monks impose on themselves this strange use of time? When I
first became a Catholic I was told they did so to ensure that
prayer was being offered while the rest of the world was asleep.
'In that case,' I thought to myself – but was too polite to say so
openly – 'they must be flat-earthers. Didn't they know that their
Christian brothers and sisters in antipodean continents would

be awake while they slept?' Well, the Caldey monks are certainly
not flat-earthers, because they regularly sing the well-known
hymn at Compline, which assures them:

> As o'er each continent and island,
> The dawn brings on another day
> The voice of prayer is never silent,
> Nor dies the voice of praise away.

There must be some other reason. Early hours of the morning
can be conducive to prayer – but 3.30 am? That's a bit beyond
my normal capacity! There are quite a number of verses in the
psalms which mean very little to me – I should certainly have
done some proper study of them long before this stage of my
life. Yet when chanted with others in a monastic setting they do
not draw me away from the attention I try to give to God himself.
The chant is already a prayer in itself. Even when I'm on my
own at home I like to chant some parts of the office especially the
evening canticle, and the *Salva nos Domine* of Compline – yes, in
Latin too! Several of the vernacular settings of biblical texts have
etched themselves into my mind and heart. I remember with affection the first English version of Compline from the composer
Anthony Milner – alas, too little utilised. I don't think we encouraged the right people early enough in the liturgical renewal.

It is valuable sometimes to reflect on what we are actually
doing when we sing the praises of our God. Someone once said
to me that God must get very bored by being praised by his people all the time. One quick response has been to turn to the
fourth weekday Preface of the Roman Rite.

> Father all powerful ever-living God, we do well always and
> everywhere to give you thanks. You have no need of our
> praise, yet our desire to thank you is itself your gift. Our
> prayer of thanksgiving adds nothing to your greatness, but
> makes us grow in your grace, through Jesus Christ our Lord.

In 1952 (I see from my notebook) I came across a passage in
Newman's preface to his *Hymni Ecclesiae:*

> The peculiarity of the psalms is their coming nearer than any
> other kind of devotion to a converse with the power of the
> unseen world. They are longer and freer than prayers: and,
> as being so, are less a direct address to the Throne of Grace
> than a sort of intercourse, first with oneself, then with one's
> brethren, then with saints and angels, nay, even the world

and all creatures. They consist mainly of the praises of God, and the very nature of praise involves a certain abstinence from intimate approaches to him, and the introduction of other beings into our thoughts, through whom our offering may come round to him. For as he, and he only, is the direct object of prayer, so it is more becoming not to regard him as directly addressed in praise, which would imply passing a judgement on him, who is above all scrutiny and all standards. The Seraphim cried to one another, 'Holy, holy, holy', veiling their faces, neither looking at nor speaking to him. The Psalms then, as being praises and thanksgivings are the language, the ordinary converse, as it may be called, of saints and angels in heaven and hearing such, could not be written except by men who had heard the 'unspeakable things' which there are uttered. In this light they are more difficult than prayers. Beggars can express their wants to a prince; they cannot converse like his courtiers.

This long extract prefaces some of Newman's fine translations of the ordinary Office hymns, which I have often used; but I'm glad this insight came to help me early on in saying the breviary.

A fair number of the Grail version of the psalms have become real favourites, and they are well suited to the chants of Jospeh Gelineau. What delighted me at Caldey Abbey was that the monks had seized on some of the fine chants of the Anglican tradition, and, greatly to my surprise, found that they sounded well, even without accompaniment and without harmonisation. I should never have believed this if I had not experienced it, for it has always been my joy to sing the Anglican chants in full harmony ever since my schooldays. There was never any time at Marlborough when I was not in the choir for the daily service. I still hasten in any cathedral city to be present for Evensong, largely for the sake of the chanted psalms. Those unaccustomed to this tradition would be right in having an impression that Evensong was non-participative for the congregation until the final hymn, but brought up in the tradition, one enters into the prayerfulness of the chant.

One of the slightly unkind stories – but inoffensive to those who know the background – is about the Catholic university chaplain of Oxford (or was it Cambridge?) who went to the university Club (Oxford/Cambridge Union) with a notice, listing the times of Mass, etc. at the chaplaincy to be posted up. 'Sorry

sir,' said the porter at Reception, 'we don't allow religious notices in the Union.' The chaplain moved away sadly, but as he
passed the noticeboard, he saw the complete list of New College
services (or Kings College at the other place). Angrily he turned
to remonstrate. 'Look here,' he said, 'you've got the New
College (King's College) services posted; why not mine?' 'That
isn't religion sir,' the porter said, 'that's concerts.' Well, you
could perhaps say that the specially performed anthem at
Evensong is a 'concert' piece; but the chanted psalms are musical prayers.

There have been frequent complaints about some of the modern vernacular versions of the psalms. Some of them may be
from the Hebrew rather than the Latin versions, and I am not
competent to judge what is literally correct. Some of the poetic
phrases of Coverdale's psalms, however clumsy at times, appeal
to me more than the possibly more accurate Grail version.

One comparison may make this clear. The versions are of
Psalm 48/49.

Grail
Hear this all you peoples
Give heed all who dwell in the world
Men both low and high
Rich and poor alike.

My lips will speak words of wisdom
My heart is full of insight
I will turn my mind to a parable
With the harp I will solve my problem.

Why should I fear in evil days
The malice of the foes who surround me
Men who trust in their wealth
And boast of the vastness of their riches.

For no man can buy his own ransom
Nor pray a price to God for his life
The ransom of his soul is beyond him
He cannot buy life without end
Nor avoid coming to the grave.

Coverdale
O hear ye this, all ye people
Ponder it with your ears, all ye that dwell in the world

High and low, rich and poor
One with another.

My mouth shall speak of wisdom
and my heart shall muse of understanding
I will incline mine ear to the parable
and show my dark speech upon the harp.

Wherefore should I fear in the days of wickedness
and when the wicked at my heels compasseth me round
about
There be some that put their trust in their goods
And boast themselves in the multitude of their riches.

But no man may deliver his brother
Nor make agreement unto God for him
For it cost more to redeem their souls
So that he must let that alone for ever
Yea, though he live long, and see not the grave.

If you add to the Coverdale version the fine chant 'Walmsley in F', you have something incomparably more prayerful than the competent and no doubt correct Grail version.

We could, incidentally, do with a 'common market' resolution of the trouble caused by the differing numbering of most of the psalms. It would almost be a heresy in England to speak of the psalm 'The Lord is my shepherd', and its several metrical versions, as anything other than 'the 23rd psalm'. Yet for Catholics it is the 22nd. Confusion can similarly be caused by the differing numbering of the Ten Commandments. Wasn't there a film entitled 'The Sixth Commandment', which proved disappointing to one whole set of Christians?

My reservations about the spiritual helpfulness of some of the psalms could be extended to a lot of the Old Testament. I notice how selectively we all use and quote from the scriptures. I have already used two quotations from the Book of Ecclesiasticus. Yet I am truly upset by the attitude expounded in Chapter 25 about women, and I am appalled at some of the suggestions for bringing up children in Chapter 30: 'Do not share your child's laughter, if you do not wish to share his sorrow and to end by grinding your teeth. Allow him no independence in childhood and do not wink at his mistakes. Bend his neck in youth, bruise his ribs while he is a child, or else he will grow stubborn and disobedient and hurt you very deeply.'

I recently discovered a passage in Dom Aelred Graham's *The End of Religion* which expresses what I certainly feel about 'biblical prayer'.

One of the duties of Benedictines is to recite or sing together in community the psalms. The practice might well be studied afresh with a view to revision. Inspired, so we are taught, by the Holy Spirit, these Hebrew poems appear, for the most part, as very much bound up with a time and place that are simply not ours. Frequently self-righteous in sentiment and rancorous in tone, they are an odd form of address to a God whose essence, according to Christian belief, is love. The best of them ... can hardly be surpassed in any form of worship but they cannot, for all their solemn impact, extinguish the critical spirit. Even the touching 23rd psalm (see what I mean? Even a Catholic monk doesn't say 22nd.) is marred for me by our being notified that the Lord's banquet is prepared, derisively one presumes, 'in the presence of my enemies'. We are here at some remove, or so I feel, from the worship due to a God who 'makes his sun rise on the evil and on the good, and sends his rain on the just and on the unjust'. And yet it is pleasant to engage in psalmody with one's monastic brethren in the early morning hours or at evening. Being at worship with those to whom one is linked by so many communal ties turns the rhythmic chanting into an agreeable lullaby, soothing one through, unnoticed, when need be, the not so agreeable words.

These are my sentiments entirely.

Dom Aelred was an Ampleforth monk who helped for many years in a foundation in the USA. He once came, during my university vacation, to St Mary's Priory in Canton, Cardiff, for a brief stay. He came to my home in Llandaff one afternoon for tea and a chat, though he was 'on call' at the parish. Somehow the phone bell wasn't heard by us in the garden, and when the Priory did catch up with us, it seemed he was supposed to be doing a baptism. A car came swiftly to collect him – I believe the candidate was from the Spanish consulate. Dom Aelred was not an absent-minded cleric, but when he wrote his fine book *Zen Catholicism*, one of his brethren said, 'Dom Aelred? Yes, he's the monk who has gone right through the Catholic Church and come out on the other side!'

I recently came across something written by Beethoven

which perhaps helps me to relate the sacred to the secular meaning of music.

> Every real creation of art is independent, more powerful than the artist himself, and returns to the divine through its manifestation. It is one with man only in this, that it bears testimony to the mediation of the divine in him.

Certainly not all composers are explicitly religious people – sometimes they seem, like Delius, to be religiously irreligious. But the effect of their music is not unlike a religious experience. James MacMillan suggests that 'music is a phenomenon connected to the work of God because it invites us to touch what is deepest in our souls and to release within us a divine force. Music opens doors to a deepening and broadening of understanding. It invites connections between organised sound and lived experience or suspected possibilities. In the connection is found the revelation, a realisation of something not grasped before. Such "seeing" offers revelations about human living and divine relationship that can affect changes in our choices, our activities and our convictions.'

On four or five occasions I have spent a week at the Cheltenham Music Festival, very conveniently staying with my brother and his wife in Cirencester. The President for many years was the composer Sir Lennox Berkeley, and the festival began on a Sunday with a fine act of worship in the best Anglican tradition. It occurred to me that there was a second Sunday when we might celebrate using the whole range of music from the Catholic tradition. Sir Lennox was a Catholic, so I put the suggestion to him, and this was passed to the Music Director. Accordingly I was empowered in 1979, and the following year, to arrange an evening Mass at St Gregory's parish church which would incorporate plainchant, polyphony, and vernacular hymnody. The parish was staffed by monks of Douai Abbey, and with the help of monks from Prinknash Abbey, and the choir from Clifton Cathedral, under my friend Christopher Walker, we put together a fine liturgy. It began with the choir's procession to a hymn by Anthony Milner, and then the monks entered with the plainchant Introit, and they led the Latin Gradual, Offertory and Communion antiphons. The Clifton choir sang Byrd's five-part setting of the Common of the Mass. The sermon was preached by Dom Gregory Murray of Downside, himself a distinguished organist, and the Bidding

Prayers were read by Sir Lennox, and myself introducing the *Salve Regina*. The Festival authorities had a detailed outline of the liturgy in the official brochure, and also leaflets for the congregation on the day. The church was filled to the doors, in large measure perhaps by those Catholics who yearned for a dignified Latin liturgy. It was a grand occasion, graciously supported by the Mayor and Mayoress of Cheltenham, and lasted nearly two hours, which meant a quick scamper across to the Town Hall for the final concert of the Festival.

Another composer I had the pleasure of knowing was Edmund Rubbra, who had a musical Fellowship in Oxford at the time of my post-war return. Both of us had recently become Catholics, with different and mutual connections with the Dominicans, and we found we had much to talk about when he came to tea in my New College rooms. From then we wrote to each other once a year. His spiritual odyssey took him beyond the confines of the church, I think, but the personal contact has imbued his music for me with some special warmth. In one letter he wrote in praise of the music of Anthony Milner, referring especially to one of my favourites, *Salutatio Angelica*. 'This is a wonderful work,' he said, 'and you see it is listed as his Opus 1.'

A quaint encounter arose in 1971, when I had not seen Rubbra for over twenty years. In that year I was back at my year of study in Cardiff. I am a man of regular habits, and each morning as I arrived at college I passed the same young man walking briskly into the city. One evening I went to the launderette near my lodgings, and he happened to be there also. Nothing very extraordinary about this. But when the academic year was over I was driving in west Wales paying my first visit to St David's Cathedral. As I walked down the nave I heard organ music, and then it stopped while the organist came to discuss something with a bearded man who I felt sure was Edmund Rubbra; by his side was that young man from Cardiff. I went up to him to reintroduce myself, and in turn Rubbra said, 'Oh yes; and this is my stepson, Adrian Yardley.' 'We haven't actually met,' I replied, 'but we share the same launderette.' Adrian and I met only once since then briefly at a Cheltenham concert, and I note with pleasure that the 'programme notes' issued with Rubbra's recorded *Sinfonia Sacra* in 1996 are written by Adrian.

Another anecdote relates to my journey in 1949 to Canada with my mother. We were staying in a Toronto hotel. As I got into the lift one morning the only other occupant was Sir Adrian Boult. I've never been short of a word on these occasions, and the link for me was with his stepson, Jonathan Wilson, next to whom I had stood for a year as a bass in the Marlborough College choir. Jonathan was a quiet, reserved young man, and a book of his poems was published posthumously after he had been killed in the war. Jumping over the years to the 1960s, Sir Adrian was conducting the final concert at the Llangollen International Festival. For some reason I called in at the Royal Hotel, and found him having breakfast. The only thing I had to say this time was to remind him that we had shared a lift in Toronto!

However it is out of little memories like this that I have built my personal world of music interest. It had begun as far back as 1936 when, as a twelve year old, I had sat behind Sir Walford Davies, the Master of the King's Music, at the Cardiff Eisteddfod where he was to be one of the adjudicators. I clutched his Book, *The Pursuit of Music,* and he wrote in it '...with Owen Hardwicke' before signing it. In later years I sat behind Francis Poulenc at the Wigmore Hall, and at my visits to the Three Choirs Festivals, watched with awe as Ralph Vaughan Williams, Herbert Howells, and other special visitors like Zoltan Kodaly, moved around among the audiences.

In 1964 at the Hereford Festival a new work by Anthony Milner, *The Water and the Fire,* was to be performed under his baton. The work described musically the symbolism of the Paschal Mystery, and I followed it with a piano score. I was extremely disappointed that no-one seemed to be present from the Catholic press. So I wrote a piece for *The Tablet* and suggested that, *faute de mieux,* it might be considered for publication. And it was. Owen Hardwicke – music critic! This was my only venture of this kind.

On a much later occasion, after Anthony's symphony had been commissioned and performed by the BBC Symphony Orchestra, Anthony and I went as audience to a Prom concert. The programme included Berlioz's *Nuits d'Eté,* a passionate favourite of mine. To my initial astonishment it was a work hardly known to Anthony, and for the first time I realised how vast the literature of music is, and how unsurprising that a composer of distinction was not acquainted with an item that a mere amateur listener like me had come across.

'And who is then your favourite composer?' people sometimes ask; a question that is not patient of a simple answer. It depends what time of day it is, which day of the week and how I
am feeling. As a schoolboy I always answered, 'Beethoven,' but
I had already thrilled to the experience of singing in the choir for
Bach's *B Minor Mass*, Mozart's *Requiem*, Haydn's *Creation*, all of
which had left an indelible mark. My Quaker housemaster, R. A.
U. Jennings (known to the boys as Jumbo Jennings) told me with
a smile that he thought Beethoven was a 'vulgar composer' – he
was trying for a reaction, I think. He said, correctly as it turned
out, that I'd grow to love the slow movements of symphonies
and quartets more as I grew older. He reckoned also that at the
end of even a very musical day, one would want some J. S. Bach
to finish.

Jennings was a fine man. Though a Quaker he attended the
daily Anglican service in the college chapel. He kept in touch
with me through and after the war and came to Cardiff for my
ordination as a Catholic priest. After Vatican II when our liturgy
began to develop, and we inserted short periods of silence at
Mass, he felt prompted to write to me again. In his retirement he
did some voluntary teaching in Salisbury at a convent school.
When there he would occasionally go to Mass with the pupils.
He wrote: 'I find that Mass gets more and more like Quaker
meeting every week!'

He was right about Bach. I would dearly love to be assured of
a cantata a day. It would take many months to get through them
all. I have never quite understood how music with such 'mathe-
matical' precision can often be so moving.

An early memory at school is of being moved by a rendering
of the song *Bist Du Bei Mir* by a young boy soprano, Peter
Heyworth. Didn't he become a leading music critic?

The Friends Ambulance Unit spawned other musicologists.
William Mann – I recall him singing in a jokey way to the slow
movement theme of Beethoven's Sixth, *'Sie haben, sie haben, sie
haben es gehabt'*, just as 'You've had it' came into slang usage in
English. Another was Julian Budden, the Verdi expert, and a frequent broadcaster. We met up one day, after 35 years gap, at
Broadcasting House. I wondered as I waited for him, 'Will I
recognise him after all these years?' Just then I saw him emerge
from the lift, look around the hall, approach an elderly man,
then stop and turn round and catch my eye. He was obviously

having the same problem as me. We had an agreeable lunch chat together.

Well, who are at least among my favourite composers, apart from the masters of classical music? Since I became addicted to opera, it has been – after Mozart, Handel and Monteverdi – the operas of Richard Strauss and Janacek. My seventieth birthday was celebrated by attending *Der Rosenkavalier* at the New Theatre in Cardiff. As a memento Deborah Parry Edwards, a member of the WNO chorus, had arranged for me to have a large poster signed by all the cast, *'Penblwydd Hapus!'*

For the rest I have rather set aside any adventures into 'new' music. I strongly approve of contemporary composers having a generous chance to be heard. I have been very taken by some of the clearly religious music of John Tavener, Arvo Part and others, and I still like to grapple occasionally even with works I don't particularly like on first hearing. I enjoyed John Amis's *Tablet* review of the 1996 performance of Schoenberg's *Moses and Aaron* (and this is by no means 'new'). He indicated that he saw Schoenberg as one of the four giants of the first half of this century's composers, with Stravinsky, Bartok and Hindemith. He went on:

'The final duet is almost the only moment during more than two hours when the sounds are at all easy on the ears. The rest of the music is atonal, thick and gruff. Schoenberg's music takes no account of the fact that, like most things terrestrial, music is subject to the laws of gravity. Our ears are conditioned to accept a suggestion of tonality in the lowest note of a phrase, chord or sequence of notes. Our ears expect a harmonic root.'

Amis was not criticising the performance, nor the competence of the composer. He said:

'The performance was, as far as I could follow it in the score and dim lighting, exemplary with such colouristic moments as there are being highlighted by the conductor … I must record that the audience was enthusiastic. I came out longing for a drink and a simple chord of D major.'

I know what he means. I'd even settle for C Major. I'm not averse however to making special efforts to stretch my ears, but with so much Mozart, Handel, Haydn, and Bach still unheard by me, as a listener I am growing less patient than I was sixty years ago with the obscurities of 'musique concrete' and the like.

And is it all, as my bishop suggested, merely a 'sensual orgy'? Certainly not, though I regret I am only a passive listener and not even a mild performer. Apart from my failure in piano playing, I took up the oboe in 1940. The school orchestra was short of an oboist and provided the music was simple and not too fast, I managed to be incorporated in the playing. On arrival in Oxford in 1942 I contacted Sir Thomas Armstrong and was given an audition for joining the orchestra to accompany the Bach Choir for a major performance of Bach's *B Minor Mass:* only two rehearsals were left. I was nervous as well as excited, and grateful for the help of a bassoonist, who had little to play, guiding me along the score. One evening I went to a concert at the Town Hall when Evelyn Rothwell (Lady Barbirolli) was the oboe soloist. That slightly depressed me. How could I ever reach that quality of tone? Then came the final rehearsal for the Mass. Who was sitting beside me as first oboist but Evelyn Rothwell! I survived, but that's all.

At one of the Cheltenham Festival Masses, of which I have spoken, I arranged for a collection to be taken for the Musicians Benevolent Fund, of which Sir Thomas Armstrong was Chairman or Patron. In forwarding the sizeable cheque I reminded him of that Oxford performance of thirty years earlier, and he sent a very gracious reply.

My great musical hero had been Leon Goossens, the great oboe player. In 1946 while still with the FAU, I had to drive and deliver a vehicle to Vienna, I can't think why. So I drove the long journey to Klagenfurt for a night's stop. The following day I set off towards Vienna and came to the end of the British occupied zone. The military guard asked me how I was going to get through the Russian zone without a 'grey card'. I'd never heard of the necessity of 'grey cards', but somehow I managed with a bribe of 200 NAAFI cigarettes to the Russian guard about 50 yards further on, to get through

On arrival in Vienna I signed in at the Officers' Transit hotel – FAU men were neither officers or 'other ranks' so we used whatever facilities were available, usually without being questioned. I then walked into a civilian, Mr Colville, who had been on the teaching staff at Marlborough. He was delighted to discover that I had a 15 cwt truck. 'Can you help me? I have to collect someone from the airport tomorrow and take him across the city to the train for Graz. I work for the British Council and we are helping to revive the Graz music festival.' 'Who is it?' I asked. 'The oboist, Leon Goossens.' I was thrilled to do this, and as we drove across the city with him in my windowless truck, with Mr Colville balancing on the battery box between us, Goossens told us about his early family memories of pre-war Vienna. I was 'de-mobbed' a month later, and back in Cardiff in September, await-ing my return to Oxford, I saw a newspaper notice that a concert at which Goossens was to play that night had been cancelled be-cause he had been struck down with flu. I hastened to the Lord Ninian Nursing Home and loaned Goossens my little radio till he was better. 'Did you tell him that you also played the oboe?' asked my father. 'Dad! Really!'

In 1961 I was parish priest when the Welsh National Eisteddfod came to the Maelor, within my parish boundaries. It was the custom for the Welsh Catholic Society, *Y Cylch Catholig,* to hire its own tent on the Eisteddfod field. I noted that the major choral work to be sung at the final concert was to be Elgar's *Dream of Gerontius.* So I commissioned a fine artist, who had painted the Stations of the Cross for our new church in Ruabon, to paint four pictures based on four quotations from Newman's fine text, but in Welsh. Then I started a search for the manu-scripts of the poem and score in the hope of borrowing them for display also. Quickly I located Newman's manuscript at the Oratory in Birmingham which Newman had founded. Father Basil Lynch's letter gave me some entertaining facts about musi-cal versions of the work.

'We shall be very glad to lend you Newman's manuscript of Gerontius for the Eisteddfod. I could send it by registered post, or bring it to Ruabon myself, if you could arrange to meet the train by which I frequently go to Chester. I am as-tonished to learn that Gerontius is being performed – I thought it was an exclusively Welsh programme. How times change! Dvorak came here in about 1896 to see the poem, which he wanted to set for the Birmingham Festival. The Festival authorities refused his offer as it was too Popish – so he wrote them a Mass instead. Elgar's Dream was written for the same festival years later, and only elicited a few growls of complaint.'

Stage One achieved. Now for Elgar's score. Somehow I found the address of his daughter, Mrs Elgar Blake, and she replied to my letter as follows:

'Thank you for your letter. What a pity the Oratory Fathers

did not tell you that they possessed the full score of *The Dream of Gerontius*. My father gave it to them after the first performance. They guard it very jealously, and I have known people having great difficulty in persuading them to lend it, but perhaps they will be kind to you. I am afraid there is nothing I can do to help. His other manuscripts are nearly all on loan or in the care of the British Museum. The second symphony is at his birthplace near Worcester. That could be borrowed if you could manage to get it and insure it. But it would not seem to be so suitable for the occasion. I only hope they will let you have Gerontius.

Yours sincerely, Carice Elgar Blake

So I won through in the end, and the Oratory Fathers graciously loaned me the poem and the score. I drove to Birmingham to collect them, and slept with these precious items under my pillow! Through the week of the Eisteddfod I spent many hours in the Cylch tent, turning the pages for people to see. I could almost say that I got to know the poem and the score upside down and back to front. Many members of the performing choirs from Rhosllanerchrugog came to have a close look. One morning quite early, and before the crowds had swarmed onto the Eisteddfod field, one choir member came back again on his own. With awe he looked at Elgar's score and his signature over the famous quotation (from John Ruskin, I think) which Elgar had put on the title page:

'This is the best of me: for the rest I ate and drank and slept, loved and hated, like another; my life was as the vapour and is not; but this I saw and knew: this, if anything of mine, is worth your memory.' Edward Elgar, Birchwood Lodge August 13th 1900

Here too was the entry and signature of Hans Richter, the conductor of the first performance:

'Let drop the chorus; let drop everybody
But let not drop the wings of your original genius.'

The viewer was silent for a while, then said to me, 'There are some moments in one's life one never forgets; and this will be one of them. May I touch it?' I found this very moving myself, and began to understand better the meaning of the veneration of relics in our tradition – though I doubt if a nonconformist from Rhosllanerchrugog would have recognised it.

At the performance on the final night of the Eisteddfod I had a good seat, and, perhaps a little ostentatiously, followed it with Elgar's score on my lap throughout. In the interval I took it back stage to show Arwel Hughes, the conductor, and some members of the orchestra.

I say it again. It is little personal items like this that actually help my attention to, and appreciation of, works of art. Music will always be at the heart of my understanding of God's creation and the fundamental goodness of the humanity he inspires.

'To listen seriously to music and to perform it are among the most potent ways of learning what it is to live with and before God, learning a service that is perfect freedom. No-one and nothing can compel our contemplation except the object in its own right. In this "obedience" of listening and following, we are stretched and deepened, physically challenged as performers, imaginatively as listeners. The time we have renounced, given up, is given back to us as a time in which we have become more human, more real, even if we can't say what we have learned; only that we have changed.' (Archbishop Rowan Williams)

'I'm sorry sir, but that's one of the things
that listeners are not meant to know.'

[Cartoon: Angelo Edwards]

'Miss Jones, Meister Eckhart said that
only the ignorant know everything.'
[Cartoon: Angelo Edwards]

Part Six

The Basics and the Future
1999 – ?

Chapter Thirteen:
With a Commitment to Unity: One Bread, One Body
A fundamental issue from the 1960s parish work days has been that of ecumenism. We have seen a leap forward in church thinking, especially through Redintegratio Unitatis, *the Vatican II document. Yet local ecumenical practice has often been slight and slow. The Bishops' Conference publication,* One Bread, One Body, *ended up with 'norms' for sharing communion that I found not only disappointing but theologically unsound. That is a dangerous assertion, so I try to explain.*

Chapter Fourteen:
In the Freedom of Retirement: A vision or a hunch?
Here I end with some incomplete reflections on where things might move in the new millennium, especially in the development of ministries and priesthood. Someone thought it might serve as a 'taster' for the whole book, so – before I had acquired the support of a publisher – it was printed in advance.

[Courtesy of *The Tablet*]

CHAPTER THIRTEEN

In Communion with Fellow Christians: One Bread, One Body

It is difficult to explain to those who have lived within one tradition of church life since childhood what it is like to leave one tradition for another. Some, alas, change allegiances because of personal squabbles or disappointment, or under some kind of social pressure. Others really do come up against doctrinal difficulties which seem to demand a move. As I tried to explain in Chapter One, my journey was more like that of one from partiality to fullness, even though there was a period of a few years after 'conversion' to Roman Catholicism when my new-found loyalty seemed to push me towards a mild denigration of the Anglicanism I had left. I had however read Père Congar's *Divided Christendom* which left an indelible mark on my understanding of the potential for real ecumenism. However it was not until Vatican II and its *Decree on Ecumenism* that things really opened up.

Soon after becoming bishop's secretary in 1954, I gave evidence of my new ecclesiastical loyalty when there was published a pamphlet by Theomemphus called *Bilingual Bishops and All That*. It was part of an internal row within the church in Wales about the significance of cultural and national identity. I largely agreed with its intention, but chose to use it as a platform from which to express a very Roman view of the relationship of the Mystical Body of Christ to the Roman Catholic Church. In a response pamphlet – and perhaps 'tract' would be a more apt description – called *Bilingualism and the Language of Truth*, I asked for a deeper enquiry into what makes the church 'catholic'. I acknowledged that all those who are validly baptised already belong to this church, but I still looked for their 'conversion'.

The pamphlet, before its publication and distribution to all the Anglican clergy of Wales, had the scrutiny of several distinguished Welsh Catholics, such as Mrs Catherine Daniel. The bishop made some helpful comments and was evidently very pleased with it. I can now see how far we yet had to travel in appreciating in theological, not just charitable, terms what the Catholic nature of the church really is. My thinking changed within a year or two, probably due to more mature reflection on Congar's exposition and I wished I hadn't written it. I hope no copies survive.

When Pope John XXIII opened the windows of the church to let in some fresh air by calling the Second Vatican Council, there was a release into openness, a re-assessment of the Catholic faith, its practice and expression. We began to take seriously many of the questions which theologians like Congar had been asking for a long time, often only privately. We all began to discover that what was referred to as 'tradition' was only post-Reformation tradition. It was largely reactive to the break-up of western Christendom by the Reformed churches, and the rise of the sovereignty of nation-states.

There was a feeling that the prime Catholic virtue was loyalty to a hierarchic structure. Now we were being asked to look at our shared responsibility for truth, and a more adequate expression of it for our times. We used to have a strong argument in 'apologetics' about the 'marks of the true Church': she was to be One, Holy, Catholic and Apostolic – characteristics which were declared to point only to the Roman Catholic Church. Now – and I think the notion was explored by Hans Küng – we were to see that these were 'tasks' rather than 'marks'. The fullness of the church was still ahead of us – none of them had yet been properly achieved. We were still on our way towards real unity, radical holiness, and catholicity in the spirit of the apostles. So we could begin to look at Christians in other traditions in a new light.

I began to notice that what I had learned about Jesus Christ, and what I had been encouraged to treat as my commitment to him in the Anglican tradition, was wholly continuous with my journey as a Roman Catholic. I didn't have to cancel anything from the past, except perhaps a few negative misunderstandings, though I had discovered there was something more to catholicism than anglicanism. There is only one church, the Body of Christ, to which I had been joined by baptism; I had always belonged to it since then. It wasn't even the case that I had moved from one 'branch' to another. I still felt that I had moved into a different and more authentically catholic institution, and the Council's documents began to make sense of this for me theologically. We have moved further on since then, but the Council was an important watershed.

In the past one was encouraged to think charitably (somewhat condescendingly) of Christians in the Reformed churches, as no doubt sincere, but mistaken, people who could be described – and I shudder now at the phrase – as 'invincibly ignorant'. Some even used the term 'unconscious' or 'anonymous' Catholics, but I could soon identify more apt candidates for that dreadful title within my new communion!

It is still not easy for some Roman Catholics to make a radical adjustment here. The real challenge, as I see it, is not so much to have a different view of other Christians, as to have a more adequate understanding of the church and ourselves. We Roman Catholics have not yet arrived at the fullness of the kingdom any more than others. We are still on the way, and as much in need of repentance and renewal for our sinfulness and faint-heartedness as anyone else, but we are increasingly glad to welcome the insights of Christians in other traditions. We are grateful for being members not only of an invisible, spiritual communion, but one which has a visible order and legitimate authority. The fullness of the church in this world must have an external, organisational face. But the real essence of the church is her dependence on the continuing presence of the Holy Spirit.

A first attempt to move things forward

What did all this amount to in practice? The personal warm relationships that grew up in my first years of parish work in Ruabon, with the Anglican and Methodist clergy in particular, were agreeable, and a basic ingredient for ecumenism. It was quite hard work however to persuade parishioners, now experiencing a local Catholic parish life for the first time, to feel the need for wider contact with other Christians. I was often openly critical of their hesitations. But by 1968/9 my impatience at the slowness of ecumenical development made me try to work out a deliberate step forward. Accordingly I drafted a little document for discussion which outlined some immediate steps which might be taken locally, even though high-level dialogue about the theology and practice of ecumenism had a long way to go. In the event, it didn't get further than my desk because of my leaving Ruabon for other fields. I think now that it was flawed in several important respects, but as an essay in practical ecumenism it had some merits, and is worth recording here.

1. We Christians recognise that we are all in a period of transition. We acknowledge that between our various church 'communions' there are at present some differences in doctrine, in moral understanding, and in traditions of worship that cannot easily be harmonised. We realise that, as members of communions which have a membership and loyalty beyond the borders of our own locality, we cannot dictate or presume immediate or long-term solutions to the consequent problems; nor can we in truth minimise their importance.

2. Yet here and now we believe that there are many of us who have really grown close in the faith we share in God, supremely revealed to us through Jesus Christ, our Lord and Saviour. We believe that the Holy Spirit is still guiding the church as the community of believers, and that he is drawing us closer in unity, to bring an end to the denominational differences that separate us as 'churches'. We believe that we cannot be wholly disloyal to the several traditions we have received, however much we reckon them to be open to radical scrutiny. They cannot simply be jettisoned, and much remains to be done at the theological and organisational level. Yet we also believe that we neglect the impulse of the Holy Spirit if we wait until, at the fullest theological and administrative levels, the newer insights of our time have dissolved all the problems.

3. Accordingly we believe that we are being most faithful to the God who continues to reveal his will to us in these new times, by accepting the unity which he has already given us as individuals, and the awareness of which he is increasingly making clear. While we shall continue to be faithful to our own communions, we pledge ourselves to enter the fullest sharing of our joint Christian heritage at every level. Firstly we express our faith that in Jesus Christ all things are made new; that we witness together to the power of Christ to transform all human life and every earthly value. We revere that freedom which God has given to each one to experience and respond to his revelation in an entirely personal way. We acknowledge that the existence of a body of traditional

Christian belief and moral principle is not of itself sufficient to convince and guide all people; that the following of Christ must always be a free and personal discovery, which is apparently not always open to others; but that it is only a wilful refusal to see and respond that could invite God's condemnation.

4. We therefore resolve henceforth to regard ourselves openly as One in Christ – members of One Church, even though this cannot normally be expressed in the fullest way across all divisions. We resolve at least to think of ourselves (even if we cannot exactly label ourselves) and to treat one another as members of Christ's One Catholic Church. Further than this, we recognise that the fullest experience of sacramental inter-communion must ultimately involve those theological and ecclesiastical factors which are not under our very personal control. The occasional expression of limited inter-communion may however be a local obligation at this time, if our common faith is to be shared according to the will of Christ. For those who feel ready for this it can become an ecumenical imperative. Such celebrations should take place with the explicit intention of finding and following the will of Christ without over-delicate analysis of 'validity' or 'status'. In the first stages it would probably be desirable that the recognised 'ministers' of those Christians taking part, should jointly celebrate an act of worship with a simple liturgy of word and sacrament. This should take place on a day and at a time and in a place which will in no way create a sense of disunity with those Christians who do not yet feel able to take such a step. It would greatly hinder the work of wider unity if we were to disturb the real faith of those Christians who have not yet felt called to these approaches. There should be no attempt to press others thus far beyond their present ecumenical understanding. The occasions should be private, without being secret.

5. It must be made abundantly clear to whoever comes to such celebrations that no new 'church' is being founded, nor any breakaway group. What measure of technical disobedience to anyone's tradition may be implied is profoundly regretted. It is indeed as a gesture – experimental if you like – towards the achievement of full ecclesial communion. It is but a first step beyond the new spirit of charity already

achieved between groups of Christians, and the joint prayer and activities which have characterised some districts already for so long as to make the whole ecumenical endeavour empty unless there is a sign of further development. It may be that this local action may assist those at 'higher' levels to take courage to move ahead with greater conviction.

6. We do not ask for permission for this experiment from our various 'authorities' for we believe that at present this would be administratively or ecclesiastically impossible. We only ask that the whole idea is not expressly forbidden in any quarter, and heaped about with sanctions. It is not a 'free for all', but an action which will express and deepen the faith of those already known to one another at other ecumenical levels, without any slide into a religious indifferentism which would be unfruitful for the church as a whole.

7. It would likewise follow that, since we recognise baptism as the normal outward sign of our incorporation into Christ's fellowship, we should seek ways of jointly celebrating the sacrament of baptism of children, in the hope that this will assist them to grow up in an atmosphere of true ecumenism. The decision in personal faith to follow a particular tradition in later life would not be seen as in any way a separation from the one communion in principle. Such a decision we do not see simply as a matter of personal choice, but one which involves objective factors which at present constitute the basis of our separateness. It would normally and rightly depend on the tradition mainly followed from earliest years but – we express the extravagant hope – those children may mature in an age when the divisions have been seen to be unnecessary.

8. Such approaches do not claim to be impervious to faults or errors. We would not wish to formalise or 'establish' them; we would wish to review them constantly insofar as we find them assisting (or otherwise) in our closer incorporation into the One Body of Christ.

Well, as I have said, the document never got beyond my desk, and I can see now that it is full of ambiguities and immature thinking. Today I would replace the word 'inter-communion' with 'shared communion'. Also to involve ordained ministers of different traditions is really saying more than what could accord with institutional truth at present. But I don't regret trying to get some thinking and doing on a local scene. There were, no doubt, many alternative experiments going on across the country, but for the most part individual priests in the Catholic Church were interpreting their reading of the official texts to meet the local pastoral needs; and greater needs began to arise as we were obviously less stand-offish with one another. Joint retreats and other 'special days' found at least Anglicans and Catholics together with a closing eucharist, and it has been widespread practice for all to receive communion together. Increasingly this did not seem to be disobedient to the spirit of the law, however unofficial the decisions that were being taken. Everyone realised that before long there would have to be some formal cognisance given to practice. In 1993 there was an important Roman Directory for the Application of Principles and Norms on Ecumenism. This was clearly going to be the official line but it had yet to be translated into the circumstances of Britain. Meantime priests, and even bishops, were often known to give a generous interpretation to official rulings. Some insisted on clear permissions being given in each instance; others encouraged people to make their own conscientious decisions. With customary British evasion, some priests discouraged Anglicans from making requests which they might feel obliged to refuse – even though they would never refuse anyone who came to the sanctuary for communion.

Moving forward, backward or sideways?
So it was with enormous hope that we knew our bishops were working on a document which would give some rulings about sharing sacramental communion in our national context. Few of us realised that the Roman Directory would so radically govern the 'norms' which were to be published. That Directory intended 'to motivate, enlighten and guide' ecumenical activity, and in some cases 'to give binding directives'. To our surprise and disappointment, our bishops seem to have felt unable to evaluate what had actually been happening over the last twenty years or so, based on the living experience of those with a fervent ecumenical spirit.

One Bread, One Body appeared in October 1998 as a 'teaching document'. It had not been run past the bishops' consultative bodies, such as the National Conference of Priests, or the Conference of Religious, before its publication. We were to be 'the learning church', dependent on those established to be our only 'teachers', the bishops. It is fair to say (and some will think it condescending to do so) that it has very much to commend it as a teaching document. That it moves us forward not one fraction in pastoral practice is an almost unbelievable disappointment. The bishops try to be compassionate when they say they are aware of the pain 'and the difficulties of not being able to share one table of the Lord with our brothers and sisters in Christ' (118). They interpret that pain as an additional motivation for working towards full unity. The 'norms' with which they end up put in writing for the first time one or two of the special occasions when Christians of other traditions may receive communion at a Catholic Mass. Even those in the Association of Inter-church Families have given a positive response to this; after all, even one tiny step forward might lead to others. The bishops say, 'Many will have hoped for encouragement of greater sacramental sharing. Others will think we have gone too far.' They suggest that the norms they have set are the only way to decide in the light of the theological principles which precede them. The impression I get is of a Roman ruling which they feel obliged to uphold, and then a theology which attempts to make it acceptable. That is why, when challenged, we hear it said, 'There is nothing new here.' We have to presume that the bishops found total consensus within their ranks, however hard that is to reconcile with views expressed more privately through the years – not to mention the notable exemptions that have been made in practice across the Catholic world, and even in the Vatican.

Because so much time and thought has been put into *One Bread, One Body*, one is obliged to justify one's criticisms. However the bishops themselves say that the document is to be a 'source of study and reflection'. My own bishop sent a covering letter to say that the document 'is offered as a response ... [It is] neither exhaustive nor exclusive and is not the last word. Its value depends on how effectively it is used by Catholics and in ecumenical groups.' That surely must allow for critical questions to be asked, and perhaps challenges to be made, if any further word is to emerge for our guidance and practice. The immediate reaction of many Catholics suggests that there is a lot more that needs to be said. There is constantly an issue about what makes up the *sensus fidelium*, how it is discerned, and the extent to which it is influential on 'the mind of the church'. There really is an unresolved issue here around the need for teaching to be 're-ceived'.

Divided churches or divided Christians?

The theology of the eucharist is clearly, even beautifully, ex-pressed, yet somehow it seems to me inadequate on several counts. If then I dislike the norms for practice which appear at first sight to follow from this theology, at what point can I validly criticise? My difficulties stem from a theological and a pastoral perspective which I have not seen noted elsewhere.

The Decree on Ecumenism (*Redintegratio Unitatis*) recognised that, while the Christian churches are *de facto* divided in a way that seems to contradict the will of Christ, their adherents are not personally guilty of the sin of separation. They have been baptised and nurtured in a situation of division. They are one in Christ with all believers, members of One and the same Body of Christ. That is the case even if the church, as an ecclesiastical in-stitution, in which they witness and worship, stands in separa-tion from the Roman Catholic Church.

Accordingly while rulings can legitimately be made about officially organised denominational sharing (especially in sacra-mental worship), that should not interfere with the discernment which individuals need to make about how, when and where to act together as fellow Christians. Normally Christians worship – especially on Sundays – in their own communities. The presence of Christians from other traditions at a Catholic Mass is there-fore always in that sense abnormal or exceptional, however frequent it may happen to be, as with inter-church couples. Consequently any decision about the propriety of their receiv-ing sacramental communion cannot be made on the basis of their denominational diversity, and should not be subject to some kind of test – least of all a test set by someone further up the hierarchical ladder. The parallel question for a Catholic, when exceptionally attending the eucharist of another tradition, cannot simply be answered by quoting the rules of that tradi-tion. Christians have to discern on the basis not only of their beliefs, and the customary directives, but of their appropriate application to their immediate circumstances. They have to be clear why they are there and what they intend to express for the sake of truth, integrity and Christian love.

In both cases, theological principles and degrees of understanding are involved. But it is surely unreasonable to presume
unorthodoxy in the visitor to a Catholic Mass, while presuming
orthodoxy for all the Catholics taking part. It is equally unreasonable to expect Catholics attending eucharist in another tradition to understand and accept the official Catholic rejection of
the validity of the orders of the presiding ministers when they
are happy to share what in many cases appears to be a rite in-
distinguishable from that of the Catholic tradition.

Of course I need to spell these arguments out, but at this
moment I simply want to say that the 'norms' reached by the
bishops' document tend to suggest that, because the churches
are divided, the Christians are. The norms therefore overlook
that fundamental unity each Christian has in Christ, and legis-
late as though we were in danger of overlooking or ignoring the
historic division of the churches.

Unity, in perfect or full communion
So we need to examine the meanings of 'unity' and of 'full communion'. The document says: 'There can be no full unity among
Christians that does not embrace unity in the eucharist.' True,
but that does not make those two unities identical. Even when
we have 'unity in the eucharist' among Catholics, insofar as we
receive communion together, we know there is often lacking the
unity of love which it symbolises and should help to create. As
the document continues, 'This communion will be complete
only in the fullness of the kingdom of God.' 'We celebrate together the communion we already share, but we are also very
aware of the imperfection of our unity, even among Catholics
gathered to share together the one Bread of life.' (44) Because of
the division of the churches we continue to celebrate the eucharist separately and with a variety of formal understandings
of what we do. Yet because of that real, though imperfect, communion we have as baptised members in the One Church, it is
difficult to see why individuals in extraordinary, however frequent, circumstances, may not celebrate that degree of communion by receiving the sacrament without special permission
being required. It may well be that the visitor might feel it
wasn't quite 'right' to do so; that depends on their own experience of the sacrament, their upbringing and the particular bond
they may have with some of their fellow-worshippers on the

occasion. Shared communion with us certainly cannot be used as a device towards the unity of the churches, but it can be a celebration by believers of their union in Christ such that they may be impelled to work harder to remove whatever still divides the churches. The final goal of ecumenical endeavour in any event is not shared sacramental communion, but unity of love in Christ. When we think about it we recognise how inadequately we make that a reality, however faithful our liturgical celebrations.

The document says, 'The Eucharist is a most precious gift of the Lord to the church' (4): it is Christ's gift, not ours. How dare we then withhold it from those who here and now on this or that occasion wish to receive, especially if there is 'a burning desire to join in celebrating the one eucharist of the Lord.' (5) That 'burning desire' may simply be implicit in the eagerness with which some of our visitors come to Mass with us. The bishops cannot be unaware that 'not refusing' communion to those who present themselves has been moderately widespread – not out of contempt for the rules, but as a considered interpretation of them.

The bishops rightly make much of the fact that 'Catholic faith in the eucharist and in the church are two essential dimensions of one and the same mystery of faith.' (10) They overlook the fact, however, that most people's understanding of both is partial. The full significance of the eucharist as uniting us with Christ and with one another is often missing; the full significance of membership of the Church is similarly lacking – or we would not have been divided for so long.

Several powerful quotations take us further into the nature of the church and her communion: 'The church is the visible unfolding here and now of God's gift of salvation, our sharing together in communion of God's life of love.' (16)

'The Church is the company of those who have been given the gift of faith, a faith by which they respond in a deep personal way to the call of Christ, and follow him as his disciples.' (17)

Now the understanding of 'church' by individual believers in the varied traditions may not be either clear or vivid, but if there is any understanding of baptism it is difficult to see how we can block the completion of the initiation of which it is but the first stage, when pastoral circumstances find us together. 'Receiving Holy Communion is the climax of initiation begun in baptism.' (18)

So far then, following the Vatican II Decree, there is a recognition of our communion in Christ. But that is not the same as 'full communion'. 'Christians are in full communion with the Catholic Church when they hold in common all the gifts of grace with which Christ has endowed his church.' (20) 'The one, holy, catholic and apostolic church of Christ is to be found in its fullness, though imperfectly, in the visible Catholic Church as it is here and now.' (21) There are then, we are to understand, degrees of communion, degrees of full communion, and degrees of perfect communion; and one seriously wonders how many of us Catholics have the claim to full, perfect communion, and therefore to automatic, unrestricted access to sacramental communion when, alongside of us there are those, raised and nurtured in a different tradition, who display the signs of commitment and holiness often way ahead of ourselves. The document struggles to explain this further: 'There are varying degrees of communion (with the Catholic Church), depending on how much Christians share together in the mystery of salvation and the means of grace. The more that is shared, the more people are in communion with one another.' (22) That would surely be an argument in favour of sharing sacramental communion when circumstances create the possibility, even though all factors for full communion of the churches are lacking. The bishops evidently fear that we should be living untruthfully if the barriers came down, because communion in the Catholic Church has ecclesiastical (i.e. institutional) as well as ecclesial (i.e. fellowship) implications. We celebrate the eucharist with institutional authorisation, not only as an immediate communion of believers. 'The unity of the universal church is a communion in truth, in love and in holiness. It is rooted in sharing the same faith and in our common baptism, in the eucharist, and also in communion with the bishops of the church united with the Bishop of Rome. The three signs and sources of unity, shared faith, shared eucharist and shared ministry, belong together.' (59)

Shared faith

So often one has heard it said that other Christians don't believe what Catholics believe about the eucharist. Yet it is difficult to be sure what precisely Catholics do believe – or at least we don't test them, once admitted to communion as children. This document may well be a help in clarifying the teaching of the church.

But are we right, and is it just, to presume that our visitors fall automatically at this hurdle? The eucharist is something we do in obedience to Christ, not only something that we believe. Yes, at least we expect some genuine sense of Christ's real presence in the consecrated bread and wine; but simply to refer to the terminology of 'transubstantiation', as though that resolved all the nuances of our Catholic faith, is to presume something unwarranted in the faith of Catholics themselves. Not many of us find that metaphysical description apt any more, especially if it purports to be some kind of 'explanation'.

We could all do with an increase in our 'reverence for the mystery of faith whereby we feed on the body of Christ in order to become more fully the body of Christ'. One of our dangers is that we reverence the presence of Jesus in the sacrament – for example by our genuflections and respectful quiet in the place of its reservation – yet fail to revere the Body of Christ in his faithful people. It is commonly said (in shameful ignorance of widespread Anglican practice) that Christians in other traditions only see eucharistic communion as a mere symbol of Christ's body and blood; the only 'change' being in the faith of the recipient. But even in Free Church practice a communion service is not merely a symbolic and commemorative rite, but a special link with Jesus as he intended.

The well-known lines from the first Queen Elizabeth ring true for many Catholics as well as others, and is healthy in its refusal to define:

T'was God the Word that spake it
He took the bread and brake it
And what the Word did make it
That I believe and take it.

Shared faith in the eucharist may in fact be more consonant with one another across the divides than the church formularies may suggest. The findings of the ARCIC commission surely attest to this. The actual practice which has been increasing through the ecumenical years whereby our visitors receive communion with us should not be dismissed as galloping indifferentism.

Shared ministry
Shared ministry is certainly something we lack, and the topic opens a Pandora's box of theological niceties, starting with the

'valid orders' argument. 'Absolutely null and utterly void' is a warning of frightening negativity about Anglican orders from Pope Leo XIII, though he believed it to express the result of historical and theological enquiry. But there is a prior difficulty which the bishops envisage when they suggest that it is a constitutive element in the faith of Catholics at the moment of communion that they are affirming membership of that visible community of the church through the priest and the named bishop and Pope. I concede that somewhere along the line of thinking there is an implication of such an affirmation, but I seriously doubt whether any Catholics advert to it. Of course it is relevant to the celebration that the Pope and local bishop are named in the eucharistic prayers as those with whom we are in communion; but that should not exclude others. Indeed, one of the formulas adds 'with all your holy people'. Catholics are not always particularly enamoured of their bishops or popes; it would have been difficult to be happy about being 'in communion' with some of the Borgias. Catholics look beyond those named in the eucharistic prayer to the visible unity of structure which would seem to have been the intention of Jesus. But in these ecumenical days why do we not sometimes include the names of church leaders of other traditions, to celebrate the measure of communion we do have with them, even though it is imperfect? For myself I have for a long time declined to limit the list to Pope, bishop and clergy, and say 'bishops, priests, deacons and all other ministers'. I dare say some people may think I am referring to our own non-ordained ministers, but my heart is reaching out to the local Anglican and Free Church ministers. Quoting the 1993 Roman Directory the bishops say, 'Baptismal communion tends towards full ecclesial communion.' (22); but that does not immediately imply 'ecclesiastical' communion, that is, acceptance of institutional structures.

Normal and abnormal
Moving towards the norms the bishops feel obliged to lay down, they say, 'Full participation at Catholic Mass through reception of Holy Communion normally implies full communion with the Catholic Church itself.'(60) The word 'normal' appears again when they say, 'Whatever exceptional sharing may be possible, only the full reconciliation of Christians can make normal the full sharing together of the sacrament of unity.' (93) Of course

the bishops are right when they say, 'When as Christians we do come together for the eucharist, we should not celebrate in a way that suggests a degree of unity which we do not have.' (78) For that reason I believe they are right to discourage as inappropriate the celebration of the eucharist at a special ecumenical gathering. It is increasingly embarrassing to find others invited to Mass as an 'ecumenical celebration' and then denied their access to communion. But that is not mainly what troubles the people of God. We are concerned with the 'abnormal' presence of individuals at our Mass, or our 'abnormal' presence at their eucharistic services. The idea that someone has to make a formal judgement to justify an exception to 'normal' practice is legalism of a damaging kind. The exceptions are 'only when a strong desire is accompanied by a shared faith, given a pressing spiritual need, and at least an implicit desire for communion with the Catholic Church.' (77) What we are likely to have is a desire on the visitors' part to share in the faith of the Catholic friends or relatives with whom they have come, anxious to share as a fellow Christian in the gift of Christ's communion of himself. To restrict their receiving communion to 'grave and pressing spiritual need' is so grudging as to be offensive. It may well be that there is, in any event – as I have read elsewhere – a misunderstanding about the proper way to translate *gravis* from the Latin Directory.

Several 'occasions' for exception to the norms almost reduce matters to absurdity. For instance, at a nuptial Mass for an interchurch couple, permission may be granted to, say, the Anglican party to receive Holy Communion on this special occasion, after due enquiries have been made about the extent of his shared faith in the eucharist. This will express the unity already shared in the two sacraments of baptism and matrimony, and seems eminently sensible. But that will probably be on a Saturday morning. The couple move off for their honeymoon, and the following day (Sunday) they wish to continue to celebrate their unity, and they go to Mass together; but this time only the Catholic may receive communion. Of course they may have flown away to a 'Catholic' country where no Anglican service would be available, in which case they will probably have another automatic exemption from the usual restrictions at home. This is patently ridiculous. The exceptions surely demonstrate that there is no ultimate theological objection to receiving communion together, except that they have to sustain the pain of church divisions. So far from the special permissions being seen as a gesture of charity or generosity, in my view they undermine the propriety of refusing the sacrament for this couple on every other occasion that they worship together. What is possible once is surely possible again, and again.

One senses that the near illogicality of the norms here occurred to the bishops. Short of saying that only 'card-carrying Catholics' should really be present at Catholic Mass, so that we wouldn't have to deny the others the right to Holy Communion, they turn to an alternative – the making of a 'spiritual communion'. The presence of others (catechumens, young children, the remarried-divorced, those with unconfessed grave sin), they say, indicates that a worthwhile celebration is possible without the reception of the sacrament . They can benefit from the liturgy of the Word, and make a 'spiritual communion' and receive a gesture of blessing. Now one knows of many devout Sunday-by-Sunday attenders who restrict themselves for one of the above-listed reasons to such an alternative; but increasingly I wonder how it can be justified in the light of Jesus' words related in John's Gospel: 'If you do not eat of the flesh of the Son of man and drink his blood, there is no life in you.'

Looking back to the origins of our eucharist, as the bishops do (3), when the first followers of Jesus met for the 'breaking of the bread', it is difficult to imagine that they excluded anyone by reason of lack of understanding or even their quality of life. Confused and disorganised as the first disciples were, including their failure to understand Jesus' words about the eucharist, but certain that they would continue to follow him – 'to whom would we go?', they so rhetorically asked – they were learning to understand by doing. The church hadn't got round to criteria for ordaining those who presided; there isn't any real sign that the Twelve were baptised; being called and chosen by Jesus sufficed. Of course our eucharist today is wholly in line with that simple breaking of the bread. We have been led by the Spirit to understand more; but let us not rule against sharing with those who come with good will to our celebration today; they should have the same chance as we do of learning by doing. This does not obliterate our need to work for an end to the divisions of the churches, but the occasional shared communion of the faithful of different traditions might lead us more quickly to some solution.

Is there room for mutuality?

Rather more controversial thoughts emerge when we try to understand the mystery of Christ's presence in the consecrated bread and wine, or rather when we ask how it comes about. We Catholics may be concerned that other traditions are relatively unclear as to what 'happens', but are we any more consistent in our belief? The re-enactment or re-presentation of the one perfect and supreme sacrifice offered by Jesus on Calvary, and completed by his rising and ascension, would seem to be central to our tradition. It enables us to unite our own self-offering to the Father, and transforms the inadequacy of this into a powerful redemptive action, as the tokens of bread and wine become the body and blood of the one victim and high priest, and feed our minds and hearts as we receive them in the sacramental meal.

Now all that is true, but it is high theology, and I am truly unsure to what extent most Catholics are theologically aware of it all. For the most part I suspect that the participation of many is likely to be much less analytical. They come 'for the grace of communion', as they might say. The real presence of Christ in the scriptures, their self-offering with him in the gifts may hardly be adverted to. There is little doubt of their devotion when they come up for communion. They are certain to be very respectful to the sacramental body of Christ; it is often for them a moment of intense closeness to Jesus, but they may well not be sensitive to the commitment they are thereby making to their fellow communicants and the world so much in need of their love. Good and dignified liturgy can help to deepen their awareness, and that is the serious responsibility of the presiding priest and his assistant ministers. Christ can more readily be heard in his scriptural Word if it is read with dignity and understanding. The liturgical Constitution of Vatican II says that Christ is also present in the presiding minister; he acts *in persona Christi*. For many that means that just as it was the very words of Christ at the Last Supper that rendered the reality of his presence in the bread and wine of that new Passover meal, so now it is the words of the priest, which are of course the recorded words of Jesus, that makes him present on our altars. But at the 'consecration' of the Mass, the priest is simply reading the gospel narrative; he is not 'miming' for Jesus. (If he were, then he would mime thoroughly, and at least break the bread as he says those words; yet the rubrical norms tell him not to break till later.) So is the transformation of the elements (or whatever words we think most fitting to use) achieved by reason of his ordained ministry? Does he really have a 'sacred power' unlike the endowments of all the other members of the church called to discipleship?

We have learned that it is the whole congregation, by their baptismal share in the priesthood of Christ, who 'offer' and 'celebrate' the eucharist. The ordained priest 'presides' and accordingly is the narrative reader. But Christ becomes present by the power of the Spirit. It is the Holy Spirit who fills the offered bread and wine with the sacramental presence of Jesus. To emphasise that what happens at Mass is what the whole people of God celebrate and experience, the 'presider' must be someone authorised to do so in the name of the church – so much wider than this little congregation here and now. His authorisation, or ordination, by a bishop provides us with the link with the family of the whole church. I have no doubt that for an authentic celebration of the eucharist the one who presides needs that authorisation. We are an 'ordered' church.

Now the problem for Catholics who attend the eucharist of another tradition is that they have been told they should question, nay deny, the authorisation of the presiding priest. The question one is supposed to ask is whether or not the priest has 'valid orders'. In this approach, if one is told that only Catholic and Orthodox priests are in the assured line of apostolic succession and have the necessary 'sacred power' to consecrate the bread and wine, then, however sacred a commemorative service may be, Christ is not really and truly present for communion. Are we expected to think – as has been crudely but sharply expressed – that they are 'firing blanks'? Of course every Catholic would have to recognise that the priest/minister has not been authorised to preside for Catholics, but s/he has been authorised within her/his own tradition for the congregation being visited; this is not a 'normal' situation. If it is the Holy Spirit, not some magical power, by which Christ is present in the sacrament, I see no reason why the Spirit should be absent from those celebrations in churches separated from full Catholic recognition. This of course is not easy to convey to people who have rigid ideas about 'validity' as some kind of objectivisation of what ordained priesthood means. Even so, if one depends on a direct line of ordination by apostolic succession, then we know that there are many Anglican bishops and priests who have, sometimes by rather odd lineage, acquired the link which could be recognised by Catholics. I find all that a lot of logic chopping. When present at the eucharist of another tradition, even viewing this with minimal criteria, I am trying to worship in fellowship with other Christians, following Jesus' command to 'do this in memory of me'. I am not required to make a theological statement on precisely what I receive at communion time; it is still an important act of worship, even if I am told not to concede that Christ is sacramentally present. Personally I have greater trust that the Holy Spirit deprives no-one of his special presence, and that means in every celebration. That in no way undermines my hope that we can reach a formal recognition of one another's ministry in due time, and I am not in favour of indiscriminate recognition. The pastoral question we face is about abnormal or extraordinary situations, even though they may for some people be quite frequent.

Perhaps I may illustrate how I dealt with a situation in one parish I served. In my first 'Unity Week' I invited a neighbouring Vicar (the parish covered six Anglican parishes) to bring his choir and people to our church to celebrate Evensong for and with us as congregation. He was so pleased about this that he said, 'Next year you must come to us for choral eucharist.' 'Now David,' I said, 'if you invite us as a Roman Catholic community, I shall have to recommend that we all obey the current discipline about our non-reception of communion.' (This was years before *One Bread, One Body* appeared.) 'On the other hand if you simply inform us, and other Christians in our area, that there will be a choral eucharist in "Unity week" which any of us is welcome to attend, then it will be up to each person to make their own decision.' This led to much informal discussion among parishioners, including the parish council, with the eucharistic ministers, etc. on the lines I have indicated in this chapter. Some were ready for a maximal, others only for a minimal interpretation of the situation about 'validity', 'authorisation', etc. About eighteen of us attended, and eight felt ready to receive communion. What particularly pleased me was the comment of one elderly Irish lady as we came out: 'Owen, I wasn't quite ready to receive communion here today,' because that assured me that she was sensitive to church teaching, to her own cultural background and the contemporary development of rapprochement with Anglicanism.

I fear that such personal discernment has no recognised place in a church that insists only on episcopal norms which function as 'rules'. I feel certain that many of the bishops would not intend this. I am eager to discover that many others agree that *One Bread, One Body* is indeed not 'the last word'.

CHAPTER FOURTEEN

In the Freedom of Retirement:
A vision or a hunch?

'As priests and as the church's representatives, don't we talk as if everything were clear? This is lying and untruth. If we talk of God, then let us tell people straight: You must never consider your life closed: you must never think that your account has reached its final figure: you must never think you can make yourself comfortable in the comprehensibility of your existence. Let us tell them you must get away from the familiarity of your existence; you are travelling towards an absolute infinity of which you can never get the measure.' (Rahner in *Meditations on Priestly Life*)

I didn't start to write this book to forecast the future. I certainly don't have a calling of that kind. I did start it to reflect on what faith, church, ministry and priesthood have meant to me through my not particularly significant life, but which has mingled in and out of the lives of a fair number of different people. I actually picked up my biro – this was before I had got anywhere near to a Word Processor – when I chose to mark my entry to official retirement in 1996 at the age of seventy-two by spending seven weeks in residence at the Cistercian monastery on Caldey Island, off the coast of Pembrokeshire. The daily discipline of rising for Vigils at 3.15 am, and therefore of retiring after Compline at 8.30 pm, fitted not too uncomfortably into the winter schedule of light and dark, for it was November/December. I valued the seven-times-a-day of the daily Office, a routine of two hours manual work each afternoon, and the communal meals in silence or while a prepared audio-tape took us through Nelson Mandela's autobiography. I was greatly helped by the lack of alternatives for recreation; writing and reading filled many hours. Now I have discarded a good deal of what I began to write there. I hope I have managed to eliminate many of those autobiographical details which are not germane to my themes, even if they were of mild interest to some specially close friends. What I wanted to convey was some reflection in developing ideas as practised.

'So are you really retired?' I am often asked, and I give the cynical response: 'I'll have a look at my diary,' because it is often absurdly full. Three years have passed and in more than two-thirds of that time I have not given any great priority to finishing these chapters. I am both pleased and annoyed with myself for allowing my time to be filled so variously. I have largely failed to confront the need to space things out, to establish real priorities and to stick to them when new requests are made for help of one sort or another. I still work too fast and with consequent inaccuracy, and the failure to attend to details. My mind roars ahead with at least two new ideas or projects to explore each night, and this is simply unrealistic. Because I have been blessed with uncommonly good health most of the time, it is only straightforward physical/mental tiredness that reminds me that there really should be sensible parameters for someone of my age.

There is a lot of tidying up I would like to achieve, not least over these reflections, and I still have three regrets in my life. Firstly, that in spite of a never failing desire for it, I have been so dilatory in really cultivating the practice of contemplative prayer as the chain-anchor of my life. I keep trying, but I could have done so much better. Secondly, that I have never mastered the Welsh language for use. In spite of several notable efforts, including some intensive courses, I have failed to keep up the exercise of what little I know, and that is rather shameful for someone who is so proud to be Welsh. Thirdly, that I have passed over the chances of developing my piano playing – largely through my impatience and the unwillingness to get down to detail. For someone as innately musical as I am, it is ungenerous to have remained a listener, instead of being able to share even private performance. Only the first of these three would immediately appear to be related to my spiritual and theological journeyings; but I know I would have done better if I had persevered in the other two also.

What then do I see, at this stage of my life, as the challenges to my own perception of Christian faith, of the church, of ministry and of priesthood? The great areas of intellectual and spiritual development go way beyond the limitations of Roman Catholicism, though I am content to start from there. Real universality stretches beyond even ecumenical endeavours among Christians. We are compelled to look at things in the context of the world's historic religions, and that fact colours the shape and form of our approaches. I see no disloyalty to the unique figure and crucial role of Jesus the Christ in looking for his earlier and later outlines in the unfolding visions of those who have not known him. I'm really not sure what I could have done about this if I had remained a parish priest with the heavy commitment of trying to deepen the faith of Christians within the expanding tradition of Catholicism.

Already we have seen the terrible sense of insecurity that some people feel since Vatican II began to move us beyond post-Reformation thinking. The so-called 'restorationists' are only responding to what they have been brought up to think of as the never changing teaching of the church. It is very upsetting for them to be reminded that it is only God who does not change. Yet in their defence it is necessary to remind myself that some people can manage change more quickly than others. Some of them are, for cultural, family or indoctrination reasons, understandably reluctant to change – a kind of temperamental arthritis. I hope I shall always remember to be patient.

As for those who try to manage the ways of the church, I fear that the factors of patriarchy and power are what predominate. We are not dealing with a benign form of conservatism which has a value in slowing down the disruption of too hastily moving ahead. We are simply experiencing the endemic affliction of every institution, the church no less than any other – the compulsion to preserve itself, and preferably in exactly the same form.

I am certain that the church will have to take many different shapes in the future. The phenomenon of base communities in Latin America can neither be simply replicated in affluent Europe, nor should they be, but even as an intermediary stage they have re-awakened a simpler model of being church which has much to say to us. Declining numbers in our western congregations, especially of young people, are beginning to pressurise us into re-scheduling the way we manage things. So far it is largely a process to ensure the provision of Sunday Mass as the minimum social requirement of Catholic faith. This is only now hitting home in western Europe on a large scale. The scandal of providing only one or two annual opportunities in some parts of the world, for a church that proclaims to be essentially eucharistic, does not seem to have been realised by those with patriarchal power. If it had been realised, their guilt would have been all the greater. For it is simply untrue that there are not people competent to preside for the eucharist, either as a temporary or permanent arrangement. What has been lacking is the willingness of church leadership to contemplate their authorisation by ordination.

It is not simply a matter of abandoning the celibacy requirement, although that has its importance. It is the determination to sustain the ordained and lay distinction as a valid concept which affects 'order', and that sometimes seems like a disguised name for clerical power. Now I have no personal axe to grind here. In spite of my unreadiness to conform at several points, I have never been treated badly. It simply disappoints me that the structure of episcopal loyalty to consensus thinking among bishops, and the wholesale submission to the rule of Peter and/or his curial assistants, makes so many good, holy and potentially innovative men into failed leaders. We are at a peculiarly sharp watershed as we enter a new millennium in the ecclesiastical climate of our time, and I am still optimistic for a great breakthrough.

After my wanderings through 'secular employment' and on my return to parish work in 1988, I found a great readiness among the people who worshipped in the two churches of the parish of Llay with Rossett to share a collaborative model. I divided the area geographically into six districts and asked representatives of these (two per district, or three if more heavily populated) to form the Parish Advisory Council. I expressed the hope that there should be a change-over of the representatives every couple of years, so that we didn't risk having a clique. While in 'line management' terms, I was canonically responsible to the bishop for the parish, I did not take the Chair of the Council. In fact I reckoned that would inhibit my expressing my views. A Chairman is supposed to facilitate the participation of others, not hog the meetings! Then, quite soon after starting this consultative method, I produced an age-list of the priests of the diocese, giving a five and ten year projection, just so that everyone could see how fragile would be the provision of priests in the near future, unless something startlingly new happened. The members immediately decided to set up a special working-group to confront the question, 'How can we assure the pastoral care of the people of this parish if, in five years' time, we cannot have a resident priest?' They met, monthly, I think – for I was not one of the group – over a period of more than a year and then turned up a document which analysed the leadership needs for good teaching, and pastoral care of the young people, the elderly, sick and housebound, and the bonding of a worship-ping community. Somewhere along the line I invited them all to design a 'Job Description' for the next parish priest, so that they could look specifically at the tasks usually expected of him, and to note how few of them actually required ordination.

They looked at the implied structures and training to achieve their purposes, and looked at the formal links they would need, as a lay 'council', to have with the bishop and especially to en-sure the provision of a Sunday eucharist. After explaining the document to me, and then to the advisory council, they ex-plained it all to a general meeting of the parish which was re-markably well attended. It was with a certain pride that I phoned the bishop to come and look at the diagrammatic pre-sentation in place on the wall of the parish hall after the meeting. He came within an hour, though he had just arrived back from Lourdes and was due in Cardiff the next morning, and was warmly congratulatory of this initiative, as well as making some pertinent comments.

In all this, perhaps what was least on the table for discussion was any decision about who was to come to preside for Sunday Mass. The people assumed, no less than the bishop, that, however he was chosen to do so, an 'outsider' would be brought in for this crucial task. It was possibly only I myself who felt uneasy about this, because I could not see how someone could satisfac-torily preside for the liturgical celebration and nurturing of a community where he had no leadership or other role.

As I moved towards retirement, and was going to be avail-able for parish 'supply' work in parishes during the absence through holidays or sickness of the parish priest, I began to sense that there was something really odd about this. What right would I have to 'preside' for a community of which I knew next to nothing? I determined already that I would try to make some advance contact with those with parish ministries. One parish across the English border, where I helped out many times, had a fulltime lay pastoral assistant to whom I 'reported' on Saturday evening. He gave me a run-down of current parish life and activities each time, and somehow gave me a picture of the community whose worship I was to lead. I even began to appreciate the comment that simply to zoom in to the task of presiding and preaching without personal contact was an act of 'spiritual prostitution'.

I began to revert to a conviction I had earlier felt that every parish needed one, or more, 'stand-by' presiders for Sunday worship in the absence of the resident parish priest. In the last parish where I served for an eight-month interregnum before moving into retirement, we had several discussion evenings to look at priestly leadership because in a period of about eighteen months they had to accept four different priests in charge. I was the third of four. That inevitably involved changes of style, and they rightly began to wonder if they had patiently to accept this. 'After all,' they correctly said, 'we are the parish.' The swift changes of priest 'made us realise the need for the people of the parish to be well organised themselves, if we are to sustain a living and united community.' They had already noted from circulating fifteen copies of the document on collaborative ministry, *The Sign We Give*, that Bishop Hollis had said in his introduction, 'It is a revolutionary insight into the way we exercise our mission which is to proclaim the Good News in today's world.' He added that what he called 'the seeds of the revolution' had been planted with the united authority of the bishops. Just before leaving the parish myself, I produced a little summary of the findings of our discussions to be shared more widely in the parish before being offered to the bishop . It had some practical suggestions to help the bishop cope with the 'shortage', including of course that the ministry of those priests who had resigned for marriage should be revived at least at this auxiliary level. I don't think many people knew that among our parishioners at that time were two men in this position!

Three and a half years later I looked again at the age spectrum of the surviving diocesan priests and wrote another little piece to stimulate discussion. While in some ways it is rather superficial, it only says what is more soundly outlined by some scholars and theologians. 'The circumstances of our day surely force on us radical questions about what a priest is, and what

ministries we need in our time and in our country.' K. Schmidt
wrote (in the collection of essays *Europe Without Priests*):

> 'The real question which needs to be put to ministries is not
> whether or not they are immutably willed by God, but under
> what form they best realise God's will with the human com-
> munity. For the ministry as such is not part of the Good
> News. Ministry is not an end in itself but a means. The pur-
> pose of church ministry can ultimately only be to help build
> up the community of Christ.'

In an interesting way, while the first outreach of ecumenism has
largely been in relation to Anglicanism which has a not too dis-
similar perception of 'priesthood', I find my mind impels me to
link up with a much less clerical, a more nonconformist, perspective on 'ministry'. I believe that it is in this direction that the
church will move into the new millennium. Globalisation in any
event will necessitate a much richer understanding of a multi-
faith world in the midst of a vast increase in powerful secular-
ism. I remain convinced that the religious spirit will continue to
flourish even though the established faith communities will
have to experience radical changes.

Where now? I certainly do not have a clear idea of how faith
in Jesus Christ is going to manifest itself in the coming years.
History shows us how a vital Christian civilisation can rise, fall
and even disappear in one part of the world only to re-appear
elsewhere. The forms in which the faith is upheld and practised
have to be as varied as the cultures and temperaments they
serve. And yet over and again we are told that the faith, and
even the church, never changes. This is to me so patently untrue
as to be a denial of the incarnate nature of the gospel. I personally
am quite excited by the unconfined way in which Catholics
increasingly are celebrating their faith; less and less are people
inclined to be confined by the discipline of clergy.

It was only recently that someone pointed out that the moment
at which Jesus said, 'It is accomplished' was not the glorious and
triumphant moment of the resurrection, but just as he died
ignominiously, yet willingly, on Calvary. What on earth did he
mean? He had proclaimed the Good News. He had demonstrated
God's compassion and love for sinful humankind, and this led
by a frightening inevitability to his own destruction as man.
Among other things it was the proclamation of the truth that
goodness will not triumph without sacrifice, that there is a nec-

essary stage of death before new life. 'Unless a grain of wheat falls into the ground and dies, it remains but a single grain.'

As he consented to die as the suffering servant, he knew that out there in Judaea were numbers of people who had been touched by the paradoxes of his teaching; that even the Twelve he had specially coached with his message had been obliged to confront their weaknesses and even betrayal in spite of their proclaimed trust in him. Most of them had now gone into hiding, forced to reconsider their mistaken expectations of a Messiah, and the reality of his description of the reign of God: 'the kingdom of heaven is like …' almost everything except what worldly kingdoms were like. The fact that his kingdom was 'not of this world' pointed to the very details of how they were to treat one another, and how they were especially to find him in the hungry, thirsty, naked and imprisoned peoples of this world.

Jesus' 'accomplishment' was to move out of the scene, to die willingly so that the Good News could find new life in his resurrection, whose power would somehow awaken his followers to start all over again. The promised coming of the Spirit to unite them to himself, and to give power to their reviving spirits was dramatically experienced in the story of Pentecost. This is often described as the birthday of the church, which becomes now the Body of Christ. All this clearly tells us that in some sense it was necessary for Jesus to die so that his lordship, his being the Messiah, the Christ, should come into being. In the acceptance of that revelation, we 'celebrate' the death of Jesus. He had planted the grain of wheat, his very human existence, to die so that new life could start. Yet we spend so much of our energy trying to preserve the shape and form of the church. We admit that the church is a human as well as a divine institution, but find it difficult to distinguish what is of God and what is of purely human devising.

So, to put it bluntly, I think that the church as we have known it in our western society, is dying and, painful though it may be, we must accept this willingly. But we should do so with the conviction that the seeds of new life have already been planted, and are already pushing up through the soil. It is the efforts to sustain older patterns as unchangeable which constitute our unwillingness to die, and holds back the work of God. This is an especially hard saying for those whose lives are seemingly committed simply to upholding an authoritative but closed corpus of teaching, an officially regulated code of behaviour and a fixed pattern of worship at whose centre they stand. They are certainly God's servants, but Jesus called us to be his friends; there was to be no upstairs and downstairs among the people of the resurrection. There is a ministry of teaching in which we may all be involved at some time or another, as parents, counsellors, or spiritual guides. Theologising, if that is not too posh a description, and the exercise of discernment, are tasks for all of us.

It would be absurd to suggest that all the clergy should somehow stand down, as though we could start again from scratch. The unchanging, undiminished presence of the Holy Spirit is our fundamental hope; it is that truth which unites us with the power of Jesus' life, death and resurrection. Those of us charged with special ministries in the visible society of Christ's followers need, of course, to confront our failures, as did the weak apostles after Calvary. We need to acknowledge that with the best will in the world, as the book of the Acts demonstrates, we are likely to give muddled and even contradictory leadership at times.

However, the formalities of a severely institutional church make it difficult to recognise new possibilities for growth and to fit everything into the same old structures, and thus difficult to undo the mistakes of the past. It has been a happy experience to notice the extent to which Pope John Paul incorporated sorrow and repentance for many of these in his proclamation of Jubilee for the year 2000. Even more startling has been his profound apologies uttered in the Holy Land for the sins of the church as institution through the centuries. As a general practice, the official Catholic Church has not been eager to admit she has been wrong nor, until Vatican II, to applaud the many elements of truth and holiness which flourish outside the visible structures of 'church'.

I am more than happy to re-iterate the words of Karl Rahner:

'Christianity is not the religion which solves all the riddles of the universe, but that which gives us courage in the grace of God to shelter ourselves and our lives in an incomprehensible mystery, and to believe that this mystery is love.' (Karl Rahner in *Meditations on Priestly Life*)